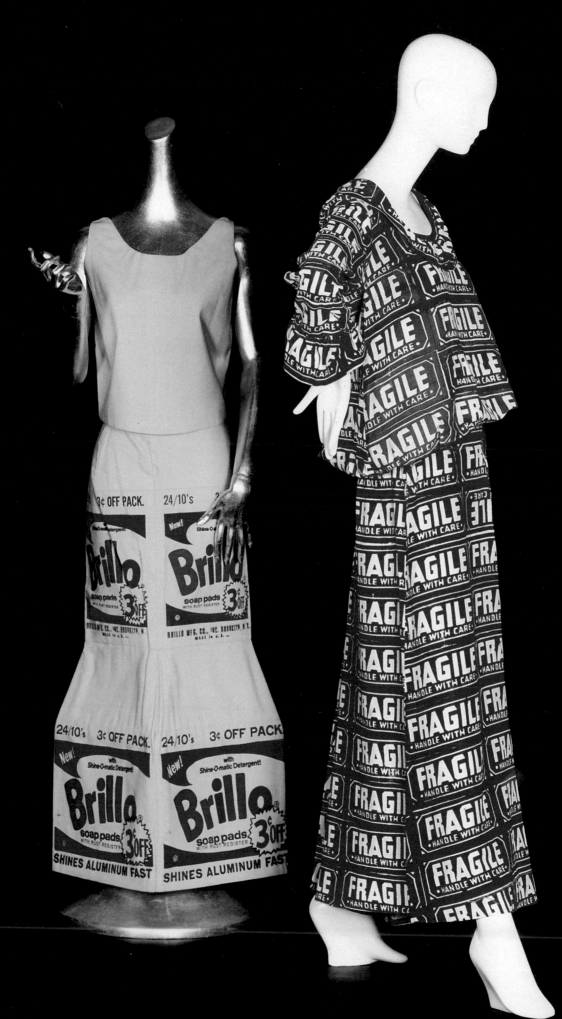

Andy Warhol, *Brillo Box* dress and *Fragile* dress

Andy Warhol, *Young Rauschenberg* blouse and *Tunafish Disaster* T-shirt

Andy Warhol, *S & H Green Stamps* blouse, signed by Warhol on left sleeve

Clothing designed by Betsey Johnson for Paraphernalia

Betsey Johnson, suit for Sterling Morrison, w___ _____ ___ming with the Vel___ ____round

Vivienne Tam, Mao dress, and unidentified Campbell's Soup Can dress

From left to right:
1. Halston, dress and scarf with images from Warhol's *Flowers* painting
2. Stephen Sprouse, jacket and hooded cape with images from Warhol's *Camouflage* paintings
3. Anna Sui, pants with camouflage design

From Warhol's collection, left to right:

1,2. Halston, cape and evening dress

3. Givenchy, bolero jacket, autographed by Hubert de Givenchy to Warhol

From Warhol's collection, left to right:
1. Arman, jean jacket with brass violin riveted on back
2. Robert Rauschenberg, jean jacket with attached necktie skirt

From Warhol's collection, left to right:
1. Norma Kamali coat
2. Gianni Versace suit
3. Jean Paul Gaultier dress
4. Comme des Garçons coat

Motorcycle jackets with paintings by Stefano of
Jean-Michel Basquiat, Andy Warhol, and Pepsi cans,
and paintings by Jean-Michel Basquiat

Left grouping: Stephen Sprouse clothing, and a motorcycle jacket with artwork by Keith Haring and others

Right grouping: T-shirts designed by Keith Haring, Kenny Scharf, and Andy Warhol, and fabric designed by Scharf

Left grouping: Clothing from Warhol's collection, including a bathrobe designed by Halston, a T-shirt with Holly Woodlawn's portrait, a robe from St. Mark's Baths, New York, and Calvin Klein men's briefs autographed by Calvin Klein to Warhol

Right grouping: Fiorucci clothing from Warhol's collection

ndy Warhol, *Brillo Box*, *Campbell's Soup Can*, and *Coca-Cola* T-shirts, *Dollar Sign* handkerchiefs and tuxedo shirt

ndy Warhol, *Energy* and *Art* T-shirts, *Fish* scarf, *Joseph Beuys* laundry bag, *Last Supper* sneakers, and *Self-Portrait* T-shirt

Composite dresses designed by Andy Warhol for 1975 "Fashion as Fantasy" exhibition,
constructed from pieces of clothing designed by Valentino, Yves Saint Laurent, Giorgio di Sant' Angelo,
Halston, Oscar de la Renta, Diane Von Fürstenberg, Stephen Burrows, and Clovis Ruffin

THE WARHOL LOOK

Cris Alexander Antonio Arman Richard Avedon
David Bailey John E. Barrett Peter Beard Cecil Beaton
Berry Berenson Richard Bernstein Mike Bidlo Manolo Blahnik
Stephen Bruce Bob Colacello Commes des Garçons
Howell Conant Candy Darling Corinne Day Simon Doonan
Sante D'Orazio George Dubose Kenn Duncan Johnny Dynell
Otto Fenn Nat Finkelstein Jean Paul Gaultier Hubert de Givenchy
Peter Greenaway Pat Hackett George Haimsohn
Philippe Halsman Halston Keith Haring Robert Hayes
Scott Heiser P. Heurtault Fred Hughes Victor Hugo
Katerina Jebb Betsey Johnson Matson Jones Norma Kamali
Bill King Gregory Kitchen Calvin Klein Lee Kraft Jill Krementz
David LaChapelle Roxanne Lowit Christopher Makos
Gerard Malanga Robert Mapplethorpe David McCabe
Elizabeth McCullough Fred W. McDarrah Barry McKinley
Patrick McMullan Steven Meisel Melton-Pippin Michael Mintz
Richard Misrach Jack Mitchell Gene Moore Paul Morrissey
Don Munroe Billy Name De Noyer Michael James O'Brien
Cornelia Parker Paige Powell Robert Rauschenberg
Matthew Rolston James Rosenquist Raeanne Rubenstein
Yves Saint Laurent Francesco Scavullo Kenny Scharf
David Seidner Stephen Shore Leila Davies Singeles
Francesca Sorrenti Alice Springs Stephen Sprouse Stefano
Federico Suro Tilda Swinton Vivienne Tam Oliviero Toscani
Emmanuel Ungaro Ellen von Unwerth Gianni Versace
Nicholas Vreeland Edward Wallowitch Bårbara Walz
Andy Warhol Albert Watson Bruce Weber Vivienne Westwood

Works by the artists listed above are included in this book, and many are also included in the accompanying exhibition.
An exhibition checklist is available upon request from The Andy Warhol Museum.

GLAMOUR

STYLE

THE WARHOL LOOK

FASHION

Mark Francis and Margery King

With essays by Hilton Als, Judith Goldman, Bruce Hainley, Richard Martin,

Glenn O'Brien, Barry Paris, John W. Smith, Thomas Sokolowski, Peter Wollen

THE ANDY WARHOL MUSEUM

A BULFINCH PRESS BOOK   LITTLE, BROWN AND COMPANY
BOSTON   NEW YORK   TORONTO   LONDON

This book was published on the occasion of the exhibition

THE WARHOL LOOK
GLAMOUR STYLE FASHION

Organized by The Andy Warhol Museum
Curated by Mark Francis and Margery King

Advisors: Simon Doonan, Richard Martin, and Thomas Sokolowski
Interview section organized by John W. Smith
Film and video organized by Geralyn Huxley

Exhibition tour:

Whitney Museum of American Art, New York
November 8, 1997 – January 18, 1998
The presentation at the Whitney Museum of American Art
is sponsored by Bloomberg News

Art Gallery of Ontario, Toronto
February 16 – May 3, 1998

Barbican Art Gallery, London
May 28 – August 16, 1998

Musée de la Mode, Marseille
September – November 1998

Museum of Contemporary Art, Sydney
December 1998 – March 1999

The Andy Warhol Museum, Pittsburgh
Spring 1999

**We are grateful to Simon Doonan and the display team of Barneys New York
for their expert assistance with the design and realization of the fashion
photographs on pages 1–31 of this publication.**

THE ANDY WARHOL MUSEUM
117 Sandusky Street
Pittsburgh, PA 15212-5890
tel: (412) 237-8300
fax: (412) 237-8340
http://www.warhol.org/warhol

The Andy Warhol Museum is one of the Carnegie Museums of Pittsburgh
and is a collaborative project of Carnegie Institute, Dia Center for the Arts,
and The Andy Warhol Foundation for the Visual Arts, Inc.

Design: Bruce Mau Design, Bruce Mau with Kevin Sugden
Project editor for Bruce Mau Design: Sara Borins

Bulfinch Press is an imprint and trademark of Little, Brown and Company (Inc.)
Published simultaneously in Canada by Little, Brown & Company (Canada) Limited

Printed by Diversified Graphics Inc. Minneapolis, Minnesota
Bound by Midwest Editions Inc. Minneapolis, Minnesota
Printed on Simpson Evergreen Matte, 80 lb.
Typeset in Adobe Akzidenz Grotesque/Grotesque Extended, and Monotype Baskerville

Cover (front): Bill King, *Candy Darling, Jed Johnson, Andy Warhol, Corey Tippin, and
Donna Jordan*, 1971; (back): Naomi Campbell wearing Gianni Versace's *Marilyn* dress,
by Ola Sirant for *Fashion File*, spring/summer 1991 collection

Contents

Foreword

Thomas Sokolowski
Director, The Andy Warhol Museum

This is what fashion sense really is — the ability to register and appreciate and remember the details of the way those around you look and dress, and then reinterpret those details and memories yourself.
Malcolm Gladwell, "Listening to Khakis," *The New Yorker*, July 28, 1997

According to ancient sources, the Greek painter Zeuxis created his image of the legendary beauty Helen of Troy by selecting the most pleasing anatomical features from among the daughters of King Heraion of Kroton, thereby achieving a composite perfection for his painting. In a sense, Andy Warhol adopted the same strategy. For Andy, this selection process could be termed "shopping," and what better arena in which to shop than the domain of fashion? (This artistic "shopping" should not be confused with its more pedestrian twin — a pursuit Warhol also adored, traversing the junk marts of Manhattan, the hallowed halls of Sotheby's and Christie's, and the various emporia of the rag trade in search of objects that might catch his fancy.) In fact, this eclectic mixing and matching was the keystone of his lifelong artistic mission. Given the myriad publications and exhibitions devoted to Andy Warhol's art, it behooves the museum that bears his name to consistently endeavor to break new ground in approaching his oeuvre; this exhibition and its accompanying publication do just that. *The Warhol Look/Glamour Style Fashion* is a cunning attempt to assess just how and why he constructed his "aesthetic shopping" and to show how and why his "look" became not merely successful but ubiquitous. In this year, the tenth anniversary of his death, his influence has never seemed stronger, as the boundaries between commerce and culture fall away.

Mark Francis and Margery King, in conjunction with their curatorial colleagues at The Andy Warhol Museum, Geralyn Huxley, Greg Pierce, John Smith, and Matt Wrbican, have fashioned the runway upon which the three and a half decades of Warhol's professional life may be viewed. Their discursive dialogue over the past three years has been fruitful: rich in its byways, insightful in its speculations, and even sometimes comical, in the unexpected results that they have collectively turned up. Curators and archivists alike have discovered that fashion is the connective tissue joining what previously appeared as disparate elements. Since the staff of The Andy Warhol Museum were neophytes when it came to the showrooms on Seventh Avenue or via Montenapoleone, we turned to two experts in the field, Simon Doonan, Barneys New York, and Richard Martin for advice; they were invaluable. Richard Gluckman gave the exhibition space itself a stunning carapace, and Bruce Mau Design fashioned the printed pages into a wondrous form.

Christopher Lyon of Bulfinch Press gave the written word a graceful shaping. The staff of the Andy Warhol Foundation for the Visual Arts, Inc., were incredibly helpful, as always. Barneys New York gave us the space and with effortless grace helped to conduct the fashion shoot for the book. David Ross and Willard Holmes of the Whitney Museum of American Art came on board straightaway and offered up their institution to host the premiere showing. To them and their counterparts at other museums on the international tour, I am grateful. To all of the lenders who so graciously parted with their artworks, and to all of the photographers who rummaged through their archives to find just the right photos, and who generously provided us with these materials, often without charge, I express my heartfelt thanks. Lastly, to Andy, who continues to teach us all how to look at ourselves, we all bow in humble and bemused admiration.

Acknowledgments

Mark Francis and Margery King

This book, and the exhibition from which it developed, was first conceived during the months after The Andy Warhol Museum opened in 1994. Since that time, the book and exhibition have grown into a very ambitious project for a young institution. We have sought the advice and drawn on the expertise of many people during its planning and realization. In particular, we wish to thank a number of individuals who encouraged us by their enthusiastic response at the outset: Sandra J. Brant, Holly Brubach, Arthur Danto, Simon Doonan, Richard Martin, Gene Moore, Ingrid Sischy, Geraldine Stutz, and Gianni Versace (with whom we met on June 16, 1997, shortly before his untimely death).

We are enormously grateful to the artists, photographers, designers, and authors represented in this publication, for their cooperation and willingness to contribute their work, and we especially appreciate those private collectors and museums who have lent fragile and valuable objects to the exhibition. We are grateful also for the support and interest from our colleagues in the other museums that will participate in the exhibition tour: David Ross and Willard Holmes at the Whitney Museum of American Art, New York; Matthew Teitelbaum and Jessica Bradley at the Art Gallery of Ontario, Toronto; John Hoole and Carol Brown at the Barbican Art Gallery, London; Corinne Diserens at the Musée de la Mode, Marseille; and Bernice Murphy and Nicholas Baume at the Museum of Contemporary Art, Sydney.

We have drawn constantly and in depth on the resources of The Andy Warhol Foundation for the Visual Arts, Inc., in New York, and we are especially grateful for the assistance provided there by Eileen Clancy, Martin Cribbs, Pier Djerejian, Scott Ferguson, Vincent Fremont, William Ganis, Archibald Gillies, Tim Hunt, Sally King-Nero, Matt Miller, Neil Printz, J. Scott Riker, Beth Savage, and Priya Wadhera.

Many others have helped us, providing advice, information, and other support. It has been a pleasure to work with Doris Ammann, Michael Auping, Amy Barraclough, Martina Batan, Marell Battle, Robert Becker, Pierre Bergé, Jill Bloomer, June Bové, Maria Brassel, Julia Brennan, Andrew Brooke, Gavin Brown, Jamie Cabreza, John Cale, Sasha Chermayeff, Beverley Coe, Susan Courtemanche, Lydia Cresswell-Jones, Patrizia Cucco, Leslie Dick, William Doig, Judith Eisenberg, Ronald Feldman, Sonja Finn, Peter Fischer, Georg Frei, John Gilliland, Brad Goldfarb, Eloise Goodman, Ruth Handel, Kelly Hardon, Gal Harpaz, Mary Haus, Stella Ishii, Cory Jacobs, Bill Judson, Jane Kallir, Ruth King, Danièle Leclercq, James Lingwood, Benjamin Liu, Sarah Lowengard, Donna Lee Lyons, Matthew Marden, Letisha Marrero, Janet McClelland, Patricia Mears, David Mellor, Dara Meyers-Kingsley,

Amy Miller, Dana Miller, Stefano Moreni, Paola Morsiani, Alberto Mugrabi, Edgar Munhall, Esty Neuman, Luis Nunez, Constance O'Neil, Mark Palmen, Chris Paulocik, Laura Paulson, Anise Richey, Natasha Roach, Andrew Rose, Jessica Sares, Ian Schrager, Kate Shela, Stuart Simons, Erica Sipos, Stephen Sprouse, Valerie Steele, Norma Stevens, Michael Ward Stout, Michael Stratton, Elisabeth Sussman, Steve Sutton, Ena Szkoda, Judith Tannenbaum, Peter Tunney, Paco Underhill, Tom Van Voorhees, Sheena Wagstaff, Debra Whitner, Peter Wollen, and Lisa Zay. We have been privileged to work closely over the past months with a highly gifted group of collaborators, who have committed themselves to the project with unlimited zeal: Carol Judy Leslie, Christopher Lyon, Karen Todd, and Ken Wong at Bulfinch Press for the publication of the book; Bruce Mau, Kevin Sugden, Sara Borins, and Catherine Jonasson for its design and production; and Richard Gluckman, Robert White, and Alex Hurst for the design of the exhibition in New York.

Our greatest debt is to our colleagues at The Andy Warhol Museum, who have all helped to complete the project within an unreasonably short schedule. Thomas Sokolowski, director, has been constantly supportive and encouraging. John Smith and Matt Wrbican have committed the archival resources of the Museum wholeheartedly. In addition, John was responsible for the *Interview* section of the book, and Matt was the Museum's creative director for the fashion photographs at the front of this book. Geralyn Huxley and Greg Pierce enabled film and video selections to be fully integrated into the exhibition. Ellen Baxter and William A. Real coordinated the conservation of many fragile and ephemeral objects. Colleen Russell managed the exhibition's public relations for the Museum. And Cheryl Saunders indefatigably oversaw the myriad registrarial challenges posed by our selections. Elizabeth Beaman and Grace Kane were enthusiastic interns.

Finally, without the incomparable contributions of Lisa Miriello, curatorial department assistant, and Jesse Kowalski, project assistant, this project would never have come to fruition. With undimmed energy, extraordinary precision, and good spirits, they have worked without respite for many months on the research and realization of the whole enterprise. They have established an unprecedented standard of commitment and loyalty to the artists represented, to this institution, and to their colleagues. We thank them, above all, for their contributions to every aspect of this project.

Clothing worn by Warhol in the 1950s

The Warhol Look

Mark Francis and Margery King

ANDY WARHOL'S last public appearance before he died was as a runway model in a January 1987 fashion show at the Tunnel club in New York. It was not an isolated occasion, as Warhol had made a career of modeling in his last years, but it poignantly recalls an aspect of Warhol's work that inflects the better-known images of Warhol as painter, filmmaker, publisher of *Interview*, photographer, author and philosopher, television producer, and socialite.

This book, and the exhibition it accompanies, is the first sustained attempt to trace and clarify Warhol's unflagging interests in glamour, style, and fashion throughout his life, from childhood to his untimely death at the age of fifty-eight. When these subjects are followed closely and sympathetically, they reveal a cohesiveness and consistency in Warhol's life and provide a deeper understanding of the influence of his work than emerge from a focus on individual groups or types of work. Glamour, style, and fashion are fundamental threads from period to period and across each of the media he touched. By observing how Warhol moved, with exceptional fluidity and ease, from making photographs, films, and paintings, to performing as a model for hire, overseeing the publication of *Interview* magazine, and going out to Max's Kansas City, or later Studio 54, a complex and nuanced picture of his achievement can be recognized.

The Warhol look is not a fixed entity. It extrapolates in different directions, and it is itself ephemeral and fleeting. It encompasses the look he engendered, expressed in fashion terms by elements identifiable with Warhol and his entourage; the way he looked, an imitable personal style; and Warhol's way of looking, his gaze, the discerning, ironical, basilisk look caught in Bill King's photograph on the cover of this book, and documented in thousands of Warhol's own photographs.

Alone among his peers, Warhol became a well-known figure beyond the confines of the art world and entered popular culture itself. During the silver Factory years of 1963 to 1968, what Warhol and his entourage wore, said, and did became just as significant as what they produced or exhibited. Their edgy style and the glamour that emanated from it have repeatedly become points of reference for designers of haute couture and for young people on the streets who reject the snobbery and cost of "designer" fashion.

The Warhol look continues to have widespread influence, evident in popular fashion television and a rash of recent magazine spreads and films (e.g., *I Shot Andy Warhol* or *Basquiat*), which have reinterpreted recent history in the light of current taste. The look of the sixties and that of the eighties have recently been in vogue, and we may expect other moments to be similarly reincarnated.

In their responses to his intense desire to be looked at, other artists, designers, and photographers can be seen to have important roles in the

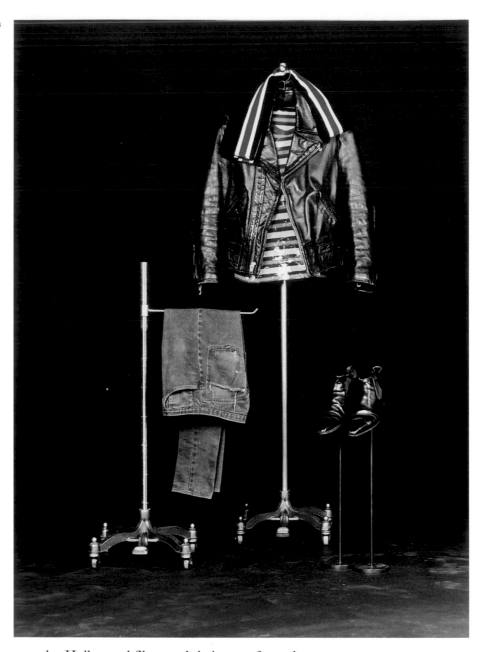

construction and definition of the styles with which Warhol is now associated; in large part they created the Warhol look. That is, Warhol engendered the look, or successive "looks," that were then disseminated and promoted by numerous photographers, personalities, and designers through the mass media of print and television. The Warhol look, a repertoire of styles, has evolved from a phenomenon associated with the artist and his entourage into a pervasive influence on taste. No other artist in the past fifty years has had such effect on the symbols and textures of urban life.

The challenge of this project depends ultimately on the ability of the recording media of film and photography, magazines, and objects such as clothing to fix the images and capture the personalities of Warhol and the other volatile characters in his world. Photographs are the principal means by which the Warhol look has been disseminated from the early sixties until today. Warhol had the foresight to recognize how photography could help create his own image when he encouraged, from 1963 onward, talented photographers such as David McCabe, Billy Name, and Nat Finkelstein to record the activities of his entourage. Many of the resulting images have become, through repeated publication, indelibly linked to our nostalgia for this extraordinary moment in cultural history. These photographs convey the mythic fantasy of the Warhol world, in part through their grainy, documentary, "hand-held" character. They are constituent parts of the Warhol narrative.

Glamour derives from the aural, iconic attraction that was projected in unprecedented ways by Hollywood films and their stars from the twenties onward. The glowing and silvery quality of film was adumbrated by Warhol in his person, his Factory, and his portraits in painting and on film. The allure of the (principally) female stars created and publicized by the Hollywood film studios was classless and democratic for the first time, and it was disseminated through Hollywood's international film distribution system and by posters and publicity stills. For Warhol, the elements of portraiture — dress, makeup, coiffure, lighting — captured in films or photographs, commingled to create collectible fetishes, objects that informed his tastes, his desires, and his own longing for fame and beauty.

Andy Warhol has long been recognized as a major innovator in avant-garde film, but his fervent desire was to create his own Hollywood-like

studio and thereby control the production of glamour. He left an enormous body of work in film, video, and television, much of which has not been distributed for over twenty years, or has only been seen briefly on cable, so its significance has been underestimated. Warhol's earliest documented enthusiasm was for relics of the stars he idolized at the movies in the thirties and forties. We can now see how this desire translated first into collections of film stills and publicity photographs, then into silkscreened paintings, and finally, by other hands, into spectacular painted, embroidered, or sequined costumes, which — to complete the circle — have been worn by a current generation of models and movie stars.

The film industry and the fashion system became templates for Warhol, providing modi operandi for his creation of art. For example, Warhol adopted the methods of film studios for his *Screen Tests*. With the notion that talent and beauty could be found on the street, and employing the lure of becoming one of his "Superstars," he co-opted the Hollywood practice of subjecting potential talent to the disciplines of makeup and lighting and then capturing them on film. The fame of the Factory in the sixties attracted dramatic beauties like Edie Sedgwick and Nico, and later such characters as Joe Dallesandro and Jackie Curtis. They performed as "themselves" in Warhol films, including *Kitchen* (1965), *The Chelsea Girls* (1966), *Trash* (1970), and *Women in Revolt!* (1974), and they also fulfilled another important function at the Factory by simply hanging out on the studio "lot," thereby creating irresistible opportunities for magazine image-makers of the day such as Cecil Beaton, David Bailey, and Bill King.

The difficulty of defining style reflects its mutability and immateriality. It is recognized by association and by signs rather than in canonical certainties. Even in his teenage years in Pittsburgh, Warhol established a distinctive style of dress and speech, hesitant and diffident though it was at first. Style was initially for Warhol a means of declaring himself "different."

One can see the evident delight with which he discovered kindred spirits almost immediately on his arrival in New York in 1949. Photographs from this period by his roommate Leila Davies Singeles show a carefree and even joyful attitude among Warhol and his friends and colleagues that was to complicate and darken as the fifties wore on. At this time he could "fit in" to the world he inhabited, yet it was in this decade that Warhol first altered his body and appearance

Clothing worn by Warhol in the 1970s

then a willingness, even a desire, for change, alteration, and embellishment. Warhol's style of dress changed from a deliberately run-down shabbiness in the early fifties, which elicited sympathy for "Raggedy Andy" in the commercial art and advertising worlds of Madison Avenue, to the more refined well-tailored suit he acquired in Hong Kong on his first trip abroad in 1956, which was more appropriate to his largely gay, cosmopolitan circle at the café Serendipity. His style continued to change; around 1963, he began to wear striped matelot T-shirts, jeans, and black leather jackets, and after 1968 he preferred more sober tailored jackets and Brooks Brothers shirts or black cashmere turtlenecks worn with jeans.

artificially by cosmetic surgery on his nose and by affecting wigs.

In his art, Warhol did not adopt a signature personal or aesthetic style that remained constant over the years. A part of his reputation was the very unpredictability of his style. He did not, for example, continue to celebrate Hollywood stars after *Marilyn* and *Liz* but widened his range with the *Flowers* and *Disasters* series (both later converted into images on clothing). His response to the idea of style was more subtle than most, insofar as he recognized its mobility (of both time and place) and instability. Early on he embraced the constancy of inconstancy.

For Warhol, a style, a look, a fashion each imply first the appraisal of taste and beauty and

In his later years he was photographed in all of these outfits and others, a testament to the relaxation of taste generally, but more specifically to Warhol's ability to project his own sensibility, even aura, whether wearing a formal evening tuxedo or (on one occasion in 1981) in drag. As a model, Warhol often wore black as a signifier of his authority and power. While never conforming to a conventional definition of stylishness, Warhol was nonetheless an arbiter of taste and style because of his own willingness to change identities, to become a chameleon of changing styles, to surround himself with acolytes attuned to the latest changes in fashion, and to be both participant and discriminating observer in the process. For Warhol, the exemplars of classic style were his close associates and confidants Fred Hughes and Diana Vreeland.

Fashion as a social system, fashion as a means of distinguishing and delighting in nuance and detail, fashion as an ephemeral, seasonal, extravagant spectacle, fashion as an index of beauty — all these were important for Warhol. He delighted in perverse and artificial sensations and in transgressing the boundaries of the different circles in which he moved. And much of this is plainly transmitted in the work Warhol did, whether making paintings and films in the sixties, or photographing and producing programs for television in the seventies and eighties. The fashion world has an omnivorous appetite for disparate inspirations, and Warhol shared this indiscriminate attitude, paradoxically refining his influences into objects for highly discriminating audiences. Many of Warhol's most important works — the *Marilyn* or *Camouflage* paintings, *Interview* magazine, or the film *Women in Revolt!* — attest to this flexible, unencumbered taste and willingness to experiment. Warhol's way of working was thus as vital, as self-confident, and as free of preconceptions as that of the best designers and editors in the fashion world.

Part of Warhol's fascination with the fashion world was the pleasure he took in attending and photographing the runway shows of Halston and other designers. Being publisher of *Interview* gave him access to these spectacles, and the magazine became an important vehicle for communicating Warhol's style and taste to a wide public. Warhol also participated in the creation of clothing, such as his cut-up dresses, made from parts of various designers' clothing, for "Fashion as Fantasy" (1975). These dresses anticipate subsequent "deconstructive" designs by Rei Kawakubo or Martin Margiela.

At present, the world of fashion has absorbed many of the qualities once attributed to avant-garde art and Hollywood. Young fashion models have become the iconic equivalents of glamorous film stars, and the outrageous and provocative behavior once expected of artists such as Warhol, Candy Darling, or Jean-Michel Basquiat can now be marketed as part of the appeal of Jean-Paul Gaultier or Stephen Sprouse, John Galliano or Alexander McQueen. Both the art and fashion worlds have a thirst for novelty and reinvention that is now slaked by the media of glossy magazines and television.

During the past decade, the extent of Warhol's cultural legacy has become increasingly apparent. His reputation as a major artist and filmmaker is now assured (except in the most conservative circles), while references to his status as a public figure, and to his notorious comments on fame, are pervasive. The influence of his work on painters, photographers, designers, editors, scholars, and curators continues to run its various courses. Warhol personified a spectacular fusion of previously distinct cultural fields, and his work embodies the complex range of associations that we expect of the greatest art. *The Warhol Look* is an attempt to investigate and understand how the great achievements and trivial ephemera connect with, and inform, each other, and how they have continued to influence contemporary culture.

Andy Warhol slipped the moorings of class, race, and gender to reinvent himself as a creative and mercurial artist. He emerged from a working-class, Carpatho-Rusyn, Catholic upbringing in Pittsburgh with an ethic of hard work which translated into an immediately successful career after he moved to New York in 1949.

It was through his self-definition within the gay milieu he discovered there that Warhol was first able to find the freedom to mix work and pleasure, business and nightlife. The narrow and apparently immutable categories of class, ethnicity, and gender imposed by his upbringing crumbled in the delirium of cosmopolitan New York. The same was true for close associates like Fred Hughes, Halston, or Edie Sedgwick. The nightclub Studio 54 became a kind of free zone in the late seventies where socialites and hustlers could mix. Warhol succinctly characterized it as "a dictatorship at the door, a democracy on the floor." All could remake their given or inherited identities in a culture that valued individual, unique, or eccentric personalities.

Though he and his predominantly gay associates initially made their contributions in seemingly marginal fields, social and cultural changes over the past forty years enable us to see that the creative "industries" of window dressing, marketing, display, and commercial illustration, populated as they were (and are) by a relatively high quotient of visible gays, have an enormous impact on popular taste. Historically, dandies have formed an avant-garde of taste, but in an era of mass culture, inheritors of these roles, like Warhol, send ripples far beyond their particular fields. Overall, the enormous profusion of his

work is hugely consequential in understanding art, fashion, and popular culture without categorical preconceptions.

For Warhol, these domains, and the creative personalities inhabiting them, nourished one another, and as his career developed from decade to decade, he delighted in the cross-fertilization that occurred as he moved from field to field. As we examined Warhol's achievement, we consciously set aside category distinctions and chronological progression in order to reflect the complex ways in which images and styles traverse fine art, magazines, publicity stunts, studio production, social life, and the popular, vernacular media of photography, film, and video. To introduce evanescent and sometimes ephemeral media into the contexts of a book and a museum exhibition, and to integrate and juxtapose them with original paintings and costumes, constitutes a revisionist approach to Warhol's work that is made possible by the availability of the totality of his production, and of his own collections, for the first time.

It is not to diminish the role of Warhol's great paintings as images, or as a form of decor, that we have consciously inverted the traditional hierarchy of archival ephemera, costume, photograph, film, and fine art. After all, it was Warhol himself who used his epic cycle of paintings *Shadows* (1979) as backdrops for a fashion shoot published in *Interview*, and who described them with his characteristic hilarious nonchalance as "disco decor."

An analogy may be found for these blurrings of categories and shifts of taste in the fate of sociological terms such as "subculture." Whereas the

Clothing worn by Warhol in the 1980s

From 1961, when he first exhibited his Pop paintings in the windows of the Bonwit Teller department store, his work entered a wide public consciousness through the mass media. Warhol retained a constantly provocative position in the media through his work, but also through a clearly identifiable persona. Pop culture seemed to appear without precedent, and Warhol's paintings of movie stars, consumer objects, and traumatic current events were identified as the quintessential Pop art. But he remained enormously prolific and inventive for a further twenty years, though the very glare of media attention obscured the real content and qualities of his achievement. Even the fact that Warhol successively took up painting, films, photography, publishing, or video contributed to the misapprehensions his work suffers from even ten years after his early death in 1987.

Andy Warhol's own books, especially *Andy Warhol's Exposures* (1979), with its mix of fashion and social commentary; the *Index (Book)* (1967), with its high contrast photographs of his "scene," and *POPism: The Warhol Sixties* (1980), with its reimagined autobiography and penetrating diagnosis of social mores, are highly suggestive of his attitude toward his pluriform activities. With his collaborators Bob Colacello and Pat Hackett, Warhol created new fusions of analysis, gossip, and photography. He subverted standard expectations in his own exhibitions, superimposing his *Mao* paintings on

dress, manner, and image of Warhol and his entourage appeared in aggressive opposition to mainstream culture of the Pop era, consumer industries have learned to absorb oppositional subcultures since the late seventies (that is, after punk). No longer do leather jackets and wraparound shades signify a biker aesthetic; drag poses, styles, and stars have emerged from cult circles; punk fashions and street styles may now be seen in suburban shopping malls. Whereas the uptown and downtown cultures of the fifties remained completely distinct from each other, now the boundaries between them are invisible. Warhol's own career is symptomatic of these radical changes, but he also helped bring them about.

decorative wallpaper in 1974, hanging portraits salon-style on glossy brown walls in 1979, and, most important, foregrounding, as if in a department store, whole cabinets of shoes, umbrellas, and historical wallpaper samples from a museum's collection in his 1969 *Raid the Icebox I.* Warhol's apparently uncritical excess was shocking at the time; subsequently, his unexpected and subversive approach to his task on that occasion has had exceptional influence on museum practice, and he continued to upset conventions in ways that have yet to be fully acknowledged.

Glamour, style, and *fashion* are loaded words. In the vernacular, they have both positive and derogatory connotations, and yet in the contemporary art world, they have been — until recently — almost exclusively terms of opprobrium. An artist like Warhol whose focus was the passing scene, and who passionately courted novelty, fascinated both by the whims of the beau monde and of the flamboyant subcultures of the city, consciously risked the denial and disdain of the "serious" art world. As his *Diaries* testify passim, Andy Warhol loved to play with his roles both within and outside this elite.

The influence of the fashion world, the glamour of Hollywood movie stars, and contemporary notions of style informed Warhol's work as a serious and significant artist, and, in turn, his work has affected style and fashion. As an artist and cultural phenomenon, he has shaped the taste of two generations. Warhol maintained these interests throughout his career, long after it was thought that he had left behind the world of commercial illustration for fine art and other arenas. Only now, by looking at the whole range

Paulette Goddard brand shoes and Clark Gable's shoes, from Warhol's collection

of Warhol's work, are we beginning to see that his fascination with glamour, style, and fashion was not a distraction from his "real" work, or a debasement of the rarefied, pure world of contemporary art, but an integral part of his multivalent life and work and a complex and productive response to the tensions between art, popular culture, and daily life.

Evening gown worn by Jean Harlow, from Warhol's collection

PHOTOPLAY

DECEMBER

INSIDE MOVIE
APRIL 1963   25¢   pdc

DEBBIE REYNOLDS

...re was a girl
..., whose eyes al-
... life was a pretty
...k: the unborn child
...th it died the little
...bbie . . . Today,
...aunted, she sits
...king back
... days

How
M...

SPECIAL ISSUE ON HOLLYWOOD WOMEN

SCREEN STARS
IND.

25¢ 30¢ IN CANADA

JUNE

HER
SECRET
PLANS
WITH
BURTON,
...EALED!

HER
EXPERIENCES
AT
HOLLYWOOD
PARTIES

WHY
WARREN
HAS TO
CHEAT
ON HER!

THE REAL
STORY
BEHIND
...ER

LANDON'S STRANGE LOVE BARGAIN

MOVIE
MAY

WHAT COLLEGE
BOYS DID TO

Hollywood Glamour

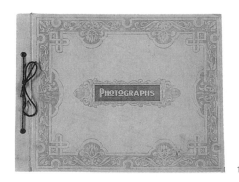

1–5. Warhol's childhood movie star photograph album, c. 1940–42

6. Autographed publicity photograph of Mae West, inscribed to "Andrew Warhola," c. 1940

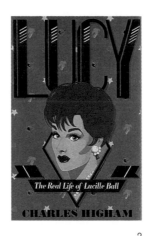

1–7. Magazines and movie posters from Warhol's collection,
1930s–1960s

1

2

3

4

5

6

7

He had one motivating idea. Absolutely central.... He was interested in the idea of glamour. Glamour fascinated him.

Robert Pincus-Witten, interview in Patrick Smith, *Andy Warhol's Art and Films*, 1981, p. 458

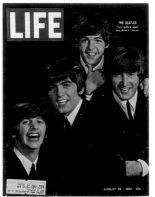

1–6. Magazines and movie posters from Warhol's collection, 1930s–1960s

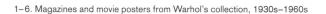

From his early childhood, growing up in Pittsburgh during the Depression, Andy Warhol was mesmerized by the glamour of Hollywood. In his youth, he collected signed photographs of stars like Shirley Temple and Mae West, whose movies he saw at the local cinemas. His fascination never faded; he remained entranced by the aura of fame, beauty, desire, wealth, and scandal that surrounds celebrities. This ideal of Hollywood glamour would in some way inform almost everything the artist did.

By the 1960s Warhol had collected large groups of press and publicity photographs of stars such as Marilyn Monroe, Elizabeth Taylor, Greta Garbo, Kim Novak, and Brigitte

1–6. Magazines and movie posters from Warhol's collection, 1930s–1960s

Bardot, and had hoarded piles of fan magazines and tabloid newspapers. (Also present in the Warhol archives are choice pieces of memorabilia, including a dress worn by Jean Harlow and shoes worn by Clark Gable). From these he culled the images that would become the sources for his paintings of Marilyn, Liz, Elvis Presley, and others. Warhol acutely chose the most iconic images of the stars who shone the brightest, but who also had a dark side. The artist's paintings have helped to lodge the images of these stars indelibly in the public consciousness.

Warhol, like so many, was captivated by the glamourous images brilliantly realized

1–5. Magazines and movie posters from Warhol's collection, 1950s–1960s

by Hollywood in the 1930s, 1940s, and 1950s. Though these images, by their very nature, were flickering and unattainable, the artist grasped them in his star portraits of the 1960s, masterfully combining iconic imagery with a complex response to the nature of stardom and beauty. In 1991 Warhol's portraits of Marilyn Monroe and Elizabeth Taylor inspired the designer Gianni Versace to give Hollywood glamour physical form in his lavish "Marilyn" and "Liz" clothing. Through his star portraits, Warhol synthesized our culture's desire for this glamourous ideal, and his images have an enduring potency. – MF/MK

1

2

3

4

1. Magazine advertisement, source image for *Hedy Lamarr*
2. Andy Warhol, *Hedy Lamarr*, 1962
3. Magazine advertisement, source image for *Joan Crawford*
4. Andy Warhol, *Joan Crawford*, 1962

When a person is the beauty of their day, and their looks are really in style, and then times change and tastes change, and ten years go by, if they keep exactly their same look and don't change anything and take care of themselves, they'll still be a beauty.

Andy Warhol, *The Philosophy of Andy Warhol*, 1975, p. 62

1

2

3

4

5

6

7

8

9

10

11

12

1

2

3

4

5

6

7

8

9

10

11

12

1

2

3

4

5

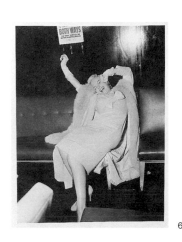

6

7

8

9

10

11

12

 1

 2

 3

 4

 5

 6

 7

 8

 9

 10

 11

 12

1

2

3

4

5

6

7

8

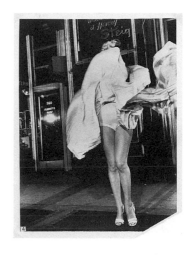

9

10

11

12

1

4

2

3

5

6

7

8

9

10

11

12

1

2

3

4

5

6

7

8

9

10

11

12

1

2

3

4

5

6

7

8

9

10

11

12

1–12. Photographs of Marilyn Monroe from Warhol's collection, 1950s

Andy Warhol, *Marilyn Monroe (Twenty Times)*, 1962

Andy Warhol, *Twenty-Five Colored Marilyns*, 1962

Naomi Campbell wearing Gianni Versace's "Marilyn" dress,
by Ola Sirant for *Fashion File*, Spring/Summer 1991 Collection

1

2

3

4

5

6

7

8

9

10

11

12

1–12. Photographs of Elizabeth Taylor from Warhol's collection, 1930s–1950s

Andy Warhol, *Liz*, 1965

David Bailey: Why do you think Andy likes all those old Hollywood stars? Mrs. Warhola: Nostalgic. He loves it. That's when he was young, he grew up with that, he loves that. That's very good. I like it too. I like er, old er, er movies and old er, I like very much old books and old er things, and old er lace, and er old clothes you get in junk shops and they become very elegant, and so he likes that the same way he likes old furs and he buys that and sets them and finally they are so very much better made. Today everything is badly made and these beautiful things he loves, like the old movies, they were better made. Maybe, maybe I don't know much about movies, but I am so scared of this television, it makes me very nervous, I can't even talk but, huh, I'm scared to death, I'm scared to death about it but um, that was better, you know, was easier, better times. Maybe not. I don't know.

Transcript of David Bailey's ATV documentary Andy Warhol (1973), p.40

1

2

3

4

5

6

7

8

9

10

11

12

1–12. Photographs of Elizabeth Taylor from Warhol's collection, 1950s

Andy Warhol, *Liz*, 1965

Gianni Versace's "Liz" jacket

1

2

3

4

5

6

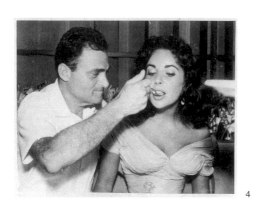

7

8

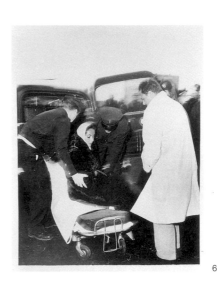

9

10

11

12

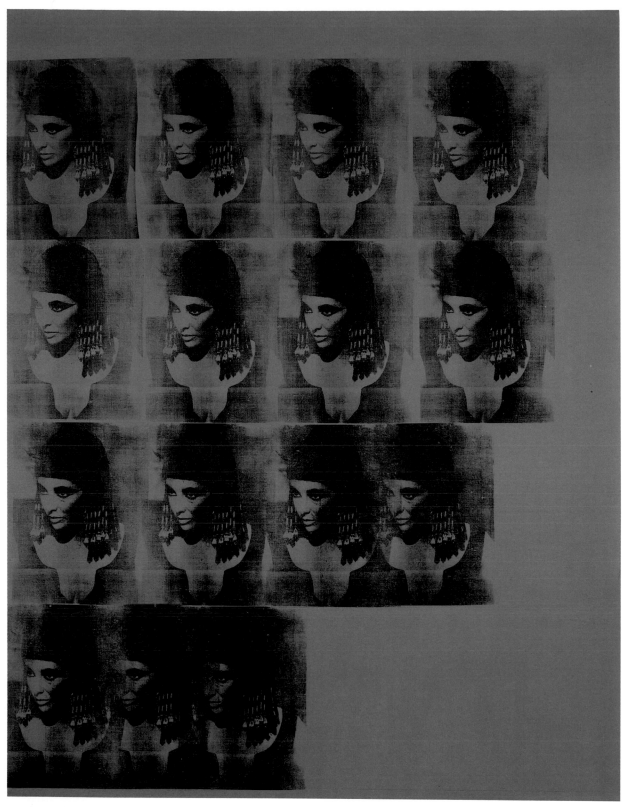

Andy Warhol, *Blue Liz as Cleopatra*, 1963

Source images for Warhol's *National Velvet*
and *Liz as Cleopatra* from *Life*, c. 1963

15 Minutes, But Who's Counting?

Andy Warhol and His Icons

Barry Paris

IN THE GOSPEL ACCORDING TO WARHOL, we live in two places at once: our real geographical spot and our "dream America, custom made from art and schmaltz," full of the glamorous icons of our own creation. When Andy was a kid named Warhola, the dream place was everywhere, but the real place was Pittsburgh, which he never loved. His ghost is surely smirking at the glitz surrounding his monument there — one of the few single-artist museums in America. He would have made fun of its grandeur, even as his ego would have adored it.

Warhol's beloved mama, Julia, hailed from the same Carpathian Mountain region that produced his father, Andrej Warhola, who in 1913 immigrated to Pennsylvania, where he worked as a coal miner. Andy, third of three sons, was born on August 6, 1928. To help support the family, Julia made paper flowers, "planted" them in tin cans, and sold them door-to-door. It was Andy's first exposure to both the manufacture and the marketing of art.

His lifelong obsession with celebrities first manifested itself at six, when he began to collect movie-star pictures — his favorites being such contemporary child actors as Shirley Temple, Mickey Rooney, Freddie Bartholomew, and Judy Garland, whom the starstruck boy worshiped weekly at the Leona Theater in Homestead. Spacey yet precocious, Andy skipped not one but two grades at Holmes Elementary School.

In 1945, at seventeen, he enrolled in the College of Fine Arts of Carnegie Institute of Technology, majoring in pictorial design. A harbinger of his talent for provocation was his senior-year painting, *The Broad Gave Me My Face, but I Can Pick My Own Nose*, which the jurors of the Associated Artists of Pittsburgh's annual exhibition declined to accept. Within a week of his graduation in June 1949, he left (with classmate Philip Pearlstein) for Manhattan and immediately found work as a commercial artist. It took a decade to develop the recipe for his Campbell's soup cans (and clean up, in more ways than one, with his Brillo boxes). They were *objets*, all right, but were they *d'art*?

They were both. He got himself a silver hairpiece and a nose job and, by 1962, his deadpan face was familiar worldwide. Andy Warhol was famous. Everybody would be, he said, for at least fifteen minutes.

The high priest of Pop art was the kinky altar boy of movies. His early pseudo-documentaries were virtually unwatchable. The later camp-sick renderings of *Frankenstein* and *Dracula* were Grand Guignol nightmares demanding an abnormally high degree of tolerance and sadomasochism.

Warhol had an abundance of both. He began filmmaking in 1963, not coincidentally the year Kennedy and the American dream were murdered. Hitherto, Warhol's *objets*

 1

 2

 3

 4

 5

 6

 7

 8

 9

 10

 11

 12

had been rather upbeat and chiefly humorous — Campbell's soup cans, Brillo pads, screen stars. Celluloid, as opposed to silkscreen, offered a greater range of perversity and psychosis.

Warhol's first films were more fun to talk about than to actually sit through: exercises in camera passivity bordering on the comatose. The greatest of them was *Sleep* — six hours of the poet John Giorno lying in bed in the act, or nonact, of sleeping. The drying of paint was spellbinding by comparison.

"I like boring things," said Warhol at the time.

The sequels to *Sleep* were equally spellbinding — *Eat* and *Haircut*, for example. My personal favorite is *Empire* — eight hours (8:00 P.M. until dawn) of the Empire State Building, which was not in an especially frisky mood when it was filmed.

"It looks very phallic," said Andy.

Warhol at a press conference read quotable raves about the building itself: "From Empire State you can see 50 miles" — *Allentown Sunday Call-Chronicle*. "There's nothing like it" — Dorothy Kilgallen. "Empire State's view is breathtaking" — Britain's Queen Mother.

In 1964, Warhol announced that his next movie would be a full filming of the Old and New Testaments; the complete version of *Warhol Bible* would run thirty days. Cardinal Francis Spellman (whose nickname, for reasons we won't explore, was "Fanny") denounced Warhol that week for his degenerate "beat mentality."

Warhol Bible, sadly, was never finished — or begun.

On the other hand, *Poor Little Rich Girl* — seventy minutes in the life of Edie Sedgwick, soon to be dead of a drug overdose — was mesmerizing, and largely ignored. Sedgwick was the Warhol-created icon who perhaps came closest to Monroe's "tragic stardom," especially as filmed by him in

13 Most Beautiful Women (1964). *Chelsea Girls* (1966) — the first of his films widely distributed — and *Lonesome Cowboys* (1968) got more attention. Put-ons or serious? Warhol's movies, like his art, were both. Therein lay their charm, outrage, controversy, and success, as they advanced to a semblance of story and a stunning array of freaks, exhibitionists, transvestites, groupies, and "beautiful people": Viva, Ultra Violet, Candy Darling, and the legendary Ingrid Superstar (who was never heard from again). It was the era when you could turn your favorite noun into a surname. Such characters, on and off screen, hovered in the twilight zone between reality and fantasy.

Some of their best hovering was in *Trash* (1970), starring Holly Woodlawn and sullen, hunky Joe Dallesandro in the saga of an "average" couple, bickering and brutalizing each other as they cope with life in New York. *Trash*, compared with *Eat* and *Blow-Job*, was *Citizen Kane*. Dallesandro starred again in *Heat* (1972), the steamy tale of a gigolo and an aging star (Sylvia Miles).

Andy Warhol's Frankenstein and *Andy Warhol's Dracula* (both 1974) — the creator's name now installed in the titles — starred Dallesandro, as usual. In *Frankenstein*, sex-starved monsters are cloned from human organs, whose donors are none too willing. At one point, somebody disembowels somebody else, yanking out the intestines a yard at a time, as if reeling in a fishing line. But then intestinal fortitude is what it was all about.

But Warhol directed neither of those pictures. On June 3, 1968, the day before the assassination of Robert Kennedy, a woman named Valerie Solanas, founder and sole member of SCUM (the Society for Cutting Up Men) entered the

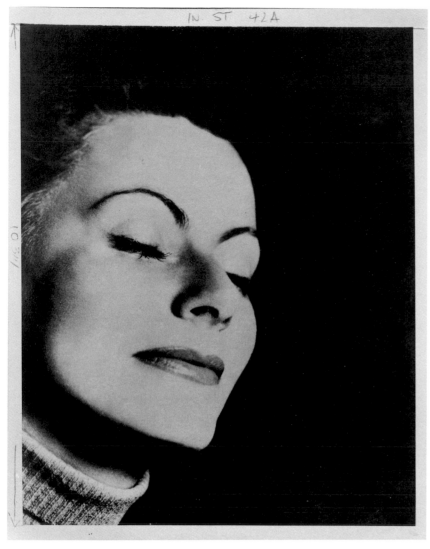

Photograph of Greta Garbo from Warhol's collection, 1920s

Factory and shot Warhol four times, nearly killing him.

After that, Warhol withdrew from active participation in his films and turned over the directing to Paul Morrissey. As the Factory had taken over his art, it took over his movies. He merely lent them his exploitable name and his weird vibes. But his enduring influence was to help legitimize nudity and explicit sex on screen, and Hollywood quickly took advantage of the groundwork he laid.

Warhol's near-assassination was the watershed event in his life. From then on, he was content to be famous just for being famous. In his last decade, he focused on alterations of such religious subjects as Raphael's Madonnas and Leonardo's *Last Supper*. He seemed to be contemplating his own impending early demise. The last of many ironies is that Valerie Solanas would become an icon, too — for nearly killing the great icon-maker himself.

The art dealer Sam Green and Andy Warhol became close and often crossed paths from the time they met in 1963. In a typical phone conversation, Green told Warhol how much

Cecil Beaton paid for the *Red Marilyn* that Andy had given him (a disappointing $400). Warhol was fascinated by Beaton and his relationship with Greta Garbo. How do we know? Because Green has this and hundreds of other conversations between himself and Warhol on tape.

The well-connected Sam served as his social hotline. "Where's the party tonight and who's gonna be there?" Warhol begins a typical conversation with Green in 1971. "I heard you were in Europe with a famous recluse [Greta Garbo]."

Green: Who told you?

Warhol: I think I read it in the papers.

Green: No you didn't!

Warhol: Yes I did, I think it was the Suzy column…

Andy hedges, hesitant to reveal his source. Green tells of "going from Paulette Goddard, with all her dresses and matching jewels and the Jaguar and the chauffeur, to meeting Garbo in her ski jacket."

Warhol: Who's Garbo making it with?

Green: I beg your pardon!

Warhol: Are you gonna marry her soon, or any other dowager?

Elizabeth Taylor has been famous for at least fifty years, for her movies, her traumatic marriages, her disastrous health, her weight problems, the ultrapublicized Hollywood Babylon scandals. Warhol was obsessed with every aspect of her melodramatic life. So are we all — still.

During a stand-up comedy performance in Pittsburgh a few years ago, Joan Rivers said, "That Liz Taylor — she puts mayonnaise on an *aspirin!*" So mean, but so funny!

Photograph of Elizabeth Taylor and Mike Todd from an unidentified magazine, c. 1957

When I asked Rivers about it after the show, she said, "Sweetheart, if I joked about how fat my *cleaning lady* is — *that* would be mean. But *Liz*? She's an *icon*, for God's sake. Dahling, can we talk? These icons set themselves up for it, and believe me, they can handle it."

The theory and practice of adorning film goddesses with fabulous jewels is moribund in the nineties — an era in which stardom rarely even lives out its Warholian fifteen minutes. Could Kim Basinger wear the Hope Diamond, and would you bother to look if she did? Show me a legendary gem such as the Peregrina pearl, and I'll show you the last great star who could put it on and pull it off: Elizabeth Taylor.

Elizabeth Taylor wore La Peregrina ("The Wanderer" — pear shaped, perfectly colored, and huge — as Desirée in *A Little Night Music* (1978), the Hal Prince film of the Sondheim musical. She wears some simple pearl strands in the early scenes, saving her pièce de résistance for the climactic confrontation of the lovers and her torchy rendition of "Send in the Clowns." When La Peregrina finally appears, it rests — no, positively *nestles* — in her cleavage, as if born (and certainly cultured) there.

Taylor links the pre- and post-studio systems — the last

great star and great icon of both — and her fabulous jewel collection reflects that. It was built with the help of husbands Nick Hilton, Michael Wilding, Eddie Fisher, and Mike Todd. But it was most augmented by Richard Burton, whose lavish gifts reflected his own sense of wit and romance. Liz wore "the Taylor-Burton Diamond" to Princess Grace's fortieth birthday party in Monte Carlo, accompanied by two detectives with machine guns — as stipulated in her Lloyd's of London insurance contract. Wretched excess, of course. But Taylor's gem transactions are now made through auctions that benefit the American Foundation for AIDS Research, of which she is founding chairman.

The jewels by themselves signify nothing. It is whom — which icons — they adorn. In Hitchcock's *Stage Fright*, Marlene Dietrich tries to blackmail Jane Wyman with her Cartier gems and then later explains to Scotland Yard, taking out a smoke from a gold cigarette case, "I'm what you call an accessory, I suppose."

In the pantheon of bejeweled actresses, the most divine is Marilyn Monroe in *Gentlemen Prefer Blondes* (1953). One of the greatest screen gems of all time is the number in which she sings, "A kiss on the hand may be quite Continental, but diamonds are a girl's best friend." Monroe does not, in fact, wear diamonds in the film. (Many other actresses, however, demanded real jewelry for their film appearances; Garbo, for one, insisted her performance would suffer if she had to wear fake jewels.)

Some Like It Hot was peak Marilyn Monroe. In 1958 she was in a state of depression following a miscarriage. Her husband, the playwright Arthur Miller, felt it would raise her

New York Mirror, August 7, 1962

spirits to make another Billy Wilder comedy after the success of *The Seven Year Itch* two years earlier. Marilyn was out of sorts throughout the whole production. Co-star Tony Curtis recalls that after each scene she called out, "Coffee!" — and was brought a thermos containing straight vermouth.

She was Sugar Kane, formerly Sugar Kowalczyk, and an ironic wah-wah trumpet played every time her derriere appeared. She and her dresses were riveting — most notably the "topless" gown she wears during "I Wanna Be Loved By You." *Some Like It Hot* made film history, as did Tony Curtis's reply when asked how it felt to make love to Marilyn Monroe: "It was like kissing Hitler."

"I never met anyone as utterly mean as Marilyn Monroe," said Billy Wilder. "Nor as utterly fabulous on the screen, and that includes Garbo…. Tony and Jack suffered because she was never on time. A scene where she had one line and they had all the rest of the dialogue, we'd have to do it eighty times because she forgot her one line. She paid absolutely no attention to anybody. She never thought, 'We're doing eighty takes and those guys are standing there. They're cramping, they're not going to get any better — in fact, it may curdle

on us.' That's what he meant when he said it was like kissing Hitler."

"Tony had his hands full with Marilyn," said Jack Lemmon. "She was ill at the time, but we didn't know that until later. All we knew then was that she was driving everybody nuts. You might do forty takes with Marilyn, or you might do one, and Billy's gonna print the one that's best for her. Billy was driven to distraction by it and said, 'I will never ever work with her again as long as I live.' "

"There's been a lot of bullshit written about that Hitler remark," noted Tony Curtis. "It was just a throwaway line. Somebody asked me what it was like making love to Marilyn, and I said, 'What do you want me to say? It was like kissing Hitler.' We would do thirty to forty takes. I'd say, 'Billy, how many fuckin' takes are we gonna do?' Billy would say, 'When Marilyn gets it right, that's the take I'm going to use.' The odd thing was, it could take her fifty takes to get out one line, but sometimes she did a whole long scene — like the one in the train berth with Jack and all the girls piled inside — on the first take. You never knew."

Monroe made only one more film, *The Misfits* (1961). Her final attempt was *Something's Got to Give* (1962), during which she was absent twenty-one of thirty-three shooting days. She was fired and died a few days later, on August 5, 1962.

That same year, Andy Warhol made his *25 Colored Marilyns* — a sensation. No one but Marilyn herself was more responsible than Warhol for turning her into an eternal worldwide icon.

The 1950s

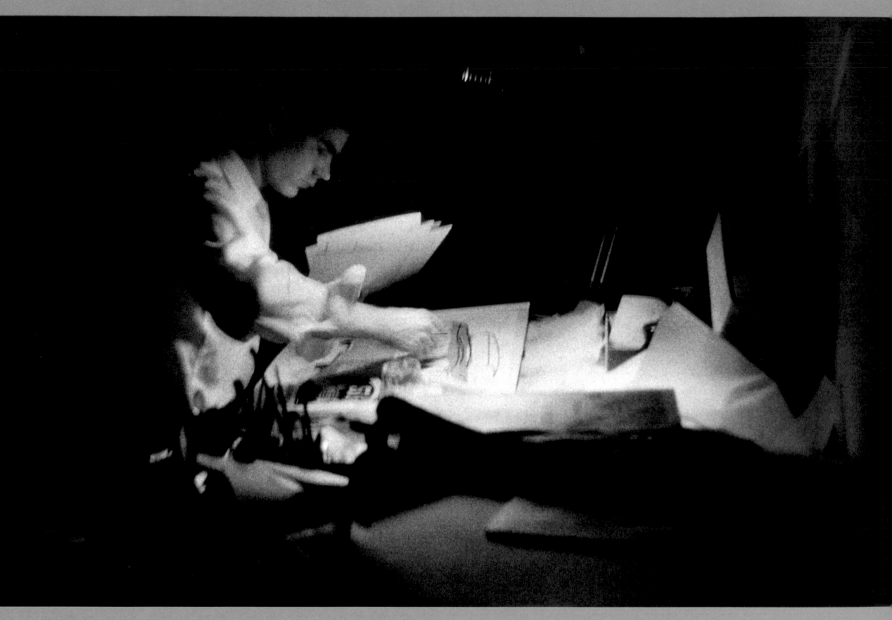

Edward Wallowitch, *Warhol working at his desk*, c. 1957

In 1949, immediately after graduating from the Carnegie Institute of Technology (now Carnegie Mellon University) in Pittsburgh, Andy Warhol moved to New York City and began working as a commercial illustrator. He quickly achieved success, with much of his work focusing on fashion illustration. His stylish drawings, which were witty, whimsical, and could even be conservative, found a market in magazines and newspapers. Clients included I. Miller shoes, for whom he created a famous series of ads that appeared weekly in the society and fashion pages of *The New York Times*. A wide range of other fashion commissions included drawings paired with Richard Avedon's fashion photos in a *Mademoiselle* magazine feature, "The Glass Slipper," and illustrations for the exotic leather company Fleming Joffe.

Warhol found himself as an artist and an individual in New York. He moved in an apparently carefree, successful gay milieu with other young illustrators, artists, photographers, and performers. He and his friends frequented the ballet, the opera, and the rococo Serendipity café, whose owner, Stephen Bruce, collaborated with Warhol on silk dresses with printed designs by the artist. Warhol created the first of

1. Warhol working at his desk, c. 1957
2. Leila Davies Singeles, *Warhol with 103rd Street Gang*, New York, 1950
3. Otto Fenn, Christmas card with backdrop by Warhol, c. 1952–54

a number of distinctive personal styles in the 1950s, a "How to Succeed in Business" look, with a touch of the gay dandy. Photographs often show him, with illustrator's portfolio in hand, in neat suits or jackets and khakis, button-down shirts, and ties or bowties. The three-button camel-colored suit he had made for himself in Hong Kong while on an extended trip to the Far East in 1956 may be the neatest expression of his new personal style.

Warhol's style of this period is recalled in the "Andy Warhol wore khakis" advertisement from a recent ad campaign for the Gap clothing stores. The artist's illustration style of the 1950s, along with his light-hearted wit, and occasionally his "blotted-line" drawing technique, seem to have returned to vogue today with the resurgence of hand-drawn fashion illustration in advertisements for Barneys New York, Neiman Marcus, and others. Warhol's experience within the nascent postwar fashion industry in New York formed the basis of his understanding of the interrelationships among illustration, photography, magazines and newspapers, advertising, publicity, and popular taste. Eventually, he moved beyond this arena's limited horizons, drawn by the power of art, movies, and pop music.

1. Leila Davies Singeles, *Warhol and others outside the Metropolitan Museum of Art*, New York, 1953
2. Edward Wallowitch, *Andy Warhol*, 1957

It must have been in the spring of 1949 when, as a budding high school artist and social climber in Pittsburgh, I began to crash exhibition openings at Carnegie Museum of Art. Interested fully as much in who was there and what they were wearing (like the society lady who affected a crystal cane) as in what was hanging on the walls, I was struck by the sight one evening of a rather androgynous, animated young man wearing a pink corduroy suit. My informants told me it was Andy Warhol, who had recently achieved notoriety with his painting titled I Can't Choose My Relatives, But I Can Pick My Nose. While I had just graduated to my first seersucker jacket, summer-weight gray flannels, and white bucks, I instantly realized how hopelessly bourgeois my ensemble appeared in contrast to Andy's unique, challenging, and truly beautiful outfit. A lady's remark that his heels were run down in no way affected my awe. Naturally, I did not introduce myself, but added the apparition of Andy to my stock of significant sightings.

Edgar Munhall, Curator, The Frick Collection, New York

1. Warhola family snapshot of Andy Warhol, Eugenia King, and Julia Warhola, c. 1954
2. Gap advertisement, 1994
3. Leila Davies Singeles, *Jones St. Sunday*, Warhol standing outside a window display in New York, 1952

Andy Warhol wore khakis.

GAP
KHAKIS

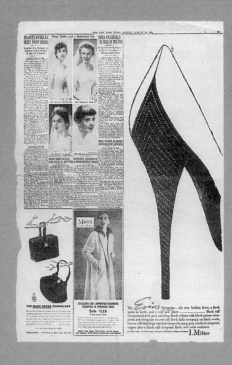

Illuminations

Warhol in the 1950s

Richard Martin

BY 1949, WHEN ANDY WARHOL ARRIVED IN NEW YORK, the age of fashion illustration was over. Erwin Blumenfeld, Richard Avedon, and Irving Penn had their cameras clicking, and a new, arguably more authentic and arguably more intense, fashion imagery was dominant. A Blumenfeld face — even if abstracted to the elements and plane of an illustrator's abbreviation — on the cover of *Vogue*'s epochal January 1950 "Mid-Century" issue, and the Irving Penn covers that followed, plainly signaled that the era of the illustrators had ended. Even *Glamour,* the Condé Nast publication "for the girl with a job," in the parataxis of its cover, was primarily a magazine of the photograph, even when Warhol published his first work there in September 1949. On commission from its art editor, Tina S. Fredericks, Warhol contributed illustrations that are anomalous in an issue dominated by vivid color and black-and-white photographs. An eight-page insert, not on the smooth stock of the magazine but on a book paper, is dedicated to "What Is Success?" as analyzed and characterized by several writers. "Success," avowed Katherine Sonntag, "is a job in New York," whereas Marya Mannes argued that "success is the men who love you." In many ways, Warhol chose the former.

Ironically, many who have documented this first publication have noted the autobiographical forecast of "Success is a job in New York" without acknowledging the other option. Moreover, the diminutive figures on the ladders of success with which Warhol illustrated the article are little different from such juvenilia as his nose-picking portrait, even if outfitted with such swank accessories as a cigarette holder, seldom evidence of real style but only of haughty pseudo-style. In fact, Warhol's success in delineating and adumbrating fifties style was owed to his lack of sophistication, his rube-like willingness to accept the quasi-elegant as if it were the real thing. In this, Hollywood met the Hudson: Warhol was a blissful follower and fabricator of the pseudo-elegant, an artist who could cover a fashion visage with jejune flowers and call it art, think it divine, and let us imagine whatever we might. Like Fran Dodsworth, the fame-seeking, frivolous wife in Sinclair Lewis's novel *Dodsworth,* Warhol was infatuated with style — fashion's or Hollywood's or camp's — however false that style might have been, and was even encouraged if the style seized on was a sham.

But Warhol's launch in New York, however astonishingly successful — for a significant career as a commercial artist followed — was a venture in anomaly and reaction to mainstream fashion sensibilities, much as his art would later defy long-held contentions of modernism. The diffident but defiant artist of the sixties had long been foreshadowed by

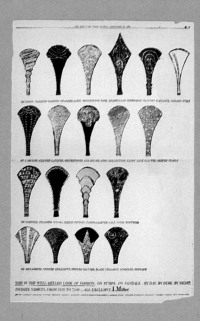

the illustrator of the fifties, who was promoting extravagance and precious sensibility in an era of fleeting, hard-glam modern fashion imagery. The *nostalgie de la soupe* of the later art is wholly anticipated in Warhol's pining memories of fashion illustration.

The first illustration of the *Glamour* insert, five shoes situated on rungs of ladders begins the ladder-of-success motif. Shoes had remained a specialty of the illustrator in many fashion magazines of the era since they were accessories and their analytical representation could assume the illustrator's license of scale even if juxtaposed with photographs whose scale is presumably authentic. Warhol's rust-colored images of pumps, here quite pedestrian, would later prance into fantasy. Through all the insert's illustrations, sweet sentiment prevails: Warhol coils the long cord of one of his recurrent telephones, affords a home-and-office image of typewriter in one hand and mop in another, and represents love proffered in a bouquet and manifest in drifting heart shapes. With the exception of the initial page devoted to the pumps, the illustrations appear chiefly at the margins, in the manner of medieval manuscript illuminations, as petty, if pretty, pictures.

The great tradition that Warhol knew and was, in a sense, condensing in the fifties was that of Erté and Vertès, earlier fashion artists whose sinuous lines and blots of color were not restricted to marginalia but commanded pages. Warhol's fashion ambition was akin to theirs. He did not aspire to make the diagrammatic little fashion drawings that accompanied patterns or co-ed and teen fashions; nor did he wish to be confined in the remaining sanctuaries of illustration in beauty and lingerie advertising and editorials — the photograph's absolutism being yet taboo in these intimate and idealized areas. Moreover, Warhol's great gift as a commercial artist was for inventory and evocation, not for direct representation of the product. Thus, in *Great Perfumes of France* (1959) for *Harper's Bazaar*, he uses the format of the flacon ten times, a model for his later repetitions without depletion of interest. Warhol sets each fragrance bottle up in taxonomy, as if counting off identical items in the manner of counting bottles, but also provides each its own interest, the actual shapes of the bottle being the visual distinction amid similarity. Illustration, in this waning moment, was being retained in the margins, literally and figuratively, for its facility in rendering easy-to-recognize details and accessories. Yet Warhol was ultimately not merely the delineator but the dreamer, the indefatigable, often reactionary optimist of fashion and glamour, however decadent, transparent, or passé.

His gloss of fantasy is most evident in a series of illustrations seen in Roger Rabbit tandem with Richard Avedon photographs in *Mademoiselle* (April 1955). The gamine Leslie Caron, on a movie poster, is transformed into the dreamer — with appropriate stars — of a Cinderella story. Inert fashion photographs said to be "inspired by M.G.M.'s *The Glass*

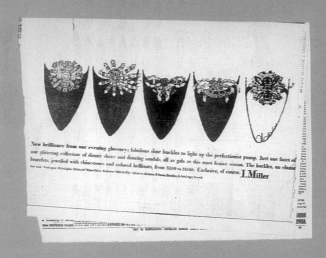

Slipper," are plied into the narrative of *Cinderella* by Warhol's deft drawings. The impression of naiveté he often created is particularly effective in this suite of advertisements, linking otherwise unconnected, inchoate styles by the slender thread of a movie. Perhaps most beguiling is Warhol's use of text in the final image of the series, where it is played around descriptions of the dresses and garments on page 46. Here Warhol assumes the style of the artist-tyke: aptly illustrating a child's tale and narrating it with puerile script, including the handwritten footnote "also available in misses sizes," added in direct juxtaposition with the printed text. Warhol marshals his images, adding stars at the beginning and end, to convey enchantment to garments probably assembled under sweatshop conditions. Without Warhol's effort to amuse and entertain, the tie-in of apparel and movie would be, at best, tendentious. Warhol imparts his mischief and magic as an illustrator to pre-existing images; he succeeds by dint of his indomitable faith in innocent illustration and in its ability to evoke a response from us, even as applied to a $70 ball gown.

Warhol's fashion vision is glamorizing and transformative, destined to take the "pretty maiden" in an "under $20" junior dress into an empyrean of fancy and imagination. What Warhol gives, he also takes. That is, he also seized from fashion its wonder of artifice and imagination. Later, the inspired *Vogue* editor Diana Vreeland would dub the category "allure," and Warhol himself would seek out Victor Hugo, Halston,

Yves Saint-Laurent, Tina Chow, and Giorgio di Sant' Angelo for that aura of fashion essence in relation to which he had become both vampire and blood bank.

Warhol's role in fashion was, after all, his favored role in life: *flâneur* and observer, not maker. For other commissions in the fifties, Warhol used the narrative terseness and suggestion found in his fashion work. But distinctive to fashion was his vision of vignettes and taxonomies built on the principles of observation and visual delight. Much later, his *Who's Who in Holiday Hats* for *McCall's* demonstrated his ability to construct character out of fashion objects. Each hat becomes a distinct individual or type, Mary Poppins unmistakable for d'Artagnan, the chef's toque distinct from the tin soldier's braided cap. Characteristically, Warhol mingles memory and the contemporary: the sweet memory of hats in a millinery era that, by 1958, was beginning to cede its authority and ubiquity to new hairstyles and a casual, unaccessorized wardrobe, together with a contemporary reference to Marshal Dillon of television's "Gunsmoke" series. Multiplicity, in its repetitions and differences, is especially rewarding in its fashion view.

After all, Warhol's fifties fashion subjects were not the couture of Dior or Balenciaga, the most demanding and the most significant fashion of the period. On the contrary, Warhol loved in fashion what was better than the ordinary, not supreme fashion art. A mock-up, a flacon, a touch of glamour would do. In *The Fifties,* David Halberstam recounts

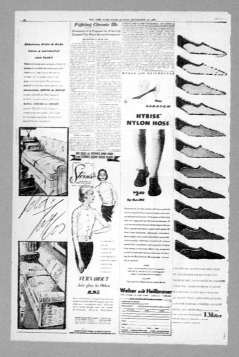

Andy Warhol, advertisements for I. Miller, 1955–59

a very telling fashion story from 1958. The First Lady, Mamie Eisenhower, was told by Mollie Parnis, one of her preferred designers in New York, that Mrs. Richard Nixon had called to inquire about having clothing made for a state trip to Latin America. Mrs. Eisenhower replied, "No, no, dear, don't do that. Let the poor thing go to Garfinkel's and buy something off the rack." Parnis created stylish, but essentially middle-class to upper-middle-class clothing. These were not, in the vernacular, "Paris originals" but homegrown American in style. But even as Mrs. Eisenhower displayed her scorn for Mrs. Nixon, she recognized the hierarchy in fashion. Even a Mollie Parnis dress was a dream to some. Today, when Giorgio Armani, Donna Karan, and Ralph Lauren are household names, it is hard to recall the out-of-reach elitism of fifties' fashion. The sensible American woman did not realistically aspire to the Evins shoes that Warhol conjured. They were icons beyond the average consumer's grasp. Warhol conspired to concoct the extravagant in fashion objects; his parvenu ignorance of good taste inspired him to a tantalizing vulgarity comprising both exuberance and theatricality.

Essential to Warhol's style in the fifties is a now hard to recreate, even harder to remember, sense of awe and amazement about objects better than the ordinary. Thus, the "holiday hats" of *McCall's* are little more than caricatures, but they are metaphors of the magical and the charismatic, rendered schematic and simple, but still Yahweh-like approxi-

mations, substitutes for the unspeakable name of glamour and fashion.

What is *High-Heeled Shoe* (1950s) but a Platonic shoe compounded of any and all fetishes and icons of foot and shoe, configured to a starlet's dainty shoe, Mrs. Lydig's unique shoes, and Cinderella's fictitious shoe? In the fifties, when the global distribution of luxury products was still a trickle compared with the flood of luxuries in the eighties and nineties, which has resulted in a far more cavalier attitude toward previously privileged styles, Warhol could still render the shoe as archetypal luxury. In his shoe personifications, he presented not only the radiant shoe but a luminary's biography as well, making icon and celebrity coalesce. His *Eight Shoes* (1950s) is more than the view of the bottom of a closet. Significantly, they are so archetypal as not to be pairs but individual shoes. Each is willfully different, from the insistently high lace-up to the variously decorated insouciant pumps. *This Is the Well-Heeled Look of Fashion* (1955), for his client I. Miller, sets heels of Byzantine splendor and monumentality as fan shapes seen consistently from center back. This architectonic series, unusual for Warhol, is consistent with his side and interior views of shoes, in seeing them as sculpture, but here with an element of abstraction. Thus, the garment as artifact played a role for Warhol. The artist who would later codify the most ordinary objects as icons of American art had long before discovered the iconic presence of fashion objects.

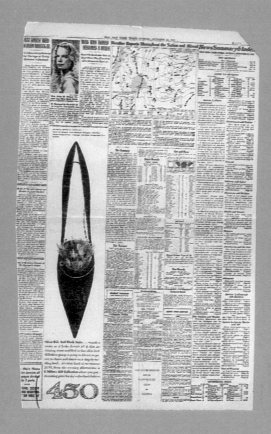

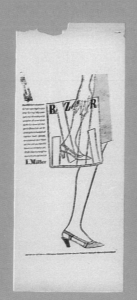

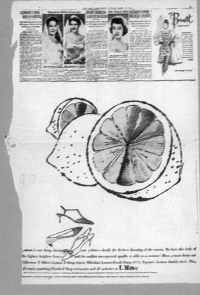

Warhol as fashion illustrator must be distinguished from others in the field. René Gruau (b. 1910), for example, a primary image-maker for Dior, allows partial representation to arise suggestively from the plane of the paper. Gruau created many familiar images indivisible from the Dior identity. For the fragrance Miss Dior, Gruau captured the ineffable, animalizing character of scent in a 1948 image of a woman's elegant hand placed languorously and seductively on a leopard's paw, a sure sign of beauty and the beast in concupiscent combination. Gruau's 1949 illustration for Miss Dior is also synecdochic: a more civilized gloved hand holding an open fan — another flirtation, but this time with mystery rather than with an identifiable animal. Gruau's sanctioned images for Miss Dior are the quintessence of fashion illustration, metaphor and message extracted from fashion, even when as intangible as a fragrance. Warhol's *Legs in Red High Heels* (1950s) perhaps comes closest to Gruau's sensibility, suggesting an ideal through a body implied by a part that is both anonymous and exemplary. Isolation of a part promotes the probity of line, allowing the drawing an enhanced aestheticism surpassing physical description.

Gruau's commercial and cordial imagery for Dior is in opposition to Warhol's tongue-in-cheek *Miss Dior* (1955), a drawing related to a Bonwit Teller window display. Here, the artist's campy, sardonic wit is his agency of abbreviation and identification, but it is clearly very far from Gruau's

ingratiating corporate image. Warhol is scarcely disarming and certainly not disingenuous, but he is profoundly different. Warhol's *Miss Dior* is not a corporate signifier but an escutcheon with interior logos and stars, *encadrement* with tape measure, a top note of fundamental Warhol shoe, and pendant mermaid-maidens. With the fleur-de-lis and French flags, Miss Dior is proclaimed. And it is no accident that after 20 inches or so, a section of the tape measure disappears from the image, only to return to the count at the very end with "68" and "69," the last surely a gibe on a sexual configuration, though both "68" and "69" must be read upside down and backward. One doubts that Gruau would have slipped into a Dior image even the smallest hint of sexuality. As the art historian Donna de Salvo has shrewdly pointed out, Warhol's *Carnet de Bal by Revillon* (1959) incorporates into the window installation an amusing reference to Matisse's *Dance*, a few blocks away in the Museum of Modern Art as well as a wish list of dance partners. The careless fifties viewer unaware of hidden persuasion in advertising might let these campy personal references pass unnoticed, yet the cognoscenti (a very fifties usage) might roar with laughter and smug approval.

Moreover, the whole Warhol image conspires to "out" Dior, as we might say in the nineties. The profile of Dior himself, rendered in a most serious Hockneyesque semi-Egyptian style, is now emblazoned Miss Dior, less the fifties fashion "dictator" than art's Rrose Sélavy. Few would have

Andy Warhol, advertisements for I. Miller, 1955–59

openly discussed Dior's effeminate homosexuality in the fifties; Warhol portrays it.

Fashion was, as many have noted, a relatively safe world for homosexual men in the fifties, even as McCarthyism and homophobia raged elsewhere and even in comparison with the world of the fine arts in New York. Warhol's own sense of security may have allowed him to "out" Christian Dior; his sense of insecurity may have made him want to claim allies, especially in a form that, overt as it is, may have been too oblique for most in the fifties. Some spectators, enthralled by the pageantry and power of Dior, could merely have seen in Warhol's deception the mind of the creator, a flattering and most Warholian combination of dress form, scissors, pins, sewing machine, and needle and thread, along with the Eiffel Tower, defining fashion as his métier and mental process. A banner made by a queen for a queen might have been little noticed as such and instead deferred to as a fashion/ fragrance likeness.

Where else in the fifties could have existed the fey, gold-leafed fetish objects Warhol made, suggestive of Cornellian keepsakes while partaking of the racket in celebrity relics? In fact, their transition in the later fifties into boy drawings demonstrates the close connection that Warhol made among his arenas of alert and blissful, eyes-closed survey: fashion, Hollywood, and homosexual imagination and desire. As the art historian Trevor Fairbrother has proved, gay visual culture

of the fifties fed into Warhol's highly successful commercial work and ultimately fed off it. These harbingers of commonplace icons are fashion souvenirs that offer value-added associations and the possibility of infinitely reflecting on the ordinary. Warhol's Midas uses in the fifties are about a luxury associated with the gold of traditional manuscript illumination, but also the luxury gold used in 1950s printing. As the design critics Ellen Lupton and Abbott Miller have rightly pointed out, Warhol the technician was keenly aware of the processes of reproduction; he is the paladin artist for the Age of Mechanical Reproduction.

The gold drawings demonstrate the style ideals of Warhol's fifties work. Warhol was indubitably familiar with Charles Demuth's *I Saw the Figure 5 in Gold* (1928) in the Metropolitan Museum of Art. While Demuth's gold is not gold leaf and is only referential, the painting's title and visual allusion to the poet William Carlos Williams are akin to Warhol's portraits through shoes. Moreover, Demuth was a gay artist whose semiexplicit and explicit images were well known in reproductions and legend in the New York gay world of the fifties; Warhol saw size 5 in gold, again and again.

A gold shoe, *David Evins* (c. 1956), celebrates the shoe's designer. The designer of expensive shoes was renowned in New York (he and his wife were significant social figures of the time), but his work would probably have been unfamiliar to anyone not acquainted with New York society or expensive

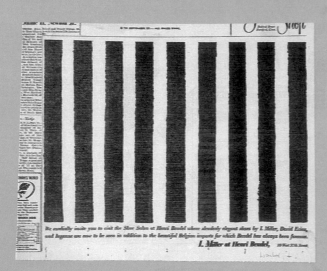

footwear. On the other hand (or leg), cognate drawings from about 1956 named after Za Za Gabor (*sic*) and Kate Smith hallow women of national recognition through television and media. His *Christine Jorgensen* (1956), depicting a pair of shoes seen from above, celebrates an early transsexual. Interestingly, Warhol's first great cultural encounters were with Hollywood and fashion; from there, and only after practice in rendering and exalting those cultures, did he attempt consumer popular culture. If Demuth had been able to express a gay man's allowable affection for a poet in *I Saw the Figure 5 in Gold*, then surely Warhol could express his admiration for a gaudy Memphis singer in *elvis Presely* (*sic*) (c. 1956).

Warhol effectively made a transition, beginning in 1955, from his commercial work for I. Miller to a personally resonant body of work, one that reflected his idiosyncratic sense of desire in objects and in fashion and media celebrities. The gold drawings of the mid-fifties move from fashion to bibelots and boys. The male *Fashion Figure* (c. 1955) is expressed in prosaic, reproduction-oriented ink and tempera, and with a commercial indifference. By 1957 gold takes the place of tempera, and Cocteauesque sensuality begins to supplant the impassivity of the earlier work. But these gold drawings in seriatim, ostensibly superficial artifacts touching on an ostensibly superficial world, are, of course, the matrix of Warhol's thinking. In the fifties, their whimsy and literary references, especially *A la Recherche du Shoe Perdu* (1955), haunted the

obvious objects, implying literary affiliations. In *To all my Friends* (c. 1956), the shoes refer not only to the illustrious but also to personal friends.

And there always was a deeper, more penetrating vision, even if that, too, was diagrammatic. One leitmotif of Warhol's work of the fifties was the X-ray-like phrenology evident in *Miss Dior*, but also seen in such works as *Female Head*. Where did Warhol get this idea of the divided and dissected brain? Advertising and the modest graphics of movie magazines (*Photoplay* and the other forties' and fifties' 'zines that Warhol adored and collected) often represented the mind in such a pattern of "ideas" visible within the head. Likewise, an untitled (1950s) all-Warhol exquisite corpse of a business card, sweetly combined with a corset, sets virtuoso "ideas" into a tattoo of clients and possibilities on the woman's body.

Furthermore, the discipline of commercial art fostered Warhol's ability to capture identity in adumbrated forms and linear brevity in a manner carried into his personal drawings of the fifties and thereafter into other work. His *James Dean* (c. 1955) renders the Cocteauesque diagram of the head lying as if asleep, conveying both desire for the handsome star and the fact of his death. In simple gestures, the signs of love and death are given: the overturned death car smashed into a wall (anticipating the *Disasters*); a memorializing tree sprouting heart-shaped leaves; and the line of Dean's sternum into neck referring both to anatomy and a cross. The fashion work of

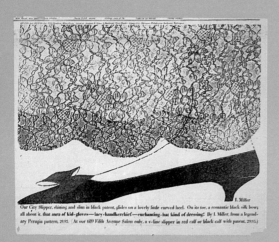

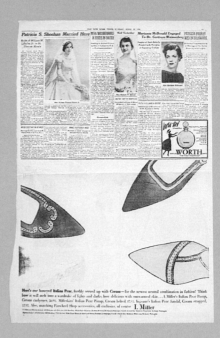

Andy Warhol, advertisements for I. Miller, 1955–59

the fifties had valued the truistic: hearts, stars, and flowers
that conveyed emotion. Thus, in *Madame Rubinstein* (1957),
a pen-and-ink portrait is given grace and sentiment by the
flower that serves doubly to suggest a feminine favor and the
scented, elegant world of beauty and makeup.

In the sixties, Warhol was drawn to new endeavors. Art
history, history, and our fascination have already guaranteed
that the new vocation was a success and more than just a
job. Nonetheless, fashion and his commercial roots in the
fifties would inhabit the Warhol enterprise for the remainder
of the artist's life. A follow-the-dot fifties advertisement,
Andrew Geller Shoe, would inspire later work. The iconic
potency of objects that Warhol discovered in fashion artifacts
would send him from specialty stores to supermarkets, from
New York culture to popular culture. The later success was
predicated on commercial imagery. Warhol's life was, as it
were, a ladder, rungs of which could all bear names from
the fifties: commercial graphics, an assimilated Hollywoodism,
fashion, beauty indeed or in sham, the beauty industry, and
a coy, safe, gay professional culture.

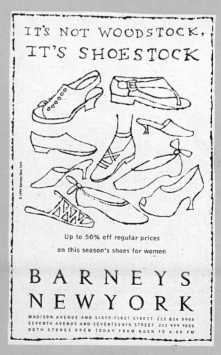

Advertisement reminiscent of Warhol's style,
The New York Times, July 10, 1994

Richard Avedon photographs, Warhol illustrations, *Mademoiselle*, April 1955

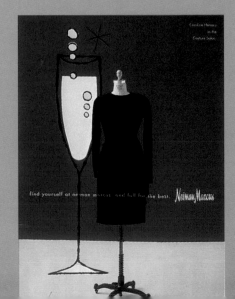

Advertisements reminiscent of Warhol's style, *W*,
left: August 1996; right: February 1996

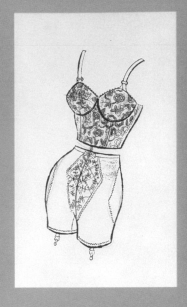

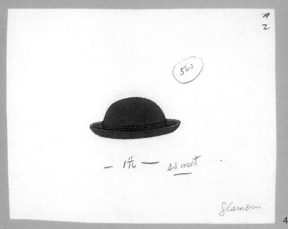

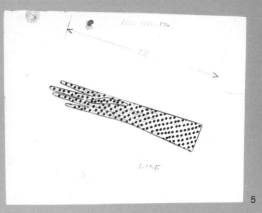

1. Andy Warhol, illustration for *Harper's Bazaar*,
   September 1955
2. Andy Warhol, *Bra and Girdle*, 1950s
3. Andy Warhol, *Purse*, 1950s
4. Andy Warhol, *Hat*, 1954
5. Andy Warhol, *Glove*, 1950s
6. Andy Warhol, *Five Shoes and Three Purses*, 1950s
Opposite: page from Warhol's portfolio, 1950s

1. Andy Warhol, *Quadrille Balenciaga*, 1950s
2. Andy Warhol, illustration for Franklin Simon shopping bag, 1950s
3. Andy Warhol, *Creme Extraordinaire*, 1950s
4. Andy Warhol, *Three Women*, 1950s
5. Andy Warhol, Hudson Hosiery print advertisement, 1950s
6. Andy Warhol, illustration for *The New York Times*, May 10, 1958
7. Andy Warhol, Hudson Hosiery promotional brochure, 1950s
Opposite: page from Warhol's portfolio, 1950s

the
first
fragrance
to bring
love to Venus will be

Bon
Voyage

Dana
PARIS — NEW YORK

1. Andy Warhol, *Shoes*, 1950s
2. Andy Warhol, *Shoe and Leg*, 1950s
3. Andy Warhol, Fleming Joffe advertisement, *Vogue*, December 1964
4. Andy Warhol, *Shoe*, 1950s
5. Andy Warhol, *Four Shoes*, 1950s
6. Andy Warhol, *Shoe*, 1950s
Opposite: page from Warhol's portfolio, 1950s

Palizzio

...CREATOR
OF THE NEW YORK LOOK

SLENDER

SPECTACULARS

*Brigadoon
and Black*

NEWS ON THREE SLIM HEEL HEIGHTS...

SKY-HIGH, MEZZANINE AND MIDWAY.

MARVELOUS TOWN FASHION SERIES,

FROM A COLLECTION STARTING AT 23.00 THE PAIR.

MATCHING PALIZZIO HANDBAG, ABOUT 25.00 PLUS TAX

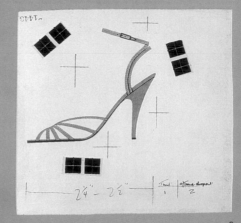

1. Andy Warhol, *All the World's a Shoe*, 1950s
2. Andy Warhol, *Shoe*, 1950s
3. Andy Warhol, *Sandal*, 1950s
4. Andy Warhol, illustration for *Harper's Bazaar*,
   July 1958
5. Andy Warhol, Enna Jetticks poster, 1950s
6. Andy Warhol, advertisement for Bonwit Teller,
   c. 1955–59
7. Andy Warhol, *Large Woman's Shoe*, 1950s
8. Andy Warhol, *Shoe*, 1950s
Opposite: page from Warhol's portfolio, 1950s

If
the
mood
is
casual...
the
casual
is
Golo!

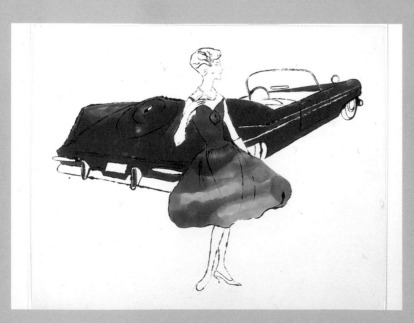

1. Andy Warhol, *Fashion Figure*, 1950s
2. Andy Warhol, *Winter Outfit*, 1950s
3. Andy Warhol, *The Exotic Calf (Fleming Joffe)*, 1950s
4. Andy Warhol, *Dress and Jacket*, 1950s
5. Andy Warhol, illustration for *The New York Times*,
   April 26, 1958
6. Andy Warhol, *Man*, 1950s
7. Andy Warhol, *Woman and Car*, 1950s
Opposite: page from Warhol's portfolio, 1950s

Treasures from India

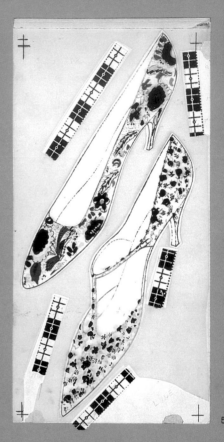

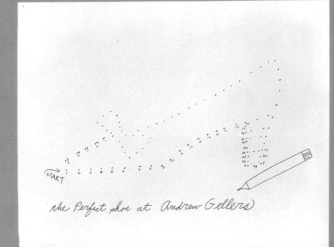

1. Andy Warhol, *Six Skirts and Two Short Pants*, 1950s
2. Andy Warhol, illustration for *Esquire*, 1950s
3. Andy Warhol, *Shoe and Angel*, 1950s
4. Andy Warhol, *Shoe*, 1950s
5. Andy Warhol, *Two Shoes*, 1950s
6. Andy Warhol, *Legs in Red High Heels*, 1950s
7. Andy Warhol, *Andrew Geller Shoe*, 1950s
Opposite: page from Warhol's portfolio, 1950s

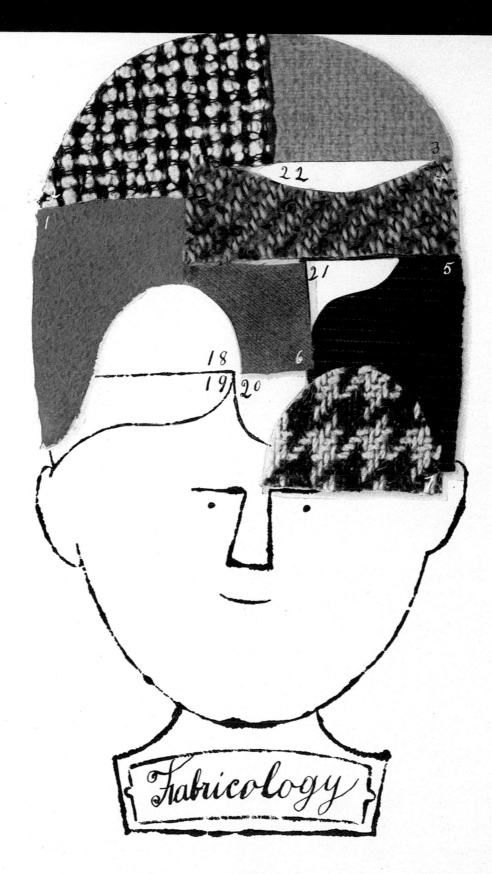

Fabricology

TEXTURE AND COLOR ARE THE KEYS TO CHIC. LOOK FOR VIVID, NEWLY SHARPENED, TWO-DIMENSIONAL TWEEDS, MANY OF WHICH SEEM HANDWOVEN; TWEEDS AND WOOLS FOAMY AND BUOYANT AS BUBBLES. EVERYTHING: LIGHT AS AIR, SPONGY, INFINITELY DRAPABLE TO CAPTURE THE LAST PRECIOUS OUNCE OF COMFORT IN THE GREAT NEW (POUFFED, ROUND, BIAS, MOBILE, RELEASED) SILHOUETTES.

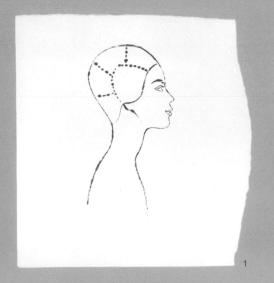

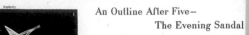

An Outline After Five—
The Evening Sandal

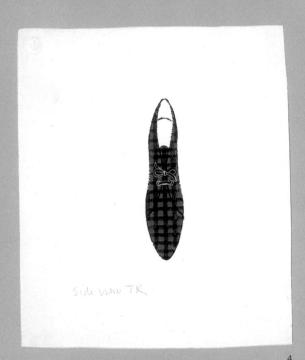

Side view TK

395

2"

INS 8 FASH.

P-80

FASH SPEC
3¼" wide

COMBINATION 70B
DROP WHITES

3¼"

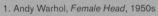

1. Andy Warhol, *Female Head*, 1950s
2. Andy Warhol, *Scarf*, 1950s
3. Andy Warhol illustration for *Harper's Bazaar*, 1950s
4. Andy Warhol, *Boot*, 1950s
5. Andy Warhol, *Boot*, 1950s
6. Andy Warhol, *Fashion Figure*, 1950s
7. Andy Warhol, *Fashion Figure*, 1950s
Opposite: page from Warhol's portfolio, 1950s

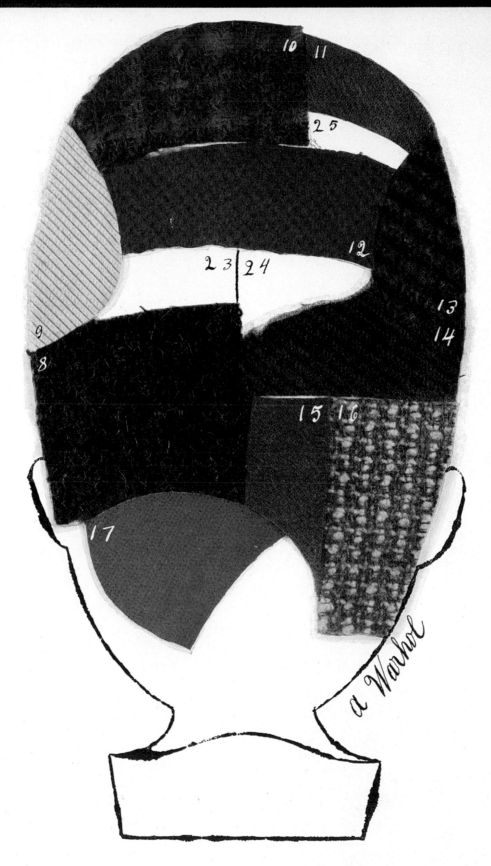

VIBRANCE IS THE CLUE TO COLOR: GREEN TWEED LIKE NEW GRASS, OPPOSITE; YELLOW LIKE PURE GOLD; KINGFISHER BLUE JERSEY, ABOVE. IN THE FRESH-AGAIN MATTER OF BLACK AND WHITE, UNBALANCE IS VITAL. NEW AS NEXT MONTH: TOASTED WARM TOBACCO COLORS; BROWN CORALS, TAWNY AS AUTUMN LEAVES. (FOR MORE INFORMATION ABOUT THESE FABRICS, SEE THE LAST PAGE OF THIS ISSUE.)

Fashion 10

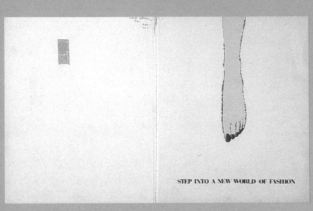

STEP INTO A NEW WORLD OF FASHION

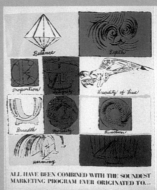

INFLUENCE YOUR CUSTOMERS BEGINNING WITH

ALL HAVE BEEN COMBINED WITH THE SOUNDEST MARKETING PROGRAM EVER ORIGINATED TO...

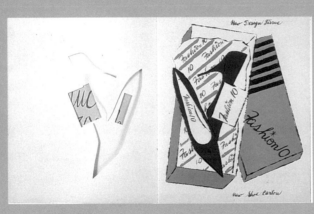

New Design Tissue

New Shoe Carton

FOR THE VERY FIRST TIME AMERICA'S LEADING FASHION HOUSES ARE RECOMMENDING A LINE OF SHOES...AND THEY ARE ALL PLANNING A... FULL MERCHANDISING PROGRAM TO INCLUDE:

FASHION 10 SHOES FEATURED IN NATIONAL ADVERTISING

HIGHLIGHTED IN MERCHANDISING PROGRAMS

INCORPORATED INTO THEIR PUBLICITY AND SALES PROGRAM

COORDINATED INTO WINDOW AND IN-STORE DISPLAY

SHOWN IN LOCAL ADVERTISING

PROMINENT SHOWROOM DISPLAY

YES...THE BIGGEST FASHION HOUSES IN THE COUNTRY WILL BE SAYING IT...AND WE'LL BE SAYING IT IN GLAMOUR, MADEMOISELLE, VOGUE, AND SEVENTEEN! AND WE'RE STARTING IT WITH

"Living Leather"

THE AMAZING NEW MIRACLE LEATHER THAT STAYS "NEW LOOKING", SOFT AND SUPPLE, 500% LONGER THAN ORDINARY LEATHER!

When She Drives

| ORDINARY LEATHER: OLD FASHIONED LEATHER STAINS, SCUFFS, BENDS, PUCKERS, PEELS, GROWS "OLD" BEFORE ITS TIME! | LIVING LEATHER STAYS "NEW-LOOKING" 500% LONGER...AND LIVING LEATHER IS NATURAL LEATHER, "IT BREATHES" |

THE MORE THAN 34,000,000 WOMEN DRIVERS WILL SEE OUR AMAZING FASHION 10 SHOES IN

MARKET III

THE MORE THAN 63,408,000 WOMEN WHO DRESS ...TO PLEASE OTHER WOMEN...TO PLEASE MEN... TO PLEASE THEMSELVES...THEIR BUY-WORD IS

Cosmetics

Foundation Garments

Ready To Wear

Why Not Shoes?

Introducing the Daringest New Way to sell Shoes

FLATTERY! THE KEY TO THE SUCCESS OF COSMETICS, FOUNDATION GARMENTS AND READY TO WEAR! SO...WHY NOT SHOES?

Flatter Her Legs

Trimmer Legs

Shapelier Calf

Slimmer Ankle

WITH THIS FABULOUS SPECIAL COLLECTION OF FASHION 10 SHOES THAT GIVE AN ILLUSION OF

TRIMMER LEG! SHAPELY CALF! SLIMMER ANKLE! THIS IS LEG FLATTERY...AS IT WILL APPEAR IN...

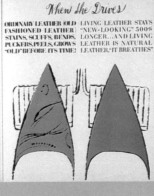

Andy Warhol, *Fashion Show Backdrop for* Glamour, 1955

Stephen Bruce, dresses with fabric designed by Andy
Warhol, early 1960s

Otto Fenn, photographs with butterfly screen projections
designed by Andy Warhol, c. 1952

97

Simon Doonan, *Andy Warhol, Compulsive Collector*, Barneys New York window display, 1989

Window Display

Andy Warhol and co-workers at Horne's department store, Pittsburgh, 1947

Store window displays transcend their practical purpose as the most immediate form of advertisement for the merchandise sold within a shop's doors. The displays arranged in shop windows are alluring tableaux meant to entice passersby. Shop windows can also very directly communicate current notions of good taste. In a fundamental sense, these displays behind glass, laid out along a store's outer walls, may be seen as a kind of museum for the street, accessible to everyone walking by.

Earlier in this century, artists like Salvador Dali and Marcel Duchamp, attracted by the display window's special allure, designed store windows. During the 1950s, a high point of visual sophistication was achieved in the conjunction of art and window display by Gene Moore, who was responsible for filling the windows of the Bonwit Teller department store and Tiffany's in New York City. Moore often hired artists to create displays, and Andy Warhol, as well as Jasper Johns and Robert Rauschenberg (under the joint pseudonym Matson Jones) and James Rosenquist all experimented with this form of commercial work early in their careers.

As an art student in Pittsburgh, Warhol had a part-time job in the display department of Horne's department store. After moving to New York, he continued his display work during the 1950s with windows that were in keeping with his popular illustration styles. In 1961, with the bravado of a young artist, Warhol created a window that set colored and patterned dresses against the ultra-contemporary backdrop of his earliest Pop paintings of advertisements and comic strips. Unlike his contemporaries, who abandoned window display after achieving recognition as fine artists, Warhol remained intrigued by this form of display. He created a window with artist Victor Hugo for the designer Halston in 1975 (in which he hawked his book *The Philosophy of Andy Warhol*), and he posed as a living mannequin in a display window for his *Invisible Sculpture* at the nightclub Area in 1985.

Throughout his career, Warhol explored the connections between art and commerce, the live body and the mannequin, the gallery, the window, and the street. This exploration continues among artists today, in window displays like Simon Doonan's for Barneys New York, in which he created a series memorializing Warhol, complete with a Warhol mannequin, and recent installations like Tilda Swinton's week-long pose in a vitrine at London's Serpentine Gallery. — MF/MK

Pat Hackett, *Andy
Warhol, Halston,
and Victor Hugo in
a Halston Window
Display Designed by
Warhol and Hugo*, 1975

Andy Warhol, Bonwit Teller window display, 1955

BONWIT'S LOVES REPLIQUE

Looking at store windows is great entertainment because you can see all of these things and be really glad it's not home filling up your closets and drawers.

Andy Warhol, *America*, 1985, p. 21

BONWITS FIRE SETS . decorated dinner tweeds and jersey tops . Sports Floor, the fifth .
Skirts by Koret

BONWIT'S LOVES POT POURRI
Lee
IMILDA
loves
SHelley Marks
Pot powne
this much
SHelley

Bonwit Teller window display with three framed drawings by Andy Warhol, c. 1955

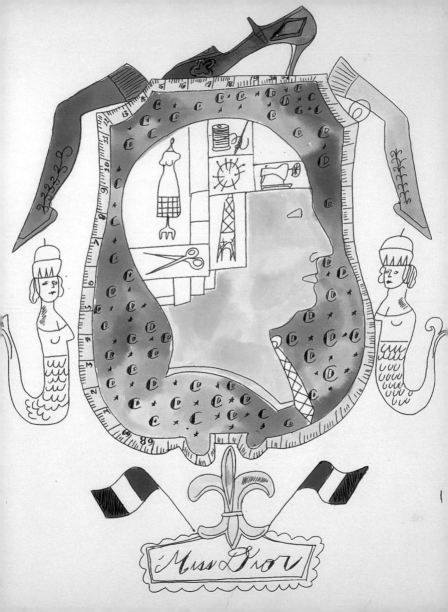

Miss Dior

Andy Warhol

esin *Larger Size*

Windows

Judith Goldman

STORE WINDOWS, AS WE KNOW THEM, did not exist until the late nineteenth century, when plate glass became available; and even then those first show windows were small and functional. They were not theatrical or decorative; they did not seduce, entice, or entertain. Their purpose was to bring light into dark, narrow shops. They also showed off merchandise, which usually sat toward the back of a window (so as not to block the light), but windows quickly became sales tools and merchandise moved up front, next to the glass, making it seem touchable, like items at an outdoor bazaar.

In the late nineteenth and early twentieth centuries, as small shops gave way to department stores, and merchandise emporiums grew larger, their windows became increasingly important. Windows glamorized merchandise, presenting the items for sale in dramatic and artistic displays. Windows were meant to stop traffic, to captivate. They were invitations to enter and shop. Windows were calling cards. They were the face a store turned to the world. They revealed style and character; they whetted appetites, created desire and need. Every aspect of a window — from its aura to the attitude conveyed by a mannequin's slouch — defined a store's image. Windows established identity: they promised quality, value, and class.

By the 1920s, store windows had become tabloids of their times, reflecting everything around them: world fairs, art expositions, and current events. Soon after Charles Lindbergh's first solo flight across the Atlantic, a lifesize dummy of him, standing above the Manhattan skyline, appeared in the window of a Paris department store. At the Galeries Lafayette, windows featuring geometric shapes made of origami paper reflected the effects of Cubism. The influence of the 1925 Exposition des Arts Décoratifs, which emphasized the modern, the mass-produced, and the new, was evident in the sophisticated graphics and rounded curves that soon pervaded urban landscapes. In Paris and New York, large, elongated sans serif letters appeared on neon signs and bold

Gene Moore, Tiffany window displays, 1956

posters. Dramatic geometric designs and repetitive mechanistic patterns marked Art Deco windows and interiors. At world fairs, material was often displayed on altar-shaped pedestals, a mode of presentation that quickly found its way into the store window.

Art and merchandising are not antithetical or mutually exclusive. Art carries connotations of style and talent; it implies connoisseurship and confers position, greatly adding to a store's image as a bastion of good taste. In the twenties, most better department stores had fine-art departments. Macy's and Lord and Taylor in New York, Halle Brothers in Cleveland,

Gene Moore, Tiffany window display, 1958

and Marshall Field's in Chicago all mounted exhibitions featuring the Art Deco style and modern French painting.

Department stores also regularly hired young painters and sculptors to work as window trimmers. L. Frank Baum, author of *The Wizard of Oz*, probably learned something about the power of dreams when he designed windows. Baum also edited *The Shop Window: A Journal of Window Trimming*. The sculptor Alexander Archipenko designed windows for Saks Fifth Avenue. The industrial designer Norman Bel Geddes, who also worked in display, wrote about windows in an essay, "The Play's the Thing." Before designing that celebrated train the Twentieth Century Limited and the Greyhound bus, Raymond Loewy worked in the display department of Macy's. In the fifties Maurice Sendak drew fantastic creatures for the window of New York toy store F. A. O. Schwarz, which so impressed that store's book buyer that he introduced Sendak to an editor. Jasper Johns, Robert Rauschenberg, James Rosenquist, and Andy Warhol all worked as window trimmers.

Gene Moore, Tiffany window display, 1957

The émigré Viennese architect and sculptor Frederick Kiesler designed art galleries and windows for Saks Fifth Avenue. He also wrote a theoretical text, "Contemporary Art Applied to the Store and Its Display," in which he attributed display's essentially American spirit to the exuberant abundance of variety stores. But the roots of display are, in fact, more French than American. In France, where fashion reigned and couture was accorded the status of art, merchandizing and art merged. In France the influence of Purism and Léger was seen in shop windows; and it was common for artists to inspire designers like Elsa Schiaparelli.

As a young woman, Schiaparelli had known Man Ray, Marcel Duchamp, and Edward Steichen; later in Paris, she knew Jean Cocteau, Francis Picabia, and Pablo Picasso. Everything that she learned from artists Schiaparelli put to the service of fashion and merchandising. As a designer and entrepreneur, she was a harbinger of Andy Warhol's Pop world. Schiaparelli made fashion accessible. Her favorite word was *amusing*. From her boutique in the Place Vendôme, with its birdcage interior designed by Jean-Michel Frank, she offered the first ready-to-wear clothes, which she called "take-out fashion." What was termed surreal then would be branded Pop three decades later. Schiaparelli designed a telephone handbag and hats in the form of a lamb chop, a shoe, and a bird in a nest. She regularly commissioned artists. Raoul Dufy drew the clothes in her collections; Cocteau's lithe, linear designs appeared as embroidery on her jackets; the Surrealist Leonor Fini designed the bottle for Shocking perfume in the shape of a dressmaker's dummy; and in 1939, when Schiaparelli brought out the men's fragrance Snuff, it was packaged in a flaçon shaped like René Magritte's pipe.

The Spanish Surrealist Salvador Dali was Schiaparelli's most innovative collaborator. Dali designed a black felt hat and a lip-shaped settee (after Mae West's lips) that recalled the giant floating lips in Man Ray's painting, as well as the lipstick markings on the cover of the second Surrealist manifesto. Together, Schiaparelli and Dali designed a tear dress, a dress with drawers (after Dali's 1936 painting *The City of Drawers*), and a lobster dress. They were well matched, the Surrealist

Gene Moore, Tiffany window display, 1962

Gene Moore, Tiffany window display, 1963

Gene Moore, Tiffany window display, 1965

with his flair for the outrageous and penchant for the limelight and the designer who trafficked in the bizarre, managing to garner as much attention as Dali when she incorporated Surrealist devices in her designs.

The Surrealist landscape was rich, fertile territory where the dream and the real merged and the subconscious reigned, and it had a transforming effect on fashion and merchandising. The Surrealists were drawn to eerily lifelike mannequins; dumb and wooden, they suggested creatures in a dreamscape. At the 1938 International Exhibition of Surrealism at the Galerie des Beaux-Arts in Paris, mannequins dressed by André Masson, Dali, and Duchamp, among others, slouched like hookers down a long corridor. Half-naked and outlandishly decorated, one had a birdcage on its head, another wore only a man's jacket, and another was wrapped in weeds. Like the mannequins, shop windows also had a hallucinatory effect on the Surrealists' imagination. Louis Aragon wrote about the spell of windows, and Dali and Duchamp both decorated them.

By the late thirties, the orderly elegance and opulent designs that characterized the Art Deco window had been replaced by complicated narratives, witty tableaux, and fantastic images. The Surrealist window was sophisticated and theatrical. In Surrealist windows, nightmares were revealed and dreams realized. In a window for Saks Fifth Avenue, the illustrator Marcel Vertés placed a mannequin on a psychoanalyst's couch, and above her head hung the dress of her dreams; in a display called "A Dream of Falling" (for a perfume named Sleeping), the Bonwit Teller display director Tommy Lee evoked the dislocation of dreams by suspending a mannequin upside down in the window.

To publicize André Breton's new book *Arcane 17*, Marcel Duchamp, Breton, and the Chilean-born Surrealist Matta

collaborated on a Surrealist window for New York's Brentano bookstore that featured a Matta painting of a bare-breasted woman and a headless mannequin, scantily clad in a chambermaid's apron. (When the display brought protests, it was moved to the Gotham Book Mart.) But the commotion caused by Duchamp's window was nothing compared with the furor surrounding Salvador Dali's 1939 windows for Bonwit Teller.

Dali was paid $1,000 for the two windows, which explored the myth of Narcissus. In the window called "Midnight Green," Dali put an old wax mannequin into a bed with a canopy resembling a buffalo's head holding a dead pigeon in its mouth. Compounding the horror, Dali wrapped the mannequin in a black sheet and placed her head on a pillow of embers. In the other window, "Narcissus White," Dali installed a wax mannequin in a fur-covered claw-footed bathtub filled with swampy water. Her hair was unkempt, tears of blood streaked down her cheeks, and around her hung hundreds of dangling hands, each holding a mirror that showed her the hideous face of self-love.

Dali worked on the windows all night, but when he

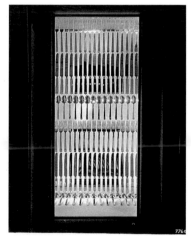

Gene Moore, Tiffany window display, 1970

Gene Moore, Tiffany window display, 1974

Matson Jones (Jasper Johns and Robert Rauschenberg), *Recreations in Dimension of 18th-Century Still Lifes*, Tiffany window displays, 1956

returned the next day, he discovered that the store's management had found his windows offensive and removed the desiccated-looking mannequins. Dali asked that his name be removed from the windows; the management demanded that he empty the tub's dirty water. Outraged, Dali entered the window, and as he lifted the tub to empty its water, it slipped and flew through the glass onto Fifth Avenue. Dali, not one to miss an opportunity, leaped through the broken window onto the street, where he was arrested, but not before his headlong dive was captured on film. Dali was well known when he began the windows; on their completion he was notorious.

Dali made shop windows famous, and by the late forties New York windows were regarded as one of the city's sights. Tourists and natives alike studied the elegant displays with their gleaming merchandise, announcing the prosperity of post–World War II America. The store window was appreciated and acknowledged; two windows appeared in the Museum of Modern Art's 1949 exhibition *Modern Art in Your Life*, which demonstrated the relationship between contemporary art and everyday objects. By then, the surreal was making its slow exit from the store window, being replaced by geometric abstractions and simpler tableaux bearing the influence of modernism and Bauhaus design. At Bergdorf Goodman, the display director Jim Buckley hung roses in midair to create stark, elegant windows. At Delman shoes, a former assistant of Buckley's, Gene Moore, designed playfully insouciant windows; in one window, Moore spoofed compulsive shoppers by heaping shoes in a pile.

Eventually, Gene Moore became display director at Bonwit Teller, where he oversaw twenty-two windows; and in 1956, he took on Tiffany's, where for the next thirty-nine years he designed windows. Moore's windows featured intricate narra-

tives and geometric designs in which something unexpected usually happened. At Bonwit's, he set elegantly dressed mannequins under scaffolds, holding buckets of wet paint, to show that fashion was an amulet against impending disaster. In another set of windows, he demonstrated perfume's power by superimposing romantic fantasies onto the eyes of the enlarged photographic faces that covered the windows. To engage his audience, Moore played games. He hid jewelry in Tiffany's windows and concealed homosexual puns in Bonwit Teller's displays. Moore also used surreal devices, but he turned them tasteful, particularly at Tiffany's, where he floated zippers, disembodied hands, and keys in space.

Matson Jones (Jasper Johns and Robert Rauschenberg), *Landscapes*, Tiffany window displays, 1957

At Bonwit's, Moore continued the tradition established by Tommy Lee and hired young painters and sculptors to design windows. Moore, who once wanted to be a painter, was empathetic to the plight of young painters; and over the course of a long career, he commissioned windows from more than nine hundred artists. But his hiring policies were strict. Although his windows paid homage to famous artists like Picasso, he

only hired unknowns. Moore gave space to artists who needed it, who had no gallery. In 1961 he turned Bonwit's windows into art galleries, where he showed Jasper Johns's *Flag on an Orange Field* and a group of Andy Warhol's early cartoon paintings. But Moore seldom invited an artist to design the entire window (as the Surrealists did); instead, he asked them to create props and backgrounds, which he then combined with merchandise.

James Rosenquist, Robert Rauschenberg, and Jasper Johns were all unknown painters when Moore hired them. Rosenquist, who painted Times Square billboards during the day and small abstractions at night, heard that Moore paid high fees

and went to see him. Impressed with Rosenquist's portfolio of outdoor signs, Moore immediately commissioned him to paint large heads of silent-movie stars. They were gargantuan: the nine-by-nine-foot black-and-white heads towered over the windows' well-dressed mannequins, creating an odd, disjunctive mood like that triggered by Rosenquist's first Pop paintings.

Jasper Johns and Robert Rauschenberg, unlike Rosenquist, never worked full-time as commercial artists. When he was

first in New York, Johns had a job at the Marboro bookshop: at the time, Rauschenberg worked as a janitor for the Stable Gallery and supplemented his income by working for Gene Moore. Rauschenberg wanted Johns to join him, but Johns, wary of commercial art, resisted until, after much cajoling, he gave in. They worked as partners, using the alias Matson Jones, and produced displays for Moore (who by this time was designing Tiffany's windows). His instructions were simple; he would ask for "a swamp" or "a cave," and they'd go off and do it. They were reliable, skilled, and imaginative, and Moore never knew who did what.

Matson Jones created meticulously crafted realistic displays. In one series, they transposed seventeenth-century still-life paintings into three dimensions, casting fruit from plaster and coloring it so it appeared both real and painterly. In another series, they made caves that looked like ice, stone, and mud, where Moore hid jewels. What, if any, effect windows had on their art is hard to know. Rauschenberg incorporated materials from Tiffany's workshop into his collages; and the icy stillness emanating from Matson Jones's winter landscapes suggests something of the silence that surrounds Johns's art.

Andy Warhol had no qualms about working as a window trimmer. He was already a successful commercial artist when Moore asked him to create windows for Bonwit Teller. He had designed book covers, received art directors' awards, and started on his prize-winning shoe ads for I. Miller. Moore

James Rosenquist, Bonwit Teller window display, 1959

James Rosenquist, Bonwit Teller window display, c. 1959

regarded Warhol as a professional. He never told him what to do or asked to see a sketch. Moore simply explained the problem and showed Warhol the merchandise. He trusted Warhol to design the whole window. Warhol understood. He knew that a window, like a book jacket, had to sell a product.

Warhol's windows were distinguished by their clarity and graphic quality. They were seldom theatrical. They were not, like those of Surrealists, filled with dreams, fantasies, and bizarre tales. His windows did not shock but gently seduced. He worked from strength, transferring his well-wrought line into his windows, where it emphasized and outlined products. In early Bonwit's windows advertising perfume, Warhol scribbled romantic doodles — hearts, flowers and love-struck cupids — onto a wooden fence. His line was innocent, irrepressible, good-natured, chic. It brought to mind Jean Cocteau's line, but it was bolder. In windows, his line embellished and sold products. In time, when the painter had absorbed the lessons of the commercial artist, he would use the line to sell himself and his art.

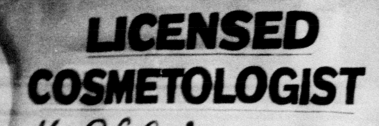

LICENSED
COSMETOLOGIST

Ms. Helaine

☆ FORMERLY OF
BONWIT TELLER

STAGELIGHT
Cosmetics

DISCOU'V
CIGARE ITE

99¢

SUGG. RETAIL $23.50

HALSTON
NATURAL SPRAY
COLOGNE

2.5 OZ. $17.⁰⁰

SUGG. RETAIL $13.50

L'AIR DU
TEMPS
TOILETTE WATER
SPRAY

1.6-OZ. $10.⁰⁰

CARTONS $9.80
TAX INCLUDED

OPEN 11-6
SUNDAYS

N° FI   D NK

Pep Col n

ST   G ARMS

Wher   Y
Rupture?

① ② ⑤

1 □
5 □

NOSES RESHAPI

25¢

3

4

5

I dropped by Patricia Field on Saturday, and found Jean-Michel Masquiat painting those wonderful $6 Tyrek (Du Pont's polyolefin fiber) jumpsuits in the store window. A one-of-a-kind original painting you can both wear and hang on your wall instead of in the closet ($28) — also check out his hand-painted sweatshirts — fabulous at $24. Patricia Field, 10 E. 8 St., 254-1699.   V.H.

Jean-Michel Basquiat in Patricia Field's store window,
Soho Weekly News, November 15, 1979

Peter Greenaway exhibition *The Physical Self*,
Museum Boijmans Van Beuningen, Rotterdam, 1991–92

Paige Powell, Andy Warhol's *Invisible Sculpture* installation at Area, 1985

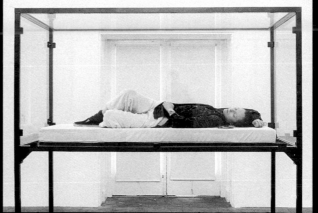

Tilda Swinton and Cornelia Parker, *The Maybe*, 1995,
installation at the Serpentine Gallery, London

Nat Finkelstein, *Edie Sedgwick and Gerard Malanga*, 1965

Silver Factory Style
The 1960s

1

2

3

Around 1963, Andy Warhol invented a new personal style. As he shifted his focus to painting, filmmaking, and the production of rock music and happenings in a new studio, his look included leather jackets, jeans, boots, sunglasses, and a silver-sprayed wig, as well as the occasional tuxedo. His studio, called the Factory, an industrial loft space with silver-covered walls and ceiling, was instantly known as the place to be. It was the site of constant creative and social activity, a heady mix of art, film, music, the avant-garde, society, celebrities, and fringe characters. Warhol and his muses and creative partners at the Factory — including the poet Gerard Malanga, the socialite Edie Sedgwick, and the Velvet Underground and its chanteuse, Nico — cultivated a look

and attitude that, along with the artist's Pop paintings, became the height of fashion.

Inspired by the glamourous movie stars he adored, Warhol created his own "Superstars," and the Warhol Factory had its own publicity machine. Visitors and regulars sat for *Screen Tests*, a changing selection of which made up the artist's *The Thirteen Most Beautiful Women* and *Fifty Fantastics and Fifty Personalities*. Edie Sedgwick, Viva, and Joe Dallesandro, among others, starred in Warhol's films, and the hip glamour of the scene was documented by the Factory photographers Billy Name and David McCabe, as well as by Richard Avedon, Cecil Beaton, and many others.

National and international media interest in Warhol and his world began at this time, generating a large amount of publicity that was both welcomed and cultivated by the artist. Warhol goings-on,

Opposite page:
1. Stephen Shore, *Andy Warhol on the fire escape of the Factory*, 1965
2. Gerard Malanga, *Nico, Taylor Mead, Ultra Violet, Viva, Ingrid Superstar, Billy Name, Andy Warhol, and others from the Factory*, 1968
3. Billy Name, *Andy, Gerard, and Chuck Playing on Couch*, 1965
4. Billy Name, *Ivy Nicholson*, 1965
5. David McCabe, *Andy Warhol*, c. 1964
This page:
1. Promotional material for Champion Papers featuring Andy Warhol and Art Kane, 1962
2. Billy Name, *Mary Woronov and International Velvet*, 1965
3. David McCabe, *Andy Warhol against the Factory Wall*, 1964

Factory happenings, and the Factory look were seen in frequent coverage of the Exploding Plastic Inevitable, the artist's multimedia extravaganzas including the Velvet Underground, and features like *Life* magazine's fashion pieces on Edie and Baby Jane Holzer. *The New York Times* covered the appearance of Warhol, Nico, and Gerard Malanga at the Abraham & Straus department store, where Nico wore paper dresses to which Warhol's silkscreen *Fragile* and *Banana* prints were applied, and the artist's films and *Silver Clouds* were used as backdrops for fashions in magazine features and advertisements. Eugenia Sheppard described the interesting mix in a *New York Herald Tribune* article on "Pop Art, Poetry and Fashion," which featured Malanga's verses.

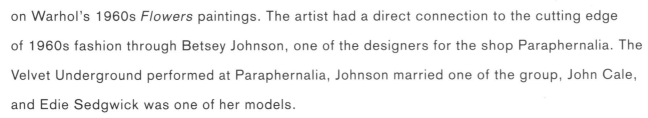

Warhol, experimenting with fashion during this period, envisioned people as moving artworks wearing clothing based on his *S & H Green Stamps*, *Fragile*, and *Brillo* images. In the early 1970s, Halston designed clothing based on Warhol's 1960s *Flowers* paintings. The artist had a direct connection to the cutting edge of 1960s fashion through Betsey Johnson, one of the designers for the shop Paraphernalia. The Velvet Underground performed at Paraphernalia, Johnson married one of the group, John Cale, and Edie Sedgwick was one of her models.

The look and attitude of Warhol's 1960s silver Factory, as well as his later 1960s studio, contributed significantly to the new style of that period. The recent revival of the 1960s look in clothing and fashion features borrows liberally from Factory personalities and photographs of the Factory scene. As so often in his work, Warhol captured the spirit of the era.

— MF/MK

1. Andy Warhol, Paul Morrissey, Baby Jane Holzer, Joe Dallesandro, Holly Woodlawn, and others from the Factory, *L'Uomo Vogue*, April/March 1972
2. Billy Name, *Andy Warhol at the Factory, Bathroom Series*, 1968
3. Billy Name, *Factory Magazine Photo Shoot (Andy with Beautiful Girls), Ivy Nicholson, Marisol, and Others*, 1965
4. Billy Name, *Fred Hughes at the Factory, Bathroom Series*, 1968
5. Billy Name, *Andy Warhol at the Factory*, 1964

1   2   3   4   5   6

7

1, 2. Andy Warhol, *Self-Portrait*, c. 1963

3–5. Andy Warhol, *Edie Sedgwick*, c. 1965

6. Andy Warhol, *Gerard Malanga*, c. 1966

7. Stephen Shore, *Andy Warhol and Ingrid Superstar*, 1966

8. Billy Name, *Jed Johnson at the Factory, Bathroom Series*, 1968

9. Billy Name, *Andy Warhol, Brigid Berlin, Gerald Malanga, and Ingrid Superstar*, 1968

10. Billy Name, *Paul Morrissey's Apartment*, 1968

11. Billy Name, *Viva and Andy Warhol at the Factory*, 1968

12. Fred McDarrah, *Andy Warhol*, 1966

8

11

10

12

9

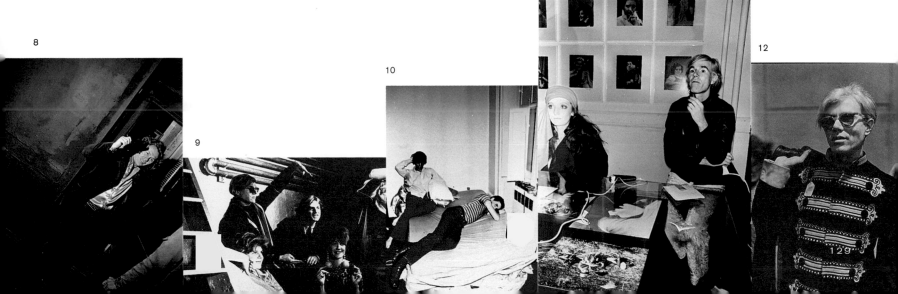

Nat Finkelstein, *Gerard Malanga*, 1965

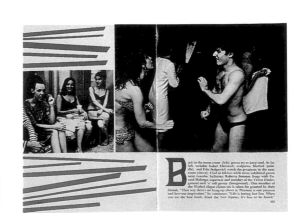

1. Billy Name, Vinyl *with Gerard and Edie,* 1965
2. David McCabe, *Edie Sedgwick and Gerard Malanga,* 1965
3. Gerard Malanga in appropriated fashion by Andy Warhol for "Poetry & Fashion" runway show, 1968
4. Article on Pop fashion and poetry, *New York Herald Tribune,* January 3, 1965
5. Article on Andy Warhol and the Factory, *Pageant,* March 1967

5

1. Arman, *Gerard Malanga wearing a silk-screened Troy Donahue shirt*, 1963
2. Francesco Scavullo, *Gerard Malanga,* 1969
3. Nat Finkelstein, *Gerard Malanga,* 1965

2

1

3

1. David McCabe, Photo session at David McCabe's studio with an assistant, McCabe, Chuck Wein, Edie Sedgwick, Andy Warhol, and Gerard Malanga, 1965
2. David McCabe, *Edie Sedgwick*, 1965
3. David McCabe, *Gerard Malanga*, 1965
4. Billy Name, *Ingrid Superstar, Ultra Violet, Paul Morrissey, International Velvet, Viva, Brigid Polk (Berlin), and Tiger Morse*, 1968
5, 6. Billy Name, *Viva, International Velvet, and Ultra Violet at the Factory*, 1968
7. Billy Name, *Ultra Violet, Paul Morrissey, Ingrid Superstar, International Velvet, Viva, Brigid Polk (Berlin), and Tiger Morse*, 1968

2   3

4

6

5   7

1. David McCabe, Photo session at David McCabe's studio with Gerard Malanga, Edie Sedgwick, Andy Warhol, David McCabe, and an assistant, 1965

2-4. David McCabe, Photo session at David McCabe's studio with Chuck Wein, Edie Sedgwick, Andy Warhol, and Gerard Malanga, 1965

1

3

4

2

My first recollection of Andy Warhol: his apparition at the Metropolitan Museum. He arrived accompanied by two or three lovely girls in outlandish clothes. They were his avant-garde as well as rampart. The looks of his entourage corresponded to his reputation — frivolous and amoral. Later talking with Andy, I discovered how serious and moral he was.

Dominique de Menil in Kynaston McShine, ed., *Andy Warhol: A Retrospective* (New York: Museum of Modern Art, 1989), p. 431

5. Billy Name, *Edie Sedgwick and Gerard Malanga*, 1965
6. Andy Warhol painting a butterfly on a model's leg, c. 1966
7. David McCabe, *Unidentified Man, Chuck Wein, and Andy Warhol*, 1965

7

5

6

Nat Finkelstein, *Edie Sedgwick*, 1965

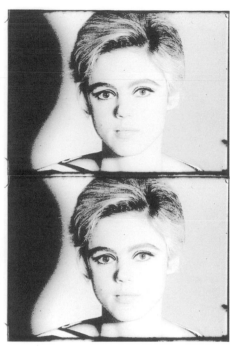

1. Billy Name, *Edie Sedgwick's* Screen
Test, 1965
2. Andy Warhol, *Edie Sedgwick's* Screen
Test, 1965
3. Billy Name, *Ingrid Superstar, Edie
Sedgwick, Bobby Schwartz, Ondine,
and Susan Bottomly making Warhol's
film **** (Four Stars), known originally
as* Since, 1967
4. Fashion spread with Factory look-
alikes, *Harper's Bazaar,* August 1995

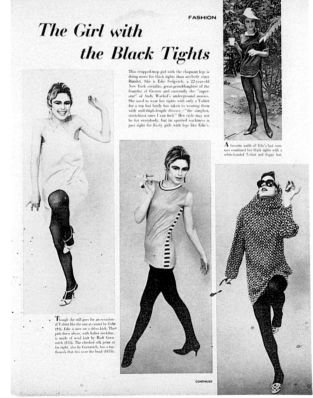

The Girl with the Black Tights

1. David McCabe, *Andy Warhol and Edie Sedgwick*, 1964
2. Article featuring Edie Sedgwick, Andy Warhol, and Chuck Wein, *The Sunday Times Magazine*, February 13, 1966
3. David McCabe, *Edie Sedgwick and Gerard Malanga*, 1965
4. Fashion feature on Edie Sedgwick, *Life*, November 26, 1965

1

1. Nat Finkelstein, *Edie Sedgwick*, 1965
2. Article featuring Andy Warhol and Edie
   Sedgwick, *Elseviers Magazine*,
   December 24, 1983
3. Article featuring Andy Warhol and Edie
   Sedgwick, *Lo Specchio*, December
   1965
4. David McCabe, *Edie Sedgwick
   Dancing at the Factory*, 1965
5. Stephen Shore, *Bibie Hansen, Edie
   Sedgwick, Pat Hartly, and Sandy
   Kirkland during the filming of* Girls in
   Prison, 1965

4

2

3

5

Long earrings are fast coming back into fashion, a fact that delights Edie because she has been wearing them all along. This set by K.J.L. ($50) is seven inches long. "I swish them the way other girls swish their hair," says Edie. Her huge rings are also from K.J.L. Edie's evening dress of matte jersey resembles a stretched-out T-shirt (Rudi Gernreich, $110). Sleeves push into folds at wrists.

3

By now we were obsessed with the mystique of Hollywood, the camp of it all. One of the last movies we made with Edie was called *Lupe*. We did Edie up as the title role and filmed it at Panna Grady's apartment in the great old Dakota on Central Park West and 72nd. Panna was a hostess of the sixties who put uptown intellectuals together with Lower East Side types — she seemed to adore the drug-related writers in particular.

Andy Warhol and Pat Hackett, *POPism: The Warhol Sixties*, 1980, p. 122

1. David McCabe, *Andy Warhol, Edie Sedgwick, and the Empire State Building*, 1965
2. Andy Warhol, *Edie Sedgwick in Poor Little Rich Girl*, 1965
3. Fashion feature on Edie Sedgwick, *Life*, November 26, 1965
4. David Bailey, *Andy Warhol and Jane Holzer*, 1973
5. David McCabe, *Richard Avedon and Andy Warhol at the Museum of Modern Art, New York*, 1964
6. David McCabe, *Ultra Violet and Andy Warhol*, 1965
7. Fred McDarrah, *Andy Warhol*, 1963

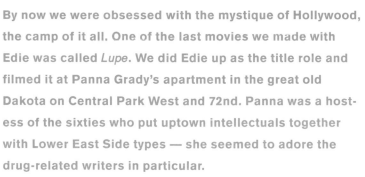

Plastics

The Magical and the Prosaic

Peter Wollen

IN THE SUMMER OF 1965, Andy Warhol had recently returned from Paris, where he had enjoyed a big success with his flower paintings and with his current superstar, Edie Sedgwick. He immediately set about shooting two new films, devised by Ronald Tavel and, of course, starring Sedgwick — *Kitchen* and *Beauty #2*. *Kitchen* was Tavel's second film for Warhol, following *Vinyl*, their first collaboration. In *Kitchen*, all the characters have the same name. "I was trying to get rid of character," Tavel later explained. Warhol had already instructed him, it seems, to "get rid of plot!" and it just seemed logical to get rid of character as well.[1] Warhol, ever the minimalist, had given Tavel another important instruction. He said, "I want it simple and plastic and white."[2]

After Norman Mailer saw *Kitchen*, he observed that you could really see only "the kitchen table, the refrigerator, the stove and the actors. The refrigerator hummed and droned on the sound track. Edie had the sniffles. She had a dreadful cold. She had one of those colds you get spending the long winter in a cold-water flat. The dialogue was dull and bounced off the enamel and plastic surfaces. It was a horror to watch. It captured the essence of every boring, dead day one's ever had in a city, a time when everything was imbued with the odor of damp washcloths and old drains. I suspect that a hundred years from now people will look at *Kitchen* and say, 'Yes, that is the way it was in the late Fifties, early Sixties in America. That's why they had the war in Vietnam. That's why the rivers were getting polluted. That's why there was topological glut. That's why the horror came down. That's why the plague was on its way.' *Kitchen* shows that better than any other work of the time."[3]

It is a bravura passage, vintage Mailer. I want to focus on a particularly humdrum and minimal detail of *Kitchen*,

which seems, in a strange way, to sum up everything Mailer remarked on in the film. Warhol wanted it to look "plastic." It was only the banality of plastic, he seems somehow to have foreseen, that could provide the rationale for Mailer's sense that the horror was soon to descend and the plague was already on its way. Warhol, of course, was fascinated by plastic. Jeffrey L. Meikle, in his magisterial work *American Plastic: A Cultural History*, [4] describes Warhol as a "plastic celebrity" who himself "evoked a sense of plastic artificiality." He notes that Warhol had undergone plastic surgery (on his nose) and had launched a road-show called the Exploding Plastic Inevitable. He comments on Warhol's *Silver Clouds,* helium balloons made of metallic polyester film. He mentions the one hundred Styrofoam boxes on which Warhol silkscreened portraits of the ten Leo Castelli Gallery artists, including himself. But most of all, he stresses the

image of Warhol as being somehow plastic.

In the summer of 1965, besides making *Kitchen,* Warhol hosted the opening party for the fashion boutique Paraphernalia, at the request of the designer Betsey Johnson. The launch was an invitation-only event complete with a guest list and a runway show, and it was photographed by Nat Finkelstein. [5] The next year, there was another party in the boutique. Warhol's films were projected on the wall, and spotlights illuminated the models, who could be seen through the plate-glass storefront by the mob of spectators gathered outside. Warhol was especially thrilled when the police showed up. The

1

Opposite page:
1–3. David McCabe, *Edie Sedgwick on the set of* Kitchen, 1965
This page:
1–3. David McCabe, *Edie Sedgwick and Co-star Roger Trudeau on the Set of* Kitchen, 1965

2

3

Velvet Underground was there as well —
the group that provided the performance
core of the Exploding Plastic Inevitable.
(Parenthetically, it is worth noting that
Betsey Johnson later dressed the Velvets
and married one of the group, John
Cale.) Paul Morrissey remembered
dreaming the name up, piecing Exploding
Plastic Inevitable together from words
in the liner notes of a Bob Dylan album.
Warhol approved.

Betsey Johnson had first met Warhol
through his then-principal acolyte,
Gerard Malanga, co-star of *Vinyl* with
Edie Sedgwick. He had suggested inviting
Johnson to the Factory to dress Warhol's
entourage for a group photograph. There
she encountered Sedgwick, who later
became her fitting model and a walking

advertisement for her clothes. Still later,
Betsey Johnson dressed Edie Sedgwick for
her starring role in the archetypal sixties-
scene film, *Ciao Manhattan*. Apparently
Malanga and Warhol were attracted to
Johnson because of her aluminum-foil
tank dresses, which matched Billy Name's
foil wall covering for the entire Factory.
The affinity between Johnson and the
Warhol world proved to be surprisingly
deep rooted. Warhol had begun his own
career as a fashion illustrator and
remained fascinated by fashion throughout his life. Johnson and Paraphernalia
combined his interest in the quintessential
sixties look with his interest in both plastics and reflective surfaces.

As described in Joel Lobenthal's
Radical Rags, the basic source book for
Manhattan fashions of the sixties and
the "beautiful people" who wore them,
Betsey Johnson's expertise in plastic clothing dated back to 1964, the year she was
employed as a college guest editor at
Mademoiselle, where she worked as assistant
to the fabric editor. There Johnson was
thrilled to discover her boss's files of
assorted fabrics: "what the industrial
people used, stuff they were making car

interiors out of, fabrics they were lining caskets with, the materials with which they were insulating spaceships."[6] Through *Mademoiselle,* Johnson was introduced to Paul Young, formerly an innovative fashion merchandizer for J. C. Penney. Young had just been lured away by another firm, Puritan, to help them acquire strength in the new sixties youth market. "I told Karl [Rosen] I'd only come to Puritan if he agreed to launch Paraphernalia,"[7] Young later recalled.

Paraphernalia brought together four extraordinary woman designers — Betsey Johnson, Deanna Littell, Elisa Stone, and Diana Dew. All four worked with unusual materials — plastics, paper, and metals — and Littell and Dew also experimented with clothes with electric lights. Elisa Stone specialized in paper dresses — they were made from paper with, in Joel Lobenthal's words, "a porous but firm weave with a pebbly texture resembling the surface of a paper towel,"[8] secured at the back with Velcro. Stone became interested in paper as a material because of her fascination with paper dolls, which were also a childhood obsession of Warhol's, perhaps even the source of his

own orientation toward fashion. In 1967, Stone's dresses made from translucent theater-lighting gels were featured on the cover of *Harper's Bazaar.* Displayed on hangers in the Paraphernalia shop, they resembled "transparent candy," in the designer's words. Stone was interested in paper because of its ephemerality, another quality Warhol liked — "I loved the idea that my clothes were not going to last."[9]

Deanna Littell, like Johnson, worked with plastics. "Someone brought me a plastic, like a leatherette, that was coated with a glow-in-the-dark film. It was used for policemen's night raincoats. They had started manufacturing it in Day-Glo purples and greens."[10] Littell used the material to make incandescent evening

1

2

3

coats, an early example of the late-sixties' light-show aesthetic that was to shape the Exploding Plastic Inevitable. Littell, inspired by Jasper Johns, also devised an American-flag shirt, with white collar and cuffs, which was never marketed for fear of lawsuits from the Daughters of the American Revolution.

As Lobenthal notes, Paraphernalia "resembled an art gallery more than a conventional retail space."[11] Its architect, Ulrich Franzen, imagined it as "a continuous Happening,"[12] with models frugging on stages under theatrical lighting, conventional window displays of the kind Johns, Robert Rauschenberg, and Warhol himself had earlier designed for Gene Moore at Bonwit Teller. Paraphernalia dramatized an element of the fashion world that was in sync with Warhol's own vision of the Factory as a place where performance, display, and art production could be combined. It also brought to New York the excitement that Warhol had earlier felt emanating from London via friends and exemplars such as Nicky Haslam, David Bailey, Jane Ormsby Gore, Jean Shrimpton, and Twiggy.

Paraphernalia stocked both Mary Quant and Foale and Tuffin, the key English fashion designers. In fact, Foale and Tuffin went on a promotional tour in the United States for Paraphernalia's wholesale division, Youthquake — another Paul Young enterprise. Earlier, in the period before Paraphernalia, Young had already launched Mary Quant in the U.S., commissioning her to work for J. C. Penney, thereby lifting her out of the boutique world into the quite different world of the American department store. In Lobenthal's words, Quant "augured the revival of the very young woman as a fashion leader, after nearly thirty years in eclipse. While the Paris couture deified soignée maturity, the English rebels of the '60s elevated the unmarried demoiselle to the most influential platform she would command during the century."[13]

Warhol's own series of superstars were plainly based on this new generation of young fashion models from London. As I have argued elsewhere,[14] he was particularly impressed by David Bailey, the London fashion photographer who had been credited with turning Shrimpton

4

and Twiggy into celebrities. Warhol used film rather than photography as a medium to blend the image of the model with that of the star. Warhol's first superstar, the socialite Baby Jane Holzer, became a much-photographed fashion icon. Edie Sedgwick rapidly became a model and cover girl as a result of Warhol's own Baileyesque star-making abilities. A number of other Warhol superstars were or had been models. Ivy Nicholson, for example, was one of the great Paris models of the fifties, photographed by Henry Clarke and William Klein, doing runway shows for Givenchy. Nico, imposed as a singer on the Velvet Underground, had also been a prominent Paris model.

Paraphernalia brought together the fashion world, the sixties youthquake, and Warhol's personal devotion to plastics. Plastics did not become a central part of American life until the post–World War II years, when Warhol was still at Carnegie Tech, finally prevailing in the fifties, during his early and formative New York years. In the Eisenhower era, mass-produced plastics became a much-publicized and increasingly central feature of

American life. New thermoplastics, such as polyethylene, made possible a whole range of innovative products with rounded shapes, textured surfaces, and cool colors. By the end of the decade, critics were already warning about the cultural dangers implicit in the new cornucopia of plastics. Poured and molded, plastic permitted the creation of unprecedented new forms and threatened to flood the world with cheap, disposable products. Advanced mold technology enabled the manufacture of endlessly reproducible multiples, which proved so appealing to Warhol.

The first plastic to enter the American home in a significant way was celluloid, developed in the 1880s as a substitute for traditional materials such as horn for combs and starched cotton in stiff collars. In 1907 bakelite entered the market, and by the end of the thirties it had been joined by vinyl, polystyrene, Lucite, acrylic sheet, and polyvinyl chloride. Vinyl and PVC were used for cheap clothing like raincoats and shoes (Ondine, the transvestite superstar, wore vinyl boots). World War II gave the plastics industry a powerful boost in the demand for mate-

Paraphernalia opened late in '65, and another trend started — stores opened late in the morning, even noon-time, and staying open till maybe ten at night. Paraphernalia sometimes stayed open till two in the morning. You'd go in and try on things and "Get Off My Cloud" would be playing — and you'd be buying the clothes in the same atmos-phere you'd probably be wearing them in…

Andy Warhol and Pat Hackett, *POPism: The Warhol Sixties*, 1980, p.115

Opposite page:
1. Advertisement for Betsey Johnson's Paraphernalia, *Aspen*, December 1966
2. Page from Betsey Johnson's scrapbook, 1960s
3. Article on a fashion show by Paraphernalia, *Status & Diplomat*, March 1967
4. Nat Finkelstein, *Andy Warhol and the Velvet Underground at Paraphernalia Party*, 1966
This page:
1. Nat Finkelstein, *Maureen Tucker, Lou Reed, and Others at Paraphernalia Party*, 1966
2. Nat Finkelstein, *Betsey Johnson and Andy Warhol Preparing Paraphernalia Party*, 1966

2

1

rials for the war effort. This was the time, needless to say, when nylon stockings replaced silk. As industry retooled for the civilian market after 1945, plastic became an increasingly ubiquitous ingredient of American culture — scarcely noticed, but not necessarily welcomed.

As Jeffrey Meikle notes,[15] the explosion of plastics was seen in both utopian and dystopian terms — either as the harbinger of an extraordinary new man-made environment, both functional and decorative, or as a deluge of tacky consumer goods heralding a decadent and homogenizing retreat from nature into a nightmare world of artificiality and impermanence. Warhol seems to have adopted elements of both attitudes in his usual paradoxical way. He exalted sameness, repetition, and mass production. He never evinced any liking for nature and positively adored the synthetic. He revered ordinary consumer merchandise — Tupperware, presumably, fell into the same category as Brillo pads or Coca-Cola bottles. He also saw plastic in negative terms — ersatz, disposable,

kitsch, and banal — even if he then elevated the terms to make them positive.

In one way, Warhol can be seen as a typical practitioner of the throwaway futurism of much of sixties' design, including fashion. The reflective silver surfaces he loved are usually described (following Warhol's own remarks) as springing from the speed-freak aesthetic, part of a druggy taste for gaudy baubles and delirious decor. But they also had their origins in the more mainstream space-age culture. Mylar, coated with reflective aluminum, went up into space with the inflatable Echo 1 satellite. Space exploration, as Meikle notes, relied heavily on "high-performance synthetics, on Mylar, Teflon, and nylon, on heat-resisting composites and form-fitting foams."[16] Moreover, the space-age aesthetic was itself intrinsically futuristic and disposable. In this sense, Warhol's taste echoed the aesthetic of Drop City and emerged parallel to, say, plastic furniture.

In the sixties, as kitsch and space-age accoutrements became fashionable, Warhol

1

2

This page:
1. Article on Paraphernalia, *The New York Times,* October 6, 1966
2. Nat Finkelstein, *Model at Paraphernalia Party,* 1966
3. Nat Finkelstein, *Edie Sedgwick,* 1966
Opposite page:
1. Nat Finkelstein, *Andy Warhol and Betsey Johnson at Paraphernalia,* 1966
2. Nat Finkelstein, *Betsey Johnson at Paraphernalia,* 1966

3

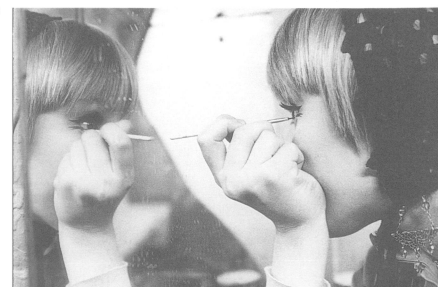

stimulated the trend and embodied it in his work. In the fashion world, reflective materials like metals and silver paper were popular — after all, astronauts them-selves had worn reflective clothing. In the world of furniture, PVC made inflatable chairs possible. The world of architecture produced Plug-In city, with plastic kitchens purposely designed to be traded in every few years like automobiles. In the Factory, too, habitués expressed the same mania for shiny surfaces and fashionable obsolescence. Perhaps for Warhol, the new ethos included the molding of artifi-cial superstars, poured into a succession of ornamental forms like plastic products, ephemeral but undeniably attractive.

Flying to the Republican convention that nominated Barry Goldwater in 1964, Norman Mailer conceptualized the plane as "another of the extermination cham-bers of the century — slowly the breath gives up some microcosmic portion of itself, green plastic and silver-gray plastic, the nostrils breathe no odor of materials which existed once as elements of nature, no wood, no stone, nor ore." He went on to characterize America as "a sick nation, we're sick to the edge of vomit and so we build our lives with materials that smell like vomit, polyethylene and bakelite and fiberglass and styrene."[17] In *Armies of the Night*, as Meikle also notes, Mailer portrays the Pentagon as "reminiscent of some plastic plug coming out of the hole made in flesh by an unmentionable operation."[18]

Mailer's ire culminated in his descrip-tion of the astronaut's capsule in *Of a Fire on the Moon*, in which the astronaut "lay in his plastic suit on a plastic couch — lay indeed in a Teflon-coated Beta-cloth (laid on Kapton, laid next to Mylar, next to Dacron, next to neoprene-coated nylon) space suit on his Armalon couch — plastic, that triumph of reason over nature." [19] We can only guess what Mailer would have thought of the Paraphernalia party, but the chasm between Warhol and Mailer was clearly vertiginous. The para-dox of plastic pits a wish to escape from the body, to cross the frontier between nature and technology, to become plastic, against one that seeks to reject technology,

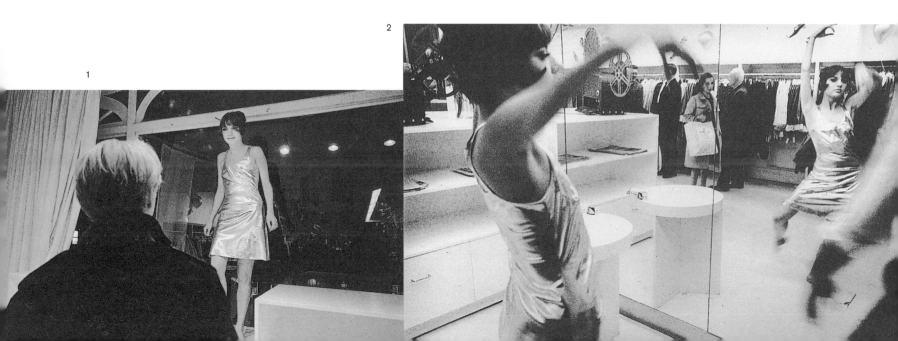

that is angered and sickened by it, that fears its implications and insists that humanity must retain its ancient place as part of nature. Plastic becomes the site of an apocalyptic cultural battle.

The exuberant creations of the Paraphernalia designers, reflecting the brash nonconformist attitudes of sixties' youth, put a newly optimistic spin on plastic, far removed from the bleakness of *Vinyl* or the paranoid pessimism that Mailer brought to his reading of *Kitchen*. Into Warhol's own world came the inspired novelty that had so attracted him in the work of other fashion designers like Rudi Gernreich and Paco Rabanne, early pioneers of plastic clothing in couture. Betsey Johnson and her colleagues provided a convincingly utopian and populist interpretation of plastic.

Their vision was not to last. Tiger Morse was the designer whose work marked the transition from plastics to psychedelia — just as the Velvet Underground did — and the final descent from psychedelia into darkness. Morse had exploded on the New York fashion scene in 1964, the year she opened her uptown

Kaleidoscope showroom. Later she specialized in fantastic multimedia parties, as well as in dresses that lit up, dresses made from vinyl, Mylar, PVC shower curtains, and so on. By the end of the sixties, Morse, who for a time had hosted the Cheetah discothèque frequented by Warhol, was reduced to waiting table at Max's Kansas City, another favorite Warhol hangout. In 1972 she died of an overdose of sleeping pills, leaving behind, as Lobenthal puts it, "her haul of silkscreen vinyl dresses and her prototype white sequin electric dress."[20] By that time, of course, Warhol himself had changed his whole lifestyle, moved uptown, and begun to associate with Halston and de la Renta. The plastic years were over.

In 1957 Roland Barthes published a fascinating essay, "Plastic," in his collection *Mythologies*, based on his visit to an exhibition of new industrial materials. For Barthes, plastics suggested "infinite transformation," bringing about "a perpetual amazement, the reverie of man at the sight of the proliferating forms of matter, and the connections he detects between the singular of the origin and

1

This page:
1. Fashion feature with Nico, c. 1966
2. Nat Finkelstein, *Andy Warhol and the Velvet Underground at Paraphernalia Party*, 1966
3. Nat Finkelstein, *John Cale*, 1966
Opposite page:
1. Nat Finkelstein, *Unidentified Woman at Paraphernalia Party*, 1966

2

3

the plural of its effects."[21] Initially used to produce inexpensive imitations of luxury materials, plastic eventually acquired currency for its own unique properties. As Barthes noted, "It is the first magical substance which consents to be prosaic."[22] It was this combination of the magical and the prosaic that attracted Warhol to Paraphernalia and that inspired his own devotion to plastic.

In the end, Andy Warhol's plastic dream was not only one of a magical world of reflective, luminescent, ephemeral fashions, but something much more intimate — a dream of being human itself as magical and prosaic, special and commonplace. "The hierarchy of substances is abolished," Barthes wrote. "A single one replaces them all: the whole world can be plasticized, and even life itself since, we are told, they are beginning to make plastic aortas."[23] Warhol, I believe, happily endorsed this vision, foreseeing a brave new world in which nature finally gave way to artifice, the particular to the general, and the lasting to the fashionable.

1. Patrick S. Smith, *Warhol, Conversations about the Artist* (Ann Arbor: UMI Research Press, 1988), p. 313.
2. Patrick S. Smith, *Andy Warhol's Art and Films* (Ann Arbor, Michigan: UMI Research Press, 1986), p. 164.
3. Jean Stein, with George Plimpton, *Edie: An American Biography* (New York: Dell, 1982), pp. 190-91.
4. Jeffrey L. Meikle, *American Plastic, A Cultural History* (New Brunswick, New Jersey: Rutgers University Press, 1995). I am indebted to Kevin Fisher's unpublished paper, "Synthetic Fashions and the Plastic Arts in the Production of Andy Warhol," for referring me to Meikle's work and molding my own thought on Warhol and plastics.

5. Nat Finkelstein, *Andy Warhol: The Factory Years* (London: Sedgwick & Jackson, 1989).
6. Joel Lobenthal, *Radical Rags: Fashion of the Sixties* (New York: Abbeville Press, 1990), p. 84.
7. *Ibid.*, p. 80.
8. *Ibid.*, p. 92.
9. *Ibid.*, p. 92.
10. *Ibid.*, p. 84.
11. *Ibid.*, p. 89.
12. *Ibid.*, p. 89.
13. *Ibid.*, p. 11.
14. Peter Wollen, *Raiding the Icebox: Reflections on Twentieth Century Culture* (Bloomington: Indiana University Press, 1993), p. 174.
15. I am indebted to Jeffrey Meikle's book for the details of most of my information about the history of plastics.
16. Meikle, *American Plastic*, p. 216.
17. Ibid., pp. 244-45. Cited from Mailer, "In the Red Light: A History of the Republican Convention in 1964," reprinted in *The Idea and the Octopus*, (New York: Dell, 1968).
18. *Ibid.*, p. 245. Cited from Mailer, *The Armies of the Night* (New York: Signet, 1968).
19. *Ibid.*, p. 246. Cited from Mailer, *Of a Fire on the Moon* (Boston: Little, Brown, 1970).
20. Lobenthal, *Radical Rags*, p. 223.
21. Roland Barthes, *Mythologies* (New York: The Noonday Press, 1972), p. 97.
22. *Ibid.*, p. 98.
23. *Ibid.*, p. 99.

1

2

1

So now, with one thing and another, we were reaching people
in all parts of town, all different types of people: the ones
who saw the movies would get all curious about the gallery
show, and the kids dancing at the Dom would want to see
the movies; the groups were getting all mixed up with each
other — dance, music, art, fashion, movies. It was fun to see
the Museum of Modern Art people next to the teeny-boppers
next to the amphetamine queens next to the fashion editors.

Andy Warhol and Pat Hackett, *POPism: The Warhol Sixties*, 1980, p. 162

3

5

4

6

Opposite page:

1,2. Billy Name, *Lou Reed, Sterling Morrison, Steve Sesnick, and Paul Morrissey on John Cale and Betsey Johnson's Wedding Day*, 1968

3. Billy Name, *John Cale and Betsey Johnson on Their Wedding Day*, 1968

4. Nat Finkelstein, *Gerard Malanga, John Cale, Nico, Unidentified Man, Danny Williams, Unidentified Woman, Sterling Morrison, Paul Morrissey, Andy Warhol, Lou Reed, and Maureen Tucker*, 1966

5. Nat Finkelstein, *Gerard Malanga, Andy Warhol, Mary Woronov, and The Velvet Underground*, 1966

6. Nat Finkelstein, *Banner outside the Dom*, 1966

This page:

1. Billy Name, *Actress and Viva on John Cale and Betsey Johnson's Wedding Day*, 1968

2. Christmas postcard to Andy Warhol from Betsey Johnson and John Cale, c. 1968

3. Billy Name, *The Exploding Plastic Inevitable*, 1966

4. Billy Name, *The Exploding Plastic Inevitable at the Dom*, 1966

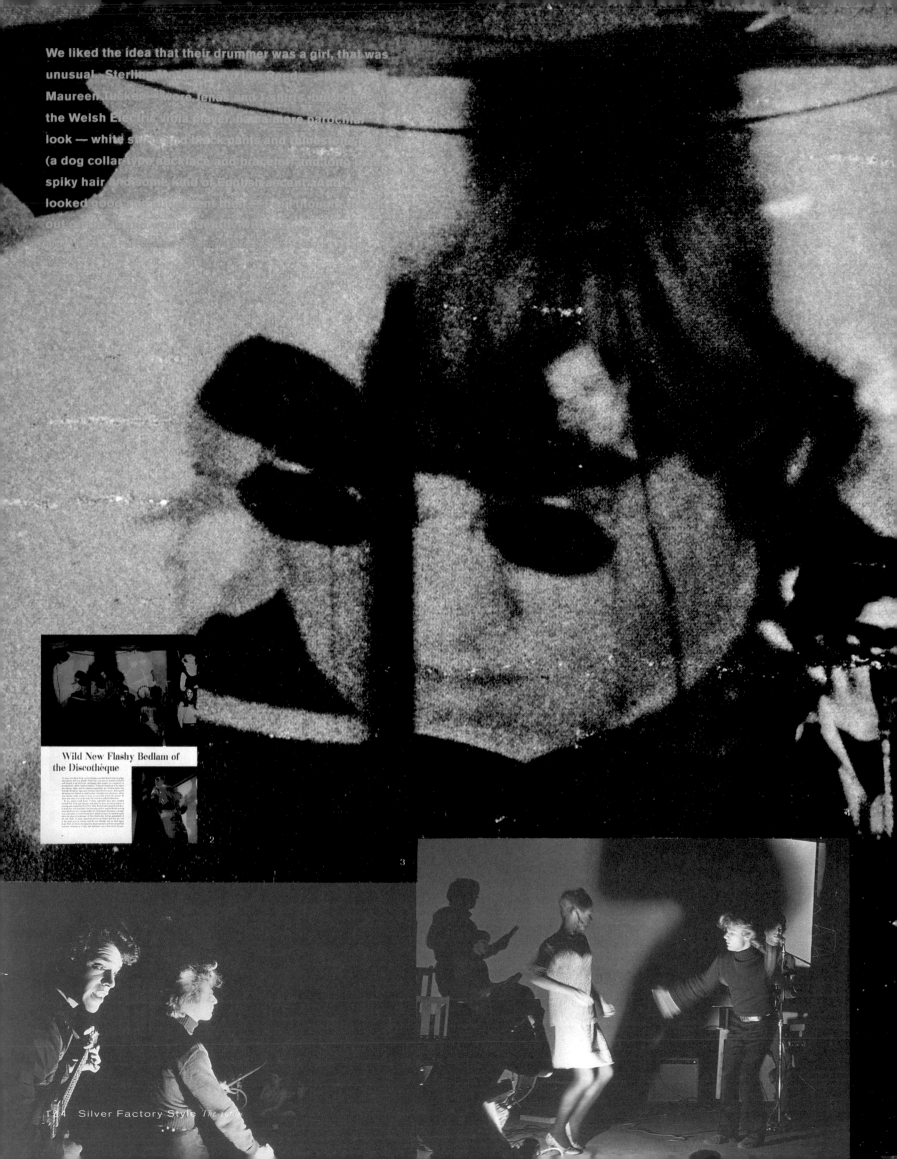

We liked the idea that their drummer was a girl, that was unusual. Sterli[n]g... Maureen Tucker... wore [tennis shoes] T-shirts [on dates]... the Welsh Electric viola player had a more parochial look — white shirt... and black pants and some... (a dog collar-type necklace and bracelet) and long spiky hair and some kind of English accent. And [they] looked good and different then — [they] flaunt[ed] out on their own...

Wild New Flashy Bedlam of the Discothèque

1. (background image) The Exploding Plastic Inevitable, *Life*, May 27, 1966
2. Article on discotheques mentioning The Exploding Plastic Inevitable, *Life*, May 27, 1966
3. Nat Finkelstein, *Lou Reed and Gerard Malanga*, c. 1966
4. Fred McDarrah, *Edie Sedgwick, Gerard Malanga, and The Velvet Underground*, 1966
5. The Exploding Plastic Inevitable, *New York Herald Tribune*, April 22, 1966

5

Nico was a new type of female superstar. Baby Jane and Edie were both outgoing, American, social, bright, excited, chatty — whereas Nico was weird and untalkative.

Andy Warhol and Pat Hackett, *POPism: The Warhol Sixties*, 1980, p.146

1. Andy Warhol, Nico in *The Chelsea Girls* reel, *Nico Crying,* 1966
2. Article with Nico and International Velvet, c. 1967
3. Article on the 1960s, with Andy Warhol and Nico, *Esquire,* August 1966
4. Andy Warhol and Nico in a publicity photograph for Pop Art Theater, 1966
5. John Cale, Gerard Malanga, Nico, and Andy Warhol, *Réalités,* 1968
6. Billy Name, *Publicity Photograph for* The Chelsea Girls, 1966

1, 2. Andy Warhol, Nico in *The Chelsea Girls* reel, *Nico Crying,* 1966
3. Billy Name, *The Velvet Underground and Nico Posing for Their First Album Cover,* 1966
4. Guess Jeans ad reminiscent of the Factory, *Interview,* February 1996

1

2

3   4

Nat Finkelstein, *Nico*, 1965

1. Fred McDarrah, *Nico, Andy Warhol, and Gerard Malanga
   Printing a* Fragile *Dress*, 1966
2. Advertisement in *The New York Times*, November 8, 1966
3. Nico, Andy Warhol, and Gerard Malanga, *Réalités*, 1968
4. David McCabe, *Unidentified Woman Wearing* Fragile *Dress,
   Andy Warhol, and Baby Jane Holzer*, 1965
5. Andy Warhol, *Fragile*, 1962
Opposite page: Fred McDarrah, *Nico*, 1966

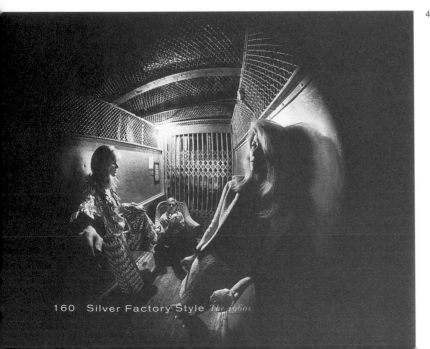

1

2

3

This page:

1,2. Billy Name, *Andy Warhol*, 1966

3. Andy Warhol, Album cover for *The Velvet Underground and Nico*, 1967

4. Article on Andy Warhol's *Banana* dress, *The New York Times*, November 8, 1966

5. Andy Warhol, *Banana* dress, 1966

6. Andy Warhol, Detail from *Coca-Cola Bottles*, 1964

7. Andy Warhol, *Coca-Cola Bottles*, 1964. The silver-sprayed bottles were made for a Warhol perfume.

Opposite page:

1. (inset upper right) Andy Warhol, *S & H Green Stamps*, 1965

2. (inset lower left) Eleanor Biddle Lloyd and Samuel Green at the opening of the Andy Warhol exhibition at ICA, Philadelphia, 1965

3. (background) Andy Warhol, *S & H Green Stamps*, 1962

5

POP PAPER . . . HIMSELF:
Andy Warhol, rhinestone-studdied scarf hanging around his neck, turned up at Abraham & Straus paper dress boutique Wednesday. He brought his long and lean blond Nicco to model the dresses while he worked. He came up with "Bananas" (see cut), giant ones pasted on. An earlier creation, "Fragile," sent Nicco scurrying for the turpentine. While the dress was being painted on her, son of Nicco, Ari, painted her legs green. Andy now works through his assistant, Gerald Melanga, who does the actual dirty work. Andy said he liked "the five-and-dime store" aspect of paper dresses. These dresses, from Mars Manufacturing Co., now come with a watercolor kit. Instant prints.

4

6, 7

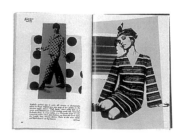

1. Fred McDarrah, *Edward Avedisian, Susanne Moss (wearing "Brillo Box" Dress), Margarette Lampkin, and Andy Warhol at Factory Party,* 1964
2. Article on Pop fashions, *Life,* February 26, 1965
3. Andy Warhol and Susanne Moss (wearing "Brillo Box" Dress) at Factory party, 1964
4. Article on Pop fashion with designs by Andy Warhol, *TV Guide,* March 5, 1966

  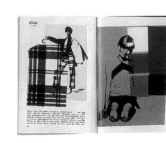

1. Andy Warhol, *Brillo Box*, 1964
2. Billy Name, *Andy Warhol with a* Brillo Box *and Billy Name's Cat*, 1964
3. David McCabe, *David Whitney*, 1964

This page:
1. Andy Warhol, *Flowers*, 1964
2, 3. David McCabe, *Andy Warhol Working on the* Flowers *Series*, 1964
4. (background image) Stephen Sprouse, *Halston fashion show*, c. 1972
Opposite page:
1. Andy Warhol, *Flowers*, 1964
2. David McCabe, *Andy Warhol Working on the* Flowers *Series*, 1964
3. (background image) Stephen Sprouse, *Halston fashion show*, c. 1972

To be successful as an artist, you have to have your work shown in a good gallery for the same reason that, say, Dior never sold his originals from a counter in Woolworth's. It's a matter of marketing, among other things.

Andy Warhol, *The Philosophy of Andy Warhol – From A to B and Back Again,* 1975, p. 151

1

2

Underground Clothes
Bizarre styles to match avant-garde movies

Reel swingers in provocative togs

3

4

1

2

Opposite page:
1. Howell Conant, Andy Warhol's *Thirteen Most Beautiful Women* projected onto one of the stars of the movie, Ivy Nicholson, 1965
2. Howell Conant, Andy Warhol's *Batman/Dracula* and *Couch* projected onto Baby Jane Holzer, 1965
3. Fashion feature with Andy Warhol's movies projected onto models, *Life,* March 19, 1965
4. Fashion feature with a silver theme, *Mademoiselle,* November 1965

This page:
1. Howell Conant, Andy Warhol's *Batman/Dracula* projected onto a model, 1965
2. Howell Conant, Andy Warhol's *Henry Geldzahler* and *Eat* projected onto models, 1965

1

2

This page:

1. Nat Finkelstein, *Andy Warhol Filming Nico's* Screen Test, 1965
2. Nat Finkelstein, *Donyale Luna's* Screen Test, 1965
3. David McCabe, Film screening at the Factory, 1965
4. Billy Name, *Ivy Nicholson's* Screen Test, 1966
5. David McCabe, *Andy Warhol behind the Camera*, c. 1964

Opposite page:

1. Andy Warhol, Dennis Hopper's *Screen Test*, 1964
2. Andy Warhol, Suzanne Janis's *Screen Test*, 1964
3. Andy Warhol, Francesco Scavullo's *Screen Test*, 1966
4. Andy Warhol, Beverly Grant's *Screen Test*, 1964
5. Andy Warhol, Gerard Malanga's *Screen Test*, 1964
6. Andy Warhol, Edie Sedgwick's *Screen Test*, 1965
7. Andy Warhol, John Giorno's *Screen Test*, 1963
8. Andy Warhol, Lou Reed's *Screen Test*, 1965
9. Andy Warhol, Ivy Nicholson's *Screen Test*, 1965
10. Andy Warhol, Brooke Hayward's *Screen Test*, 1964
11. Andy Warhol, Ann Buchanan's *Screen Test*, 1964
12. Andy Warhol, Imu, *Screen Test's* 1964
13. Andy Warhol, Baby Jane Holzer's *Screen Test*, 1964
14. Andy Warhol, Paul Morrissey's *Screen Test*, 1965
15. Andy Warhol, Billy Name's (Billy Linich) *Screen Test*, 1964

4

3

5

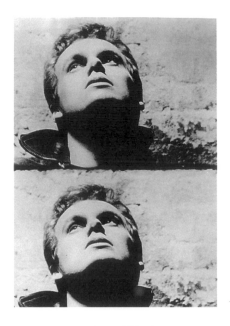

1

3

Diesen Film werden Sie nie vergessen!

Joe Dallesandro

in

Andy Warhol's
TRASH

mit Jane Forth · Holly Woodlawn

Buch, Kamera und Regie: Paul Morrissey

Eine Andy Warhol-Farbfilm-Produktion
Constantin-Film

Nach »FLESH«
der neueste Film der Factory

2

Paul Morrissey

4

5

6

1

2

3

4

1

2

3

4

5

1. Nat Finkelstein, *Andy Warhol and Baby Jane Holzer,* 1965
2. Article on Baby Jane Holzer, *Life,* March 19, 1965
3. Article on Andy Warhol and his society friends, *Town & Country,* May 1973
4. Article featuring Jane Forth, *Life,* July 4, 1970
5. Fashion feature with Jane Forth, c. 1970
6. Billy Name, *Publicity Still of International Velvet for The Chelsea Girls,* 1966
7. Publicity photograph of Nico, Mary Woronov, Andy Warhol, and International Velvet, c. 1966
8. Billy Name, *Castelli Gallery* Flowers *Show with Baby Jane Holzer and Andy Warhol,* 1964

7

6

8

1. Billy Name, *International Velvet Performing in Andy Warhol's Film **** (Four Stars)*, 1966
2. Article featuring Andy Warhol and women of the Factory, *Avant-Garde*, May 1968
3. Brigid Polk (Berlin) being interviewed by Andy Warhol, c. 1968
4. Billy Name, *Andy Warhol, Brigid Polk (Berlin), and Rodney Kitzmiller at the Factory, Bathroom Series*, 1968
5. Lee Kraft, *Andy Warhol and Viva*, 1968

1

2

3   4

5

1. Fred McDarrah, *Jed and Jay Johnson and Andy Warhol,* 1969
2. Jack Mitchell, *Jay and Jed Johnson,* 1970
3. Cecil Beaton, *Andy Warhol and Jed and Jay Johnson,* 1969
4. Andy Warhol, *Jed Johnson,* c. 1974
5. David McCabe, *Andy Warhol at Philip Johnson's Glass House, Connecticut,* 1964
6. Article on Andy Warhol with Ingrid Superstar, Jed Johnson, Gerard Malanga, Geraldine Smith, Warhol, Candy Darling, and Brigid Polk (Berlin), *Esquire,* December 1969
7. Philippe Halsmann, *Factory Crowd,* 1968
8. Fashion feature with Factory look-alikes, *Elle,* June 18, 1990

8

7

6

1. Raeanne Rubenstein, *Factory Crowd and Cecil Beaton*, 1969
2. Cecil Beaton, *Ultra Violet, Andy Warhol, Brigid Polk (Berlin), Candy Darling, and Unidentified Woman*, 1969
3. Raeanne Rubenstein, *Andy Warhol and Cecil Beaton*, 1969
4. Cecil Beaton, *Cecil Beaton and Viva*, 1969
5. Calvin Klein advertisement reminiscent of Richard Avedon's 1969 photograph of the Factory crowd, 1994

Richard Avedon, *Andy Warhol and Members of the Factory*, 1969

Richard Avedon, *Andy Warhol*, 1969

Richard Avedon, *Viva, Actress*, 1971

Drag and Transformation

Andy Warhol, *Untitled (Manicure Station)*, 1982

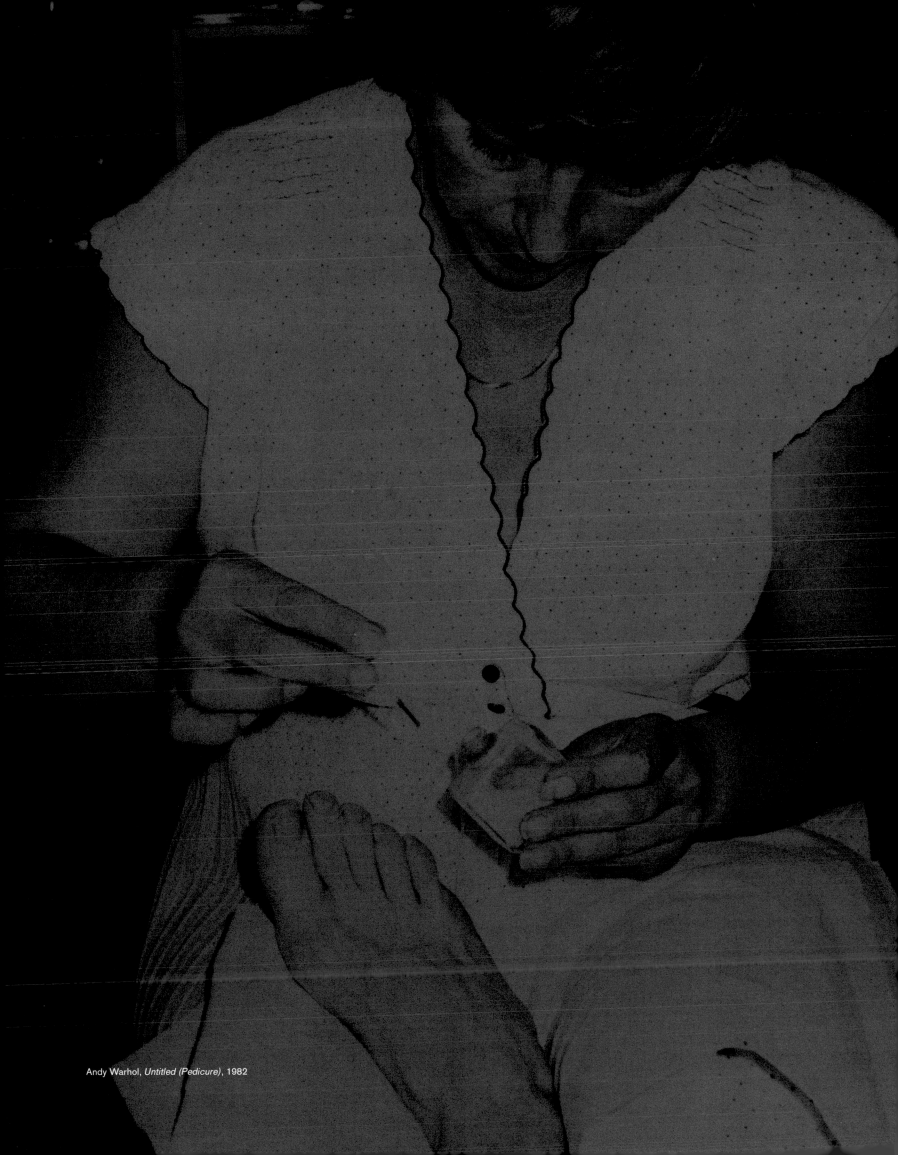

Andy Warhol, *Untitled (Pedicure)*, 1982

Warhol's wig, 1970s

Andy Warhol, *Framed Wig*, 1987

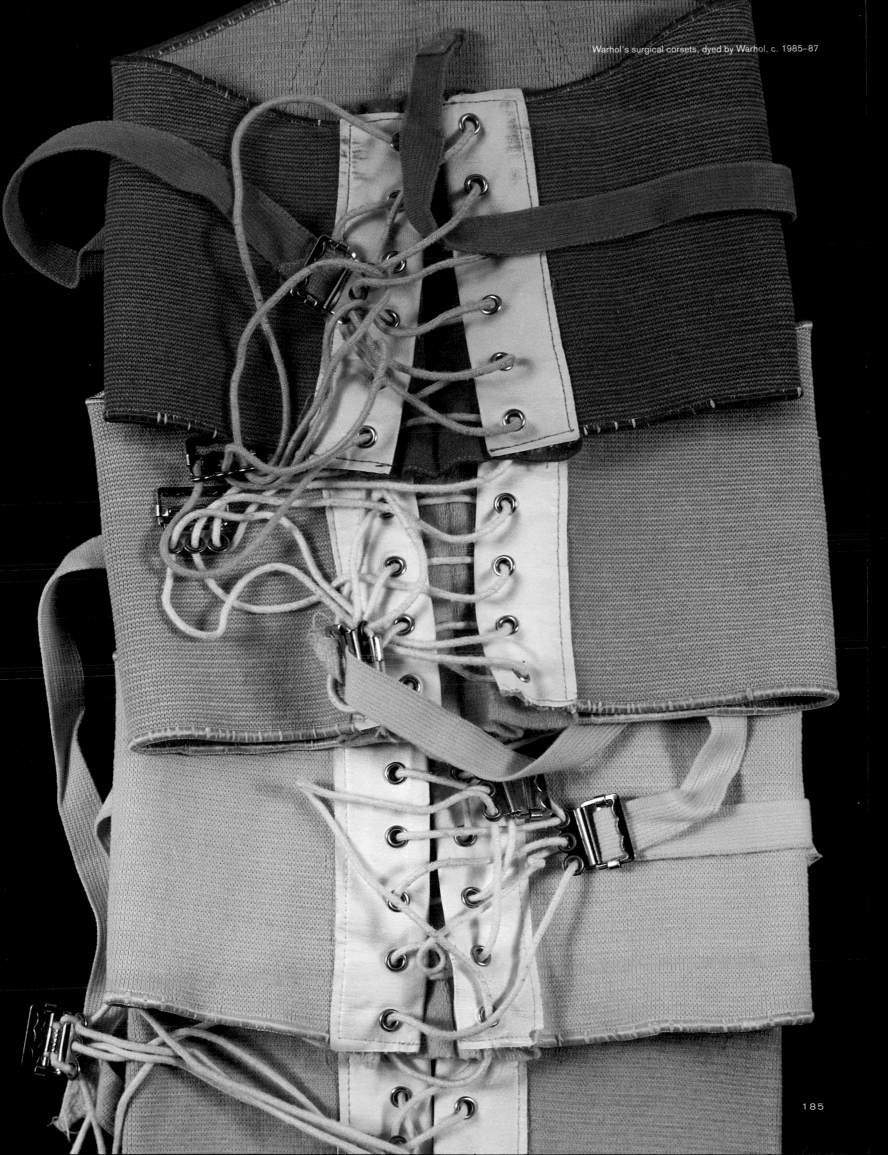

185

Another way to take up more space is with perfume. I really love wearing perfume. I'm not exactly a snob about the bottle cologne comes in, but I am impressed with a good looking presentation. It gives you confidence when you're picking up a well-designed bottle.

Andy Warhol, *The Philosophy of Andy Warhol (From A to B and Back Again)*, 1975, p. 150

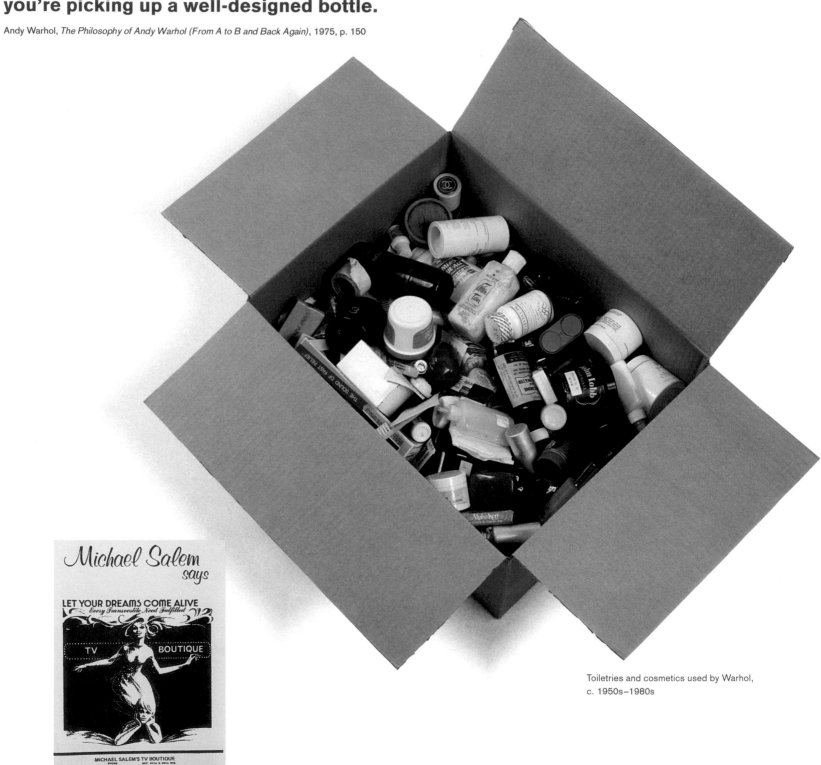

Toiletries and cosmetics used by Warhol,
c. 1950s–1980s

Michael Salem Says,
transvestite boutique catalogue, 1973

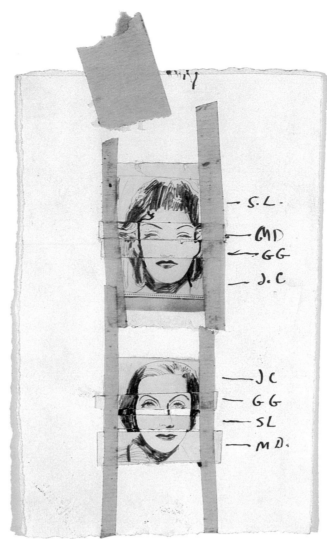

Andy Warhol, *Female Movie Star Composite*, c. 1962

Throughout his career, Andy Warhol was drawn to the flamboyant subculture of drag, and this interest found a wide range of expression in his work. Whether in full-dress drag or by subtler personal changes, through clothing, makeup, wigs, or surgery, the artist explored these related transformations in both his life and his work.

Warhol first treated the subject of drag in the 1950s, when he created sensitive pen-and-ink drawings based on photographs of his friend Otto Fenn in drag. During the 1960s, the artist filmed the outrageous performances of Jack Smith and Mario Montez, who camped up the "moldy glamour" of faded Hollywood queens. The transvestites Candy Darling, Holly Woodlawn, and Jackie Curtis were regulars in Warhol's later 1960s Factory. All three starred in Warhol and Paul Morrissey's film *Women in Revolt!*, which followed the escapades of their "women's" liberation group. Candy Darling, who seemed an incarnation of the ultraglamorous Hollywood star, was a captivating presence, both on screen and off. Her seductive yet tragic persona intrigued numerous photographers, including Francesco Scavullo and Bill King, who featured her

Andy Warhol, *Female Movie Star Composite* mechanical, c. 1962

in a fashion shoot on "Celebrity Underground Tweed" for the English magazine *Harper's and Queen*.

In the mid-1970s, Warhol again focused his work on the subject of drag, creating portraits of black and Hispanic drag queens he met in New York City in photographs, paintings, and prints with the double entendre title *Ladies and Gentlemen*. Keeping in mind the relationship between drag and other personal transformations, one may also appreciate the coded games of Warhol's early 1960s paintings *Wigs* and *Before*

Andy Warhol, *Female Movie Star Composite* photostat, c. 1962

and After. Similarly, his *Lips* book, filled with images of lips that have been shaped by the artist, and the diamond-dusted high heels in his *Shoes* paintings of 1980, are tributes to these accoutrements of drag and transformation. Perhaps Warhol's most idealistic exploration of the possibilities of personal transformation are the movie-star collages he created in the early 1960s. These works combine individual facial features of stars — Greta Garbo's eyes, Sophia Loren's lips — in what seems an effort to piece together the ideal star.

Andy Warhol, *Make Him Want You*, 1960

Andy Warhol, *Wigs*, 1960

Warhol's own transformations were clearly visible in his dress, as he moved from young 1950s professional, to hip 1960s art star, to business artist in the 1970s and 1980s. Like Candy Darling, Warhol had altered photographs of himself as a young man. He began to physically transform himself in the 1950s, when he had cosmetic surgery on his nose and first wore a hairpiece to cover his advancing baldness. The artist's wigs grew ever bolder, culminating with the hard-to-miss 1980s shock of white hair that seemed more a fashion accessory — a prickly muff or Phillip Treacy hat — than a method of hiding baldness. Warhol was also armed with a wide array of cosmetics (to smooth his mottled skin), scents, and unguents, and had worn a corset to support his midsection ever since he was shot and seriously wounded in 1968. In the early 1980s, the artist used heavy makeup and an array of wigs to transform himself into a variety of near-female personae, expressing in his own person the close connection and interplay between beautification, reinvention, transformation, and drag.

Andy Warhol, *Before and After 3*, 1962

Source for *Before and After* series, *National Enquirer*

1. Otto Fenn, self-portrait in drag, c. 1952–54
2. Otto Fenn, contact sheet, self-portraits in drag, c. 1952–54
3. Andy Warhol, *Otto Fenn*, 1950s
4. Andy Warhol, *Man with Earring*, 1950s
5. Otto Fenn, contact sheet, self-portraits in drag, c. 1952–54

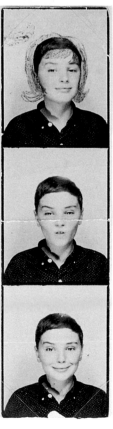

1. Cecil Beaton, *Andy Warhol and Candy Darling*, 1969
2. Otto Fenn, *Andy Warhol with altered nose*, c. 1952
3. Melton-Pippin, *Portrait of Andy Warhol*, c. 1952
4. Candy Darling, photobooth photographs with alterations, c. 1954

Francesco Scavullo, *Candy Darling and Michael J. Pollard*, 1969

1–3. Fred Hughes, *Candy Darling*, c. 1969
4. David Bailey, *Candy Darling*, 1973
5. Francesco Scavullo, *Candy Darling*, 1973

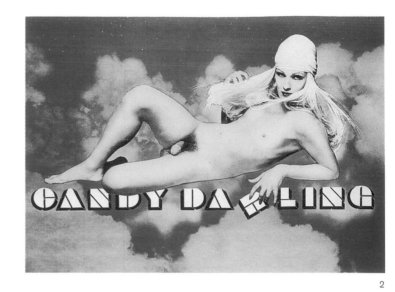

1. George Haimsohn, *Portrait of Candy Darling*, 1972
2. Richard Bernstein, *Candy Darling*, silkscreened poster, c. 1971
3. Publicity photograph of Candy Darling inscribed to photographer George Haimsohn, c. 1972
4. Andy Warhol, Candy Darling on a David Bailey photo shoot, *Factory Diaries*, 1972
5. Francesco Scavullo, mock-up design for *Cosmopolitan* with Candy Darling as covergirl, November 1972
6. Kenn Duncan, publicity still for *Some of My Best Friends Are . . .*, 1971
7. Fred McDarrah, *Candy Darling*, 1970
Opposite: Bill King, contact sheet, *Candy Darling and male model*, 1970
Opposite (inset): Candy Darling and male model in *Harper's Bazaar*, 1970

CELEBRITY
UNDERGROUND
TWEED

Celebrated Underground
Superstar Candy Darling
and a combined David Elliott
and Jim O'Connor outfit. Dove-
tail tweed battledress suit with
trouser trim, £55 5s, under, by
David Elliott. Blue silk shirt with
leaf on the sleeve,
£10 19s 6d Jim O'Connor, who
works with Zandra Rhodes. All from David
Elliott's exciting new shop/at 17
Shepherd Street, W1.

197

1

1. Candy Darling, Holly Woodlawn, and Jackie Curtis,
Vogue, June 1972
2. Advertisement for *Women in Revolt!*, *The Village
Voice*, February 24, 1972
3. Poster for *Women in Revolt!*, 1972
4–7. Publicity photographs for *Women in Revolt!*, 1972

2

3

4-7

Francesco Scavullo, *Holly Woodlawn*, 1969

I'm fascinated by boys who spend their lives trying to be complete girls, because they have to work so hard – double time – getting rid of the tell-tale male signs and drawing in all the female signs. I'm not saying it's the right thing to do, I'm not saying it's a good idea, I'm not saying it's not self-defeating and self-destructive, and I'm not saying it's not possibly the single most absurd thing a man can do with his life. What I'm saying is, it is very hard work. You can't take that away from them. It's hard work to look like the complete opposite of what nature made you and then to be an imitation woman of what was only a fantasy woman in the first place. When they took the movie stars and stuck them in the kitchen, they weren't stars any more – they were just like you and me. Drag queens are reminders that some stars still aren't just like you and me.

For a while we were casting a lot of drag queens in our movies because the real girls we knew couldn't seem to get excited about anything, and the drag queens could get excited about anything. But lately the girls seem to be getting their energy back, so we've been using real ones a lot again.

Andy Warhol, *The Philosophy of Andy Warhol (From A to B and Back Again)*, 1975, pp. 54–55

Holly Woodlawn poster

1. Richard Bernstein, poster for *Cabaret in the Sky*, 1974
2. Bill King, source photograph for *Cabaret in the Sky* poster, 1974
3. Letter from Holly Woodlawn to Andy Warhol, 1975
4–6. Photographs from Jackie Curtis's wedding, 1969

1

2

3

5

1. Jackie Curtis, c. 1969
2. Article on Jackie Curtis, *Esquire*, May 1971
3. Jackie Curtis, c. 1975
4. Billy Name, *Mario Montez*, 1965
5. Fred McDarrah, *Jackie Curtis*, 1974
6–8. Divine, *Andy Warhol's TV*, 1981

4

People don't even know the meaning of the word "transvestite." I don't live in drag. Now, Candy Darling was a transvestite, and a beautiful one. But I don't sit around in negligees and I don't wear little Adolfo suits to lunch. Of course, if I had a couple of Bob Mackie outfits, things might be different...

Divine, interview by Hal Rubenstein, *Interview* magazine, February 1988

6–8

Andy Warhol, *Shoes*, 1980

Source for *Shoes* series

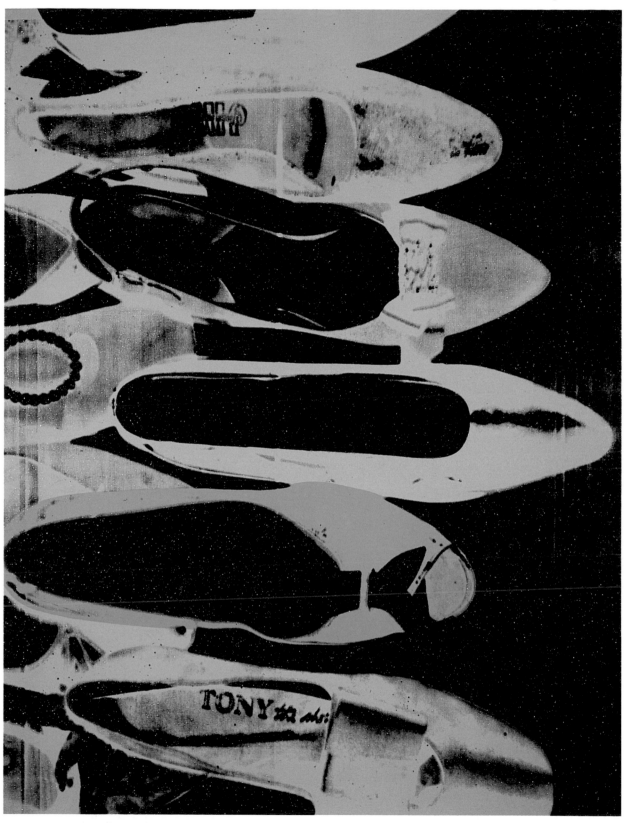

Andy Warhol, *Shoes*, 1980

Andy Warhol, *Ladies and Gentlemen*, 1975

Andy Warhol, *Ladies and Gentlemen*, 1975

Andy Warhol, *Ladies and Gentlemen*, 1975

Andy Warhol, *Ladies and Gentlemen*, 1975

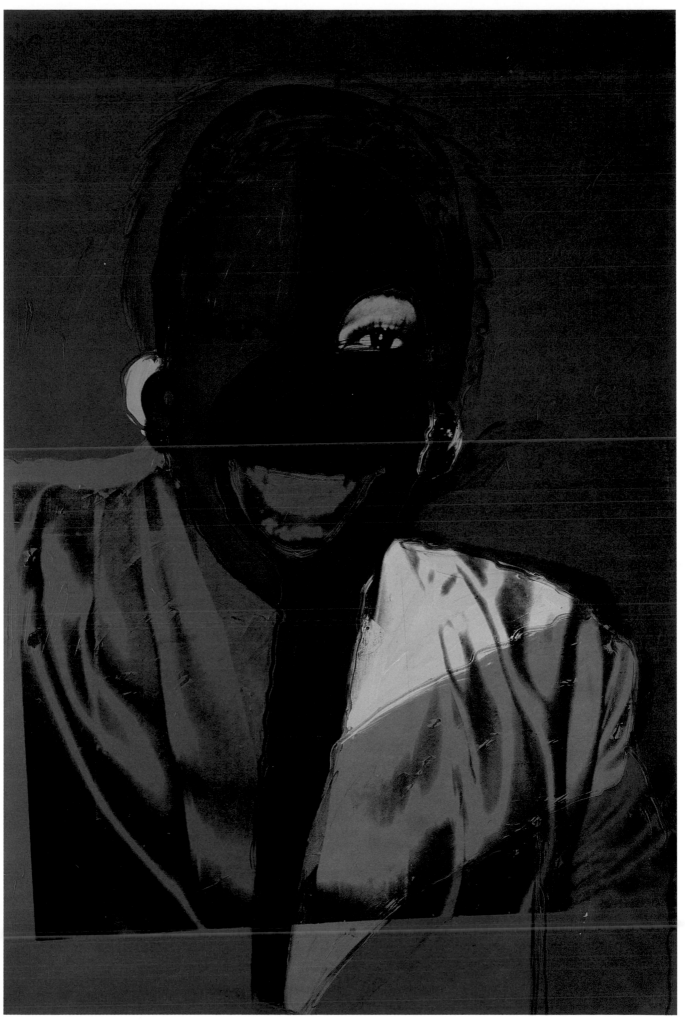

Andy Warhol, *Ladies and Gentlemen*, 1975

Andy Warhol, *Lips* book, c. 1975

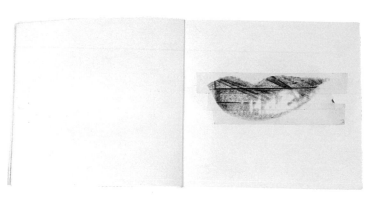

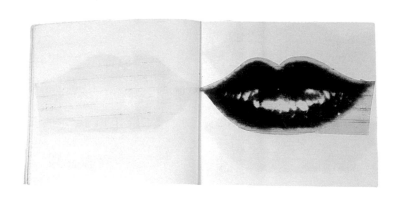

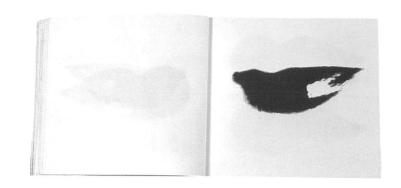

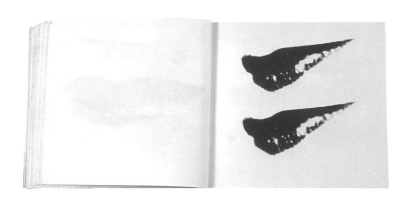

Andy Warhol, *Mick Jagger*, 1972

Andy Warhol,
Mick Jagger, 1975

Andy Warhol, *Mick Jagger*, 1975

HOW TIRESOME — AND RATHER QUICKLY, TOO — the various "life with" books by Andy Warhol's cohorts become when read one after another, the memoirs numbering now in the tens or twenties, a cottage industry whose silver-foiled eaves shimmer with overexposure. The same story many times over, written or spoken by devotees with theatrical-looking names — Baby Jane Holzer, Ultra Violet, Viva, Holly Woodlawn — whose imprimaturs are less impressive, somehow, without "superstar" attached, a fact many of Warhol's self-mythologizing associates now seem painfully aware of. Evidence of their attempts to impress is their susceptibility to recalling, in print, or for the benefit of eager young funded filmmakers, the years preceding Warhol's great media moment — his near-death by gunshot in 1968 — years these superstars and other doomed party-goers spent with Him.

In the various memoirs, the same story told with different degrees of intensity: suburban parents, prep school, Catholic school, drugs; Daddy's money, penury, nervous collapse, Silver Hill; and then the search, in New York, for a more socially skewed patriarchal figure to encourage their somewhat contrived naughtiness. These children, after their years with Warhol, their skin now slack, spend their time interpreting the value of their long-ago play space, the Factory — and its lights, cameras, multiple portraits, publishing ventures — with the acuity of fourth-generation Freudians who relegate the Factory to a symbol, an empire only a dad could have built and maintained, since dads, in their silence and decisiveness, are covetous of the imaginations of children, creating situations in which their children's greed can be acted out in order to be looked down upon, or owned and resented.

What Warhol memorists fail to consider for a moment, or in the time it took them to write their tell-alls, is that the person Warhol resonated as in their unconscious — when he resonated as any kind of person at all — was the somewhat more complicated figure of Mom, she of the bad wigs, humility, patience, attention, and jealousy. "If my left foot is dancing a good step, my right foot gets jealous," Warhol once said to his transcriber, Pat Hackett. He was pointing out, at least in this remark, that he levelled his vindictiveness at himself, cast as a joke — a not uncommon female tendency, as was Warhol's desire to be absent, a philosophical turn with a girly cast, since being considered

Mother

Hilton Als

Andy Warhol, *Candy Darling*, 1969

"nothing," or protean, many women regard as morally correct social behaviour, followed by bitterness at having adopted this attitude in the first place. Becoming "nothing" is the route moms have often followed in order to *be* Mom, she who defines herself through her children's becoming superstars. The first stage in becoming Warhol-as-she was to become "nothing," a nothing who projected an "affectless gaze" and who had an "unearthly pallor" — the journalist's quick view of the mask Warhol-as-she wore to shield the world from her prodigious forbearance.

As a mom, Warhol-as-she was often "left." Her progeny abandoned her once they began to accept the skin they were in. Such acceptance resulted in marriage first and then in flight from Warhol's perceived nest or tether, betrayals that fitted Warhol's idea of love. Love was more interesting to him when his body rejected its possibilities — expansion, comfort — by becoming "nothing," the better to experience romance in his head. For Warhol, love was pure thought.

By the time Warhol began adopting his children — or being adopted by them—he had already engineered a series of betrayals against his own mother, all of which were an outgrowth of his fury at not being "just like" anyone, least of all her, the ultimate "somebody" or superstar. Sometimes he tried to make an artist of the first Mrs. Warhola by employing her to letter words and phrases on the surface of his commercial drawings executed in the fifties and early sixties. Sometimes he didn't talk to her at all — a version of matricide. He could never forgive his mother for being the first and only Mrs. Warhola. To duplicate her on canvas (as he did with nearly all his subjects) would be to maximize, visually, the psychic failure he lived with, a failure based on not being her.

When Warhol-as-she began taking on those children who rose out of the elevator shaft at the Factory on Union Square, the protracted adolescent needs of her charges were immediately apparent. Their needs bound them to Warhol-as-she. Early on, she must have gleaned that she could never meet any of their demands, on camera or off. In effect, Warhol-as-Mom knew that her actual presence — aside from her role as producer — didn't make a difference one way or another, since each of her children was explicitly in search of what they all knew: the cruelty and indifference of dads, something Warhol-as-Mom could not offer, having no model for it, never having "really" known his father.

And in any case, Warhol-as-she thought of men as essentially thinly charming, stupid, or business minded, one-dimensional dupes without the wit to want to be moms, ever.

Warhol-as-she cultivated her role as a plain female — funky wigs, no makeup, broken-down shoes — as a way of not interfering with her children's beauty. Moms try not to be beautiful. They do not call attention to their physical attributes until their children do. If moms comment on the attention they pay to maintaining their physical well-being, they may maim a child's sense of self. Moms, in effect, cannot exist as independent entities and expect their children to develop selves of their own. No child can accept a mother's self-interest made apparent.

Also, in making herself appear unattractive, Warhol-as-she deflected the possibility of her most pressing and traditional emotional need being satisfied — a husband who could not only handle the children and their toys — the spikes, 45s, videotape machines, not to mention the toys nestled between their legs — but a husband who could finally discipline Warhol-as-she into believing that she — the Catholic girl's worry — was doing the right thing. In being physically less of a self, ghostly gray, Warhol-as-she was declaring a secondary desire, that of being made more of by a real man's imagination — a sinfully vain wish. It was a desire Warhol could never admit to, since the woman he modeled his "ghostly pallor" on was his mother, she with her unadorned self-sacrifice, Catholic view of the world and, by extension, goodness. In certain photographs, Warhol's mom appears to be a few inches shorter than her son. Like her son, she wears spectacles. Often her white-gray hair gave the impression of just having been washed and set. The freshness of her hairdo suggests that the silver clips with teeth used to create waves in her hair had moments before been placed in a plastic container nestled somewhere in her dresser drawer. That plastic container may also have contained a hair net and some bobby pins. Perhaps Andy, her son, reaching into that drawer to feel her cotton underwear, or to retrieve something else, came across this plastic container and, wishing that he had hair other then his own — thinning, mousy, brown — imagined himself in a wig more or less the same color as his mother's, hers being short and easy to maintain, an older woman's hair, the hair of a woman, the hair of a woman who was prodigious in her forbearance, since she survived bringing Andy Warhol into the world. That was the

Andy Warhol, *Jane Fonda and Candy Darling*, 1969

Andy Warhol, *Candy Darling*, 1969

Andy Warhol, *Jackie Curtis*, 1969

only hair Warhol knew of for such a long time that its significance cannot be underestimated, certainly not for an artist like
the real first Mrs. Warhola — Andy — who was a visual journalist,
a painter who transferred his sadness about being born the wrong
sex onto other women, like the subjects in *Nancy* and *Tunafish
Disaster* — homely girls glamorized either because they are car-
toons controlled by one's sense of humor, or disasters. One cannot underestimate the power in Warhol-as-she having her wig
manufactured first, and then putting it on: it was the only sartori-
al statement about his feminine life that Andy Warhol was ever
to make. The leap from having thinning hair to wearing synthetic
white hair was as much as he could do to drag out the secret
internal space Warhol-as-she projected from. Her extravagances
were minuets.

Warhol-as-she documented other people in the act of becoming exaggerated versions of themselves — the drag queens in the
Ladies and Gentlemen portrait series, certainly — but he reached his
apotheosis as a mom encouraging theatrical offspring — especially
the theatrical daughter — when he began promoting Candy
Darling in films, on video, and on the lecture circuit, she of the
too carefully applied lipstick and the intellectual process based on
cross-cutting and deep focus. Candy Darling's intense movie love,
movie interest, was an outgrowth of her love for those actresses
whose overbearing theatrical expressiveness in the films they
made in the forties and fifties (and that Candy saw as a child on
TV, on the *Million-Dollar Movie*) transformed their star vehicles
into epics.

Candy Darling believed until the end in a Candy Darling
epic being produced just for her. (The only actor who could play
Candy Darling now would be Meryl Streep who, as Sophie in
the film *Sophie's Choice* bears an uncanny resemblance to Candy
Darling.) Her expectations were commensurate with the extensive
work she had put into becoming Candy Darling. But no movie
could ever be produced that would be epic enough to meet all
her expectations, just as no girl could be girl enough to embody
and represent Warhol's interior girlishness. Bad hormone pills let
cancer loose in Candy Darling's small, white, titless frame. She
died, her dick still intact, with much the same mindset Warhol
was victimized by: a will, which could not give girlishness up.

Months before her death, bitterness had begun to consume
Candy Darling, her ravishing   and too often on film

ravished girlishness. Candy Darling's girlishness, no matter how concentrated on, perfected, could never qualify her for the role she felt she was born to play, a role in another bad movie, but one legitimized by having been made in Hollywood — *Myra Breckenridge.*

Candy Darling's acting style — in *Women in Revolt!*, among other vehicles that Paul Morrissey directed and Warhol produced — was that of a woman made of make-believe; she did not speak her lines but emoted her feelings about the lines originally scripted for and spoken by Lana and Joan and Kim — women whose reactive stance Candy Darling's body commented on, sitting on one set or another, legs crossed, not speaking, eyebrows ready for their closeup, and for that epic that never materialized.

Candy Darling could have been cast in any number of films that her heart and greed would have been perfect for. She should have played anything but herself. Despite the dedication and rigor Candy Darling applied to being Miss Darling, self-doubt nibbled at her heels flecked with Factory filth. That doubt was embodied in her bad teeth, which Warhol-as-she never paid her enough to fix, preferring instead the imperfections of Candy Darling's bleeding gums in that perfectly shaped Candy Darling face, a toothy metaphor that hurt as it spoke of our "wrong" world and the wronged in it.

Candy Darling's self-doubt does not play well on screen. In most of her Warhol vehicles, her anxieties come across as stilted, a camp performance of pathos. There were other aspects of her screen persona that could have been exploited. Had she been available to other directors, they might have worked with the fact that Candy Darling, like Warhol, was an American class-conscious snob with thick ankles, who wore stockings with runs in them; Candy Darling, like Warhol, was interested in the "nothing" lives of rich people, the overindulged whose greatest efforts are reserved for trying to disguise how little care they take with other people's lives. Candy Darling's most interesting performance was captured in a still by Peter Hujar; in that Hujar photograph we see her in full makeup, lying in bed, seemingly rich and overindulged, and dying.

Toward Candy Darling, Warhol-as-she expressed her most tender feelings, perhaps because neither Warhol nor Candy believed they were being directed at a real person. Candy Darling was the girl Warhol-as-she felt herself to be — strange, feminized,

Andy Warhol, *Candy Darling and Gerard Malanga*, 1969

Andy Warhol, *Divine*, 1974

languageless — or could have become, had Warhol not respected fear more than anything else.

Candy Darling did not live to write her memoirs; she did not live long enough to oversee the recent publication of *My Face for the World to See: The Diaries of Candy Darling*, which has not been dedicated to Mother. These diary jottings and drawings and musings do not take her Warhol years into serious consideration; nor do they recount the days spent working as a barmaid for Jackie Curtis's grandmother, Slugger Ann, dressed in nothing more than a slip and fantasy. Like the Candy Darling we see on screen, her book is a nonverbal demonstration of her will's need to uphold the idea of self as fantasy, a conviction she demonstrated for the first time, publicly, when she went into her mother's bathroom, out there on Long Island where she was raised, in order for Jimmy Slattery to introduce his mother to Candy Darling, she of the platinum hair, rayon dresses, chunky forties' shoes, big and little toes poking through black fishnets, and red lips. Candy emerged from the bathroom and walked into the living room where her mother sat watching a big color TV. She implored her mom, in her needy, actressy voice, to understand this woman with the movie-star eyes whom Mrs. Slattery had no biological relationship to. In that moment — a small feminine moment in the larger world — Candy Darling had yet to be discovered by her real mother, who also had a fondness for platinum hair, standing off alone somewhere, waiting for more and more girl to overtake him, obscuring his boy self from the world.

Something extremely interesting was happening in men's fashions too – they were starting to compete in glamour and marketing women's fashions, and this signaled big social changes that went beyond fashion into the question of sex roles.

Andy Warhol and Pat Hackett, *POPism: The Warhol Sixties*, 1980, pp. 208–209

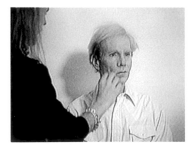

Andy Warhol, *Factory Diary*, 1981

Christopher Makos, *Altered Image*, 1981

Andy Warhol, *Self-Portraits*, 1981
Opposite: Christopher Makos, *Altered Image*, 1981

Andy Warhol, *Self-Portraits*, 1981

Andy Warhol, *Self-Portraits*, 1981
Opposite: Christopher Makos, *Altered Image*, 1981

Bianca photographed by Scavullo
Yves Saint Laurent by Bianca
Alan Bates by Andy
plus
Romano Mussolini, Massage Parlors,
Ed Sullivan, The Definitive Ray Davies,
Susannah York, Lena Horne

January 1973

Andy Warhol's

Interview

jan 73

50¢

UK 25p

Knight in White Satin
Cecil Beaton talks to Penelope Tree

m, LOVES OF ONDINE

LOVES OF ONDINE, another view

Joe in the unreleased SURF.

LONESOME COWBOYS

14

1. Joe Dallesandro, *Interview*, November 1972;
   photographs: Paul Morrissey and
   Francesco Scavullo
2. *Interview*, April 1973
3. *Interview*, April 1974; photographs: Horst

***Interview*, founded by Andy Warhol in 1969,** is the apotheosis of the artist's infatuation with glamour, style, and fashion, and it has been an important vehicle for defining and disseminating his views on these subjects, both during Warhol's proprietorship and under subsequent publishers. Originally a monthly film journal, the magazine quickly expanded its focus to encompass all areas of popular art and culture. An amalgam of tabloid newspaper, fan magazine, and art journal, *Interview* pioneered the concept of the celebrity interview by having prominent personalities interview other ones, creating an intimate conversational style that had

1. *Naomi Sims Astride a Crocodile, Interview,* 1973; photograph: Peter Beard
2–3. August 1970

15

seldom been used in journalism.

By the early 1970s, fashion and celebrity features had eclipsed film as the principal interest of the magazine. The first major fashion spread appeared in May 1972, an interview of Halston by Pat Ast, with sketches of Halston, Loulou de la Falaise, and Elsa Peretti by the fashion illustrator Joe Eula. Designers have continued to appear frequently in the pages of *Interview*, as have others in the fashion industry, including models, retailers, and makeup artists, contributing to the celebrity status of many in the fashion world today. During the 1970s and early eighties, Bob Colacello's monthly "OUT" column

1. Halston, *Interview*, May 1972
2. Elizabeth Taylor in Iran, *Interview*, July 1976;
   photograph: Firooz Zahedi
3. May 1972

ILLUSTRATIONS
BY JOE EULA

gave readers an insider's view of society, revealing both
its glamour and its narcissism.

Photography has always played a critical role in
Interview's success. Early issues of the magazine were
liberally illustrated with glamorous publicity photographs
of movie stars and stills from Hollywood films, like the
ones Warhol had collected as a child. In 1972, when
the first photographs by Francesco Scavullo appeared
in *Interview*, the magazine became a major force for
promoting the work of fashion photographers. Marc
Balet, *Interview*'s art director from 1975 to 1988, commissioned the work of talented young photographers,

HALSTON

by Robert Colaciello and Pat Ast

Halston: Do you have that on? (the tape recorder – ed.)

RC: Of course.

Halston: All right, now I won't talk.

Pat Ast: Do you find that inhibiting? I don't. I'm an actress. You're an actor. God knows you're an actor.

Halston: Ask me some questions. I'm much better if I have questions to answer.

Pat: Oh, can't we argue instead?

Halston: Don't make me argue Pat. I'm really not that way at all. I'm a good guy.

Pat: WMCA.

Okay, my first question is very abstract. You can argue over the answer. What does fashion mean to you?

Halston: Oh not that. I guess it's a reflection of the times. It has to do with personal adornment. Fashion starts with fashionable people. People who attract attention. They can be from almost any walk of life. They can be Pat Ast or Donna Jordan or Mrs. Onnasis or Mrs. Paley or a movie personality. People who command the public eye as well as having their own personal taste. I strongly believe in fashion being for fashionable people. It is not for everybody. It is for people who set the pace. That's how trends start. It usually takes a little bit of money. But more imagination. Don't you agree Pat?

Pat: I think it's a lot of hard work.

Halston: No it isn't really. Is it hard work for you to be you?

Pat: I meant for you as a designer.

Halston: That wasn't the question.

Is it hard work?

Halston: Well, as a designer we only suggest. We don't set trends at all. People set trends. We make a collection and if you have a fashionable public that comes and selects it may very well become the fashion. But it may not. It may not wear well. No designer has ever made fashion alone. People make fashion.

Do you have any favorite people right now? Any trend setters?

Halston: Well I could give you an international who's who of who I think is fashionable. Like a Mrs. Agnelli in Italy. I think she's a really sensational looking woman, great personal taste, beautiful woman, beautiful manners, everything. In France there are so many glamorous women. The Vicomtesse de Ribes has always been sensational, more before than now. I think Lulu de la Falaise has great personal chic, always did. I think Betty...

Pat: I think DD Ryan.

Halston: DD Ryan. Yes. All the obvious ones. You know, you have a beautiful woman like Mrs. Paley. For her age group and social group she sets the pace for those ladies. They all want to look like she looks. I think people like Donna Jordan certainly set a trend. Marisa Berenson. Berry. Elsa Peretti for sure. I think people like Garbo set trends. People like Katherine Hepburn always did. Even Liza Minnelli in a funny way.

Garbo came into your shop recently, no?

Halston: Yes. I used to make things for Garbo years ago. Hats.

What's she like? She's probably the most private movie star around, which is why she's so fascinating.

Halston: Oh, she is fascinating. She always has been. The first time I met her I just came to New York and I was working for Lilly Dashay. And Garbo came in to the salon and I was the one to take care of everybody and she really asked if she could be alone in the salon. She wanted to be alone. She's really shy. I think that was twelve or fourteen years ago, my first meeting with her. Now, I saw her as someone completely different. Pat brought out a side I never knew, that funny sense of humor.

What was it like to sell her something Pat?

Pat: Well I didn't exactly sell her. You know, she was brought in. They called me to see if I would wait on her. Sam Green called. She came in and said she wanted a pea jacket.

Halston: I think she was very amusing. As a woman, she's an amusing woman. She was with her friend, Cecil de Rothschild. In a business like that, I know it sounds show-offy when you hear all the names, but it is interesting the way the people everyone is talking about drop into your life from time to time. Yesterday we had Jackie Onassis in. She really is a charming, lovely, sweet woman, a little bit shy. One of the dressmakers from upstairs said she had heard so many nasty stories about Jackie Onassis that she was really pleasantly surprised to see that she is quite pretty, she couldn't be nicer.

Pat: She could not.

Halston: Couldn't be plainer, couldn't be more polite. You know, she was just enjoying herself. I think sometimes the press is a bit irresponsible with these people because they don't really give them a chance.

Well we just turn on the tape recorder and let everyone say what they want. It's the New New Journalism.

Halston: Yes, but even then one says different things on different days depending on your mood, the environment, who you're with...

How did you get started?

Halston: At the beginning. No, I just started making things. Like how did you get started? You just started writing and liked it for one reason or another and you continued.

Pat: Did you go to college?

Halston: No, not for fashion design. I went to Indiana University, the Art Institute of Chicago, and then the University of Chicago.

You're from Chicago?

Halston: No, I was born in Iowa. I only lived there for five or six years, then I moved to Indiana. That's where I grew up, Indiana. I'm a Midwestern boy. But now I'm a New Yorker. I think you have to live in New York for about fifteen years in order to be a New Yorker. It really is your town then. I really don't like to leave New York. Except for maybe a weekend. Nothing else is interesting to me at all.

What interests you in New York other than the fashion?

Halston: It's not necessarily just fashion, it has to do with everything else you do in the business life. I really like what I do, it doesn't always have to do with clothes. It has to do with people who come in that I like, not necessarily to buy, or people who I have working for me like Pat... I have found doing it.

Do you like to go to the movies, clubs...?

Halston: Oh, I like the movies once in awhile. I don't think there are that many good movies around anymore. And then if they are terribly good there's a long line. I think what I really enjoy my friends more than anything. I love dinners with friends, talking about anything interesting really. I love private parties where you might invite all sorts of friends that you have and you see all different types. I love big parties. But not too often. Like every couple of weeks. I wish more people would give them. I think people are afraid. It's just so hard today because there are so many interesting people that one wants to invite. And so many hangers-on. I think one has to edit those invited very carefully. I think it's fabulous for different friends who do different things to meet each other... writers, actors, artists, fashion people, whatever, it's amusing. An exchange of ideas! That's a new thing in New York. This large group that gets together from time to time. It's always interesting. And the women are always fabulous. That helps to make a good party. I like everything to be a bit glamorous.

Do you go to Europe a lot?

Halston: I used to go for three weeks twice a year for business. Sometimes three times a year. Because Paris was certainly the center of all fashion. We bought a great deal when I worked for Bergdorf Goodman. We were the biggest buyers in Paris. It was really interesting for me. And I used to take a winter holiday there and a summer holiday, but now I don't like it so much.

Do you think the center has moved from Paris to New York?

Halston: I don't think there is any center anymore. Fashion can come out of London, out of Japan, out of New York. We don't have the fashion structure that we used to have. With the end of Balenciagaw is the end of a whole era, of one person setting the trends for a large public. That just doesn't exist anymore. Now you can be anybody as long as you have an idea and so as long as somebody good buys it. I think that's where it is at now.

Who do you think are the best among the European designers?

Halston: St. Laurent is the most influential one, without a doubt. But I think that the greatest craftsman is probably Givenchy. He has the best ateliers. He has all those fabulous workers from Balenciaga who are the best dressmakers and tailors in the world.

What do you think of Valentino's clothes?

Pat: Next.

Halston: Well, I like Mr. Valentino. I think he's just alright.

Pat: If you like V's you're in. If your name is Virginia or Veronica or Veruscka.

Halston: Well, I never understood the idea of wearing someone's initials. But it's good business. Good businessman. He had his V's everybody's waist so they were walking ads for him. It's hard about other people's things you have, your own point of view and mine is, that at this particular moment, I don't have any heroes. Maybe I'm too old, maybe I've outgrown it that sort of... But I always had that idea that there's someone you look up to. No I don't that so much.

Who were the people you looked...

Halston: I think the obvious ones really did the numbers like Balenciaga, Chanel, even Charles James. There's always such a finesse there that no one else ever got.

Pat: Tell us about Stephan Burrows.

Halston: I think Stephen is really one of the unrecognized geniuses of the world, I really do. I gave Women's Wear the talk about it the other day. I think Stephan gives the most of anyone in America today. And the thing is the cut.

What do you think of the fashion...

Halston: I think they're wonderful.

Pat: Next...

1

1. Charles James, *Interview*, November 1972; photograph: Cecil Beaton
2. Diana Ross, *Interview*, December 1972; photographs: Bill King

2

27

providing David LaChapelle, Matthew Rolston, Herb Ritts, David Seidner, Bruce Weber, Ellen von Unwerth, and many others with early and prominent exposure. Photographers were encouraged to produce innovative, experimental work for *Interview*, which might not have been welcomed by mainstream fashion magazines.

Throughout its history, *Interview* has offered a provocative and seductive vision of fashion and celebrity. Although it chronicles the lives of the fashionable and the rich, at its core, *Interview* is a celebration of popular culture and an embodiment of Andy Warhol's belief in the democratic nature of fame. — John W. Smith

Fashioning
Interview

Glenn O'Brien

Sometimes, when Andy Warhol was asked why he started *Interview* magazine in 1969, he answered, "Umm, to give Gerard something to do." Gerard Malanga, a poet, photographer, and Andy's former painting assistant, was the creator of *Interview*'s first issue. Sometimes, when Andy didn't want to credit Gerard, he said, "To give the kids something to do." Sometimes he

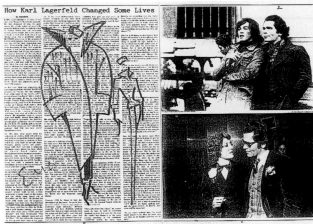

gave other answers, like "So we could get tickets to the New York Film Festival." That always seemed to be the most likely answer to me, because as charming as Gerard was, and as much as Andy liked "the kids" who worked for him, it didn't seem Andy's nature to start a business just to give someone something to do.

From the beginning, *Interview* was a tool, a key, a foot in various doors. I'm sure that later Andy saw it as something that might make money someday. But

Yves Saint Laurent talks to Bianca Jagger

What is on your mind, Yves?

Many things . . .

Always pretty.

I can't say.

Do you think you can speak in front of this machine? It's not really the right time.

(In English) I would like to be sit . . .

(In English) There–Voilà, that's a perfect place. Monsieur Saint Laurent . . . (She laughs.)

Mrs. J. (They both laugh.)

Why have you chosen women as your inspiration? (In English) To find something new? Do you find in your work that women have disappointed you?

Disappointed? No, not at all. Certainly not. Definitely not.

Do you feel that you can give everything you want to?

With women?

Aren't there any women beyond your fantasy and imagination?

No, not at all. Because I don't at all search for an ideal woman, but several ideal women.

Several ideal women?

Yes, each model I have represents a type of ideal women to me.

But the epitome . . . a few women . . .

Yes, in a certain sense . . . Why so few women?

No, these few women.

Few? Why I know at least six. (They laugh.)

At least! If you weren't a fashion designer what would you do?

Nothing. Live.

Have the people you've gotten emotionally close to influenced your creations?

Yes, alot.

Yes? Your vision of woman?

Yes, absolutely. Completely transformed by certain women I have known, friends . . . For example, when I knew Thalita Getty–Thalita–You know her?

Yes.

. . . my vision completely changed.

Your idea of woman?

Yes, absolutely.

And men, do they have any influence on your work?

Absolutely not at all.

Not at all?

Absolutely not.

Absolutely not! But from time to time in your life there have been women who have become your . . . your . . . your ideal and inspiration.

Ah, yes, absolutely. There are women who have completely transformed my view of fashion and if I hadn't known them I would never have arrived at this point in fasion, you see.

What do you do if you find that you must design something for a woman without any beauty of face or form?

I try not to put myself in that situation, poor things. I try to only be in agreeable circumstances.

Do you have a definite view of men and of women, of two sexes, or are the two variations of one, or is it something ambiguous–Woman?

Why are you always asking me about women? Because I'm a couturier?

No, it's not a question of women, it's more general: you have people, you define them . . .

No.

No?

No, not at all.

That's what I was saying . . .

No, absolutely not. No, for me they are human beings, that's all. I love them, I'm attracted to them, physically, or psychically, or morally. . . . Classification isn't part of it.

Do you like daring people?

Yes, sure.

What about people who talk about fashion.

Oh, yes. I detest that. I detest fashion ultimately. I adore clothes but I hate fashion.

And talking about it?

Yes. (They laugh.)

I'll think of something else to ask you about. I like you because you have an extraordinary sensitivity.

Yes.

. . . and because you are one of those rare creatures always searching for beauty in the things you do.

Yes, that's what I'm always looking for. I'm an aesthete.

You are always looking for perfection–are you aware of that?

Absolutely, I can't avoid it. I'm constantly looking for perfection.

What have you been most deceived by?

I'm not deceived by people because I don't pay attention to people.

Aren't there qualities you look for in people?

No, because ultimately the qualities I see in people are what I perceive them to be. It is my vision of people that counts. It's all projection. If I am deceived it's my own doing. What interests me is my vision of others.

One of the things I admire most about you is that you always give credit to people.

I am for all the people I'm in contact with.

What do you think of Erte?

Oh, I adore him. I think he's marvelous. I feel very close to him. I have no jealousies.

I know. That's one of the things I admire most about you.

I'm very sure of myself–what I do and what I like.

That's a rare quality in your world, fashion, where people are so unsure and intriguing.

You know me very well. (Laughs.)

I've got a good eye. I've seen that you would like to be above merely material things. You live in a bit of a dream world.

Yes, possibly. Yes, certainly, I'd really like to be in closer contact with life, I'm a little too distant, I guess, I like to place myself outside.

Has there been a woman or women in your life that you've been truly in love with?

Yes, one or two.

What did they represent to you?

They didn't represent anything aesthetic. They weren't muses at all. It was for me a completely new sentiment. It had nothing to do with fashion.

It didn't enhance your creative life?

No, I couldn't love a woman who inspired me to be totally disinterested. If I fell in love with a woman for an artistic reason, or from the point of view of my work, I think it would [...]

What do y[...] America.

I adore Am[...] country. A [...]

You don't fe[...]

No, do you? [...]

Well, I'm a h[...]

I love the [...] home. I'm w[...]

I like Ameri[...] surprised–[...] social-climb[...]

But people [...] There are [...] here.

There are [...] because of o[...]

People seem [...] an extrac[...] really.

You like tha[...]

Oh, yes–'ca[...]

I'm always [...] rapid rappo[...] any country [...] instant. Whe[...] to like the[...] sudden.

It depends o[...] work it's mo[...] in your favo[...]

But you mu[...]

Yes. (They both laugh.)

Aren't you a bit annoyed when women make themselves too available to you?

On the contrary, I adore it.

Not embarrassing?

No.

Does the fact of having revolutionized fashion and having arrived at the summit at such a young age upset you?

Possibly–I would surely have liked to know other things, more interesting, more real, less superficial. . . .

Yes, and after this, what would you like to do?

Afterwards? I would like . . . I would very much like to write. I would very much like to write a book . . . A very, very beautiful book that would be a summation of everything I love, of all my thoughts about life, women, men, beauty . . . It would be a memoir . . . But I don't have the patience right now to write it. I'm waiting 'til I have the time.

You should do it now.

I can make notes.

Are you always making notes? Tapes every night?

I'm a little like that–although I do it in a different way.

I've seen some extraordinary drawings you've done. Do you have any plans to publish them?

Yes, definitely.

When?

I've no idea whatsoever.

The trouble with most designers . . .

. . . is that they have an idea of women that they try to impose on them. I can all of a sudden forget the idea I'm working on when confronted with the body of the woman I'm dressing.

What's good about you is that you have an understanding of the people, of the women, for whom you're making something: 'a meeting of minds.'.

Continued on pg. 44

11

Opposite page:
1. *Interview*, January 1973; photograph: Francesco Scavullo
2. *Interview*, March 1973
3. December 1972
4. Subscription form featuring Geri Miller, *Interview*, January 1973; photograph: Ronnie Cutrone
This page:
1. *Interview*, April 1975
2. June 1972

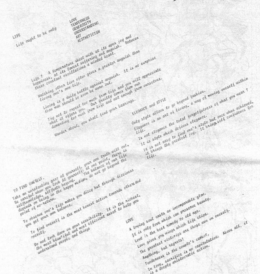

What we imagine may be very beautiful but nothing replaces reality.
Yves Saint Laurent

THE PHILOSOPHY OF YVES SAINT LAURENT

1

Andy Warhol's *Interview* june 72 50¢

subscribe

2

233

he realized early on that having a magazine was a great way to meet people and get invited to things. For the first year of its life, *Interview* was an underground film magazine. It got Andy Warhol and Paul Morrissey into film festivals and screenings. It promoted Andy's own productions, like *Flesh* and *Trash*. And it quickly proved to be an effective way to get the attention of the film stars, directors, and producers Andy and Paul wanted to meet. They discovered that the words "Can we interview you for our magazine, *Interview*?" worked surprisingly well. Later *Interview* was a good foot in fashion-world doors, art-world doors, even White House doors.

I went to *Interview* in 1970 to work with my Columbia film school friend Bob Colacello, who had been hired by Andy and Paul to edit the magazine. Bob was hired after his review "Andy Warhol's *Trash*" had appeared in *The Village Voice*, comparing it to the work of Michelangelo (Buonarroti, not Antonioni). Andy and Paul liked Bob because he was smart, middle class, ambitious, and wasn't a drug addict. From the beginning, Bob and I worked hard to make it more professional. We redesigned it to make it look less underground. We tried to find real writers who would work for $25. We initially wanted to make it a real film magazine by reviewing every film released in New York and by turning *Interview* into a magazine of actual interviews, not self-indulgent articles by "superstars." We also got Andy to do one interview each month.

Interview gravitated toward fashion

ELSA PERETTI

Intro: Elsa Peretti otherwise known as "Vicious Venus". Born Florence. Designs exquisite jewelry - sculpted silver, diamonds by the yard etc. etc. First shown with Halston collection. Coty award winner. Now featured at Tiffany and Co. Interviewed in and around New York city by art-sweet-artist Victor Hugo.

In the Bowery.

VH: What do you think about Americans?
EP: Tres fantastic.
VH: Do you feel you must pursue beauty all times?
EP: Always.
VH: How do you feel about your marriage with Tiffanys?
EP: We are going to have a few babies as soon as possible.
VH: This is a stupid question, but do you want to get married one day?
EP: I am afraid it is very stupid....
VH: How about Italy's situation today?
EP: Very sad.

[That night over the phone]

VH: How do you feel about your success at Tiffanys? Richard Bernstein told he asked one of the salesgirls how she felt about it and she said she didn't even have time for a coffee break.
EP: I prefer tea.

[Finally]

In an airplane on the way to Fire Island, after a heavy duty interview with Newsweek which delayed the plane three times that day....
VH: Do you have fun?
EP: Ma...aaaaa.....
EP: When can I smoke?
VH: Wait after the plane takes off darling. Four minutes, no one.
(Elsa had to read some questions over my shoulder because with the noise of the plane we could not even use the tape recorder.)
VH: What car do you like?
EP: "Morgan."
I have a girlfriend who used to like to get raped in Morgans.
VH: Animal?
EP: My dog, "Hero."
EP: Give me a cigarette, darling.
VH: Stone?
EP: Coral.

[Volare-oh-oh!]

VH: Food?
EP: Rice.
VH: Climate?
EP: Warm.
VH: Color?
EP: Black.
VH: Shape?
EP: Round.
VH: Time?
EP: From twelve on.
VH: Music?
EP: Mozart *(Mozart-oh-oh!)*
VH: Man?
EP: I don't know.
VH: Woman?
EP: Me. Look at the sky! So beautiful!
VH: Child?
EP: A lot.
VH: Clothes?
EP: Halston and cashmere
VH: Country?
EP: Country.
VH: City?
EP: New York.
VH: Store?
EP: Bloomingdales.
VH: Building?
EP: Empire State, Coliseum, Parthenon.
VH: Flower?
EP: Calla Lily.
VH: Boat?
EP: Sailing boat.
VH: Cigarette?
EP: Kent.
VH: Teeth?
EP: Clean.
VH: Foot?
EP: Clean and bare.
VH: Shoe?
EP: Comfortable.
VH: Liquor?
EP: Vodka.
VH: Size ass?
EP: Ma que es eso? Burro!!
VH: Size tits?
EP: Big.....ha ha ha ha.....
VH: I understand darling. Mood?
EP: Mood . . . mood . . . . mood . . . . enthusiastic!
VH: Sky?
EP: Blue!!! Like this one.
VH: Light?
EP: Good one.
VH: Elevator?
EP: Otis.
VH: Knife?
EP: Chriss.
VH: Mother?
EP: I wish I could say mine.
VH: What about keeping a man?
EP: No!
VH: Money?
EP: A lot!!! *[$]*
VH: Machine?
EP: I don't like machines.
VH: Thinking....We are about to land and will have a better 'tête à tête.'
VH: Any change in your work?
EP: Different material, but the same shapes.

[Beside the pool]

VH: Here we go again Elsa. The interview is not finished so get ready. Joe Eula has told me that you have been called the Vedette of Tiffanys.
EP: (Nice laugh) I LOVE it

VH: Miss Peretti, you always talk about tradition. How do you feel about it in your life being Latin?
EP: Very important.
VH: Do you like frivolity?
EP: Yes.
VH: Do you like plastic things like food, flowers, love . . . . etc.
EP: No.
VH: What do you think about Womens Lib?
EP: Vaffanculo!!! *— eh!*

VH: OK, NEXT....How do you see yourself: a business woman or Mother Nature?
EP: Mother Nature.
VH: How do you feel after you made it in the Big Apple?
EP: I didn't make it yet. OHHHHHH, look at the blue of the swimming pool!!!!
VH: Its pure plastic, sweetie.
EP: Don't call me sweetie.
VH: OK, Miss Peretti.

[The morning after the night before.]

VH: (Elsa's boyfriend was taking his morning walk on the beach. Elsa was morning dreaming.)
VH: Buon giorno carissima.
EP: Do you think that is the right man for me?
VH: I don't know.
EP: I don't remember what I told you.
VH: How do you feel about the Italian artist who sells shit as an art object?
EP: If people buy it, why not.
VH: Do you like real people like Bernice the lamp seller?
EP: Yes I like her very much.
VH: Do you like amyl nitrate?
EP: Depends when.
Tape 201 — Carry On With Larry Rivers and the Hairy Pie with La Peretti, Halston, Alejandro Reino, Four Dogs and Victor Hugo.
H: Do you have it on? Just turn it off, Victor. It's so off putting. Come on . .
VH: No . . . . . Come on leave it on.
H: It's off putting.
LR: (To chauffeur) Make a right.
EP: It's difficult if we know . . . It's difficult if we know

VH: I'm not tricky.
LR: Somehow always something goes wrong....
H: I'm always afraid to say something to be printed.
VH: It's for Interview . . . I'm doing an interview . . .
LR: It never comes up to your expectations. There's always something wrong. Richard Volt is doing it all the time . . .
EP: We have eight miles . . . Really let's do it . . . We have eight miles then we hear it in the restaurant . . . Come on, do it . . . really then . . . ask questions, then ask questions.
LR: Oh that kind of thing . . . . O.K.
VH: Art . . . Art . . . My dear!
EP: Fantastic!
H: I think you have to be tricky like the Pre . . . Pres . . . President Nixon.
EP: Listen . . . what is that restaurant . . . That restaurant, is it nice?
LR: The Greek restaurant. They have very few dishes and the're really not even that sort of traditional . . . Steak with Shishkebab and all that. They have a MOOOOO-SAAA-Kaaa which is fabulous, if you like Musaka . . .
EP: I don't remember what it is.
LR: . . . And you don't even have to like Musaka. It's so marvelous . . . . Musaka is, you know. Shepherds Pie . . . but with the most fantastic, kind of, they do it with cheese and it looks like a kind of square . . . It's kind of nice looking . . . And it actually has . . . like hairs!
EP: HAIRS????!!!!
LR: It's like . . .
H: Pretty . . .
LR: From the cheese . . . The way they do it . . .
EP: Ahhhh . . . From the cheese.
H: Hairy Shepherds Pie!
LR: Hairy Shepherds pie that you eat your head off . . . So like . . . so like a cheese MOOOOUUUUSSSSEEEE . . .
VH: Do you have hairy dreams?
LR: Hairy dreams? My dreams are rarely attractive . . .
EP: Sometimes I dream . . .
LR: I don't know what dreams mean, I don't . . .
EP: Do you still dream that you fall down . . . it's awful . . . that is . . .
FIRE ISLAND PINES Tape 202
Clump clump . . . walking on the boardwalk toward "tea time"—with Elsa's dogs. *woof woof*
VH: Why don't you leave them loose?
EP: Because they will get killed. I love your shoes that I'm wearing . . . Clack, Clack, Clack.
VH: I made them especially for "Tea Time."
EP: I don't know how I feel. One shoe One color,...The other shoe another color. I cannot see my feet.
VH: Miss Peretti would like to end the interview doing an ad about her favorite spaghettis. 1 . . . 2 . . . 3
EP: "La pasta Barila, La pasta perfecta."
H: Marlboro sono buoni . . .
VH: Don't buy interview, don't buy Elsa Peretti jewelery, don't buy Halston dresses . . .

Andy Warhol's *Interview* may 73 50¢
dali by darling
billy dee williams
pink flamingos

Dali by Darling

photographs & additional dialogue by francesco scavullo

1

2

Opposite page:
1. *Interview*, November 1974;
   photographs: Alejandro Reino
2. May 1973
3. *Interview*, May 1973;
   photographs: Francesco Scavullo
This page:
1–2. *Bianca Jagger, Interview*, January 1973;
   photographs: Francesco Scavullo
3. April 1973
4. April 1974

3

4

2

naturally and quickly. After Andy was shot, he became more and more interested in hanging out with rich, successful people and less interested in hanging out with sex-and-drug extremists. Fred Hughes was an unusually elegant figure in this late-hippie period, and under Fred's influence the whole Factory and *Interview* crew wore their hair long, put on jackets and ties, and looked radically clean for the early seventies. Fred even made the Best Dressed List in *Women's Wear Daily* and, along with Andy, became a fixture in its gossip column. Bob Colacello, who had aspired to a career in diplomacy when he was a student at Georgetown University, was impressed by Fred's soigné style, began to dress better and court rich ladies who might purchase portraits. Andy's friend Nelson Lyon called Fred and Bob "the head waiters." And as Bob got more into art sales and the idea of being Warhol's Boswell, he went to work directly for Andy, and I took over editorship of the magazine.

Displacing the coterie of speed freaks and drug queens in the Factory stable of superstars was a new group of fashion-world oddities — the teenage models Donna Jordan and Jane Forth, glamour girls Patti D'Arbanville, Maria Smith, and Geraldine Smith. The new

3

Max's Kansas City Pinups
by anton perich

Andy Warhol's Interview

Oct. '73
50¢

UK 25p
5 FR

DUSTIN HOFFMAN
BARBRA STREISAND
POINTER SISTERS
JAMES GUERCIO
HARLEM, DON MURRAY
& JUICY GOSSIP!

Opposite page
1. October 1973
2. *Lauren Hutton, Interview*, October 1973;
   photograph: Francesco Scavullo
3. *Interview*, May 1973;
   photographs: Anton Perich
This page:
1–3. *Interview*, March 1973;
   illustration: David Croland; photographs:
   Andy Warhol, Francesco Scavullo, and
   Catherine Milinaire

1–3

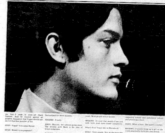

237

glamour boys were the models Corey Tippin and Jay Johnson, the pretty-boy twin brother of Andy's new roommate, Jed Johnson. The Factory had always been about glamour, but glamour was changing.

Interview interviewed hot designers like Halston and Giorgio di Sant' Angelo and established designers like Charles James and Rudi Gernreich. The Rudi Gernreich piece ran with a famous picture of Peggy Moffitt in the topless bathing suit, and this was a few weeks after Paul Morrissey had ordered me not to run any nude pictures in the magazine. Paul tried to fire me, but Fred and Andy talked him out of it.

Bob Colacello was fascinated by the fashion scene, and he convinced the famous fashion photographer Francesco Scavullo, the man behind the *Cosmopolitan* covers, to do the covers of *Interview* every month. Scavullo also did lots of celebrity portraits for *Interview,* and with the makeup artist Way Bandy in his corner, he had a way of making people look retouched without retouching. Scavullo was brilliant at what he did, but I was interested in a little variety and something new, and when I became editor of *Interview,* I used the rising young star Chris von Wangenheim to shoot the model Appolonia von Ravenstein for the cover. I felt as if Scavullo was out to get me after that, but I didn't care, and Bob and I stopped speaking directly.

It wasn't long after that incident, in 1973, that I was told that Rosemary Kent, the accessories editor and gossip columnist of *Women's Wear Daily,* a Texan Bob Colacello described rather kindly as "fat and happy," was brought in to work with me to make the magazine

LEE

by andy warhol

Sunday February 2, 1975 1:00 pm. AW, alone, arrives at the Fifth Avenue apartment building where Lee Radziwill lives. He gives his name to the doorman who takes him up in the elevator to LR's floor where LR's maid, Maria, is waiting beside the Francis Bacon painting in the hallway. Maria takes AW into the living room. The room is furnished mainly in a range of rich reds; English hunting paintings on the walls, a floral Bessarabian rug on the floor, orchid plants flowering by the red velvet couch where AW sits down.

Maria: Your name is Mr. Howard?
AW: No. Andy. I've never seen orchid flowers this big.
Maria: Yes. Very big.
(she starts to leave the room, re-checks the name)
"Andy Hughes"?
AW: No. Warhol.
(Maria leaves the room and AW picks up from the coffee table "The Romantic Egoists: A Pictorial Autobiography from the scrapbooks and Albums of F. Scott & Zelda Fitzgerald" / Charles Scribner's Sons / New York. He leafs through while waiting for LR. In a few moments LR calls out from another room, "Fred?", and then walks in wearing a black wool pullover, straight cut black wool pants, a very wide soft black leather belt by Halston, low black heels, a gold snake chain around her neck. LR is surprised to see AW: she thought it was Fred Hughes who had arrived, but FH is late so AW is alone.)
AW: It's just me. Your orchids are great, they're the biggest I've ever seen.
(kiss-kiss)
LR: They've been looking this good for a month, and they're meant to look like this for another month.
AW: (holding the Fitzgerald book) You know, I love this book.
LR: It was given to me. I think it's the kind of thing you look at just once. It's just like the COLE book—telegrams and letters.
AW: Well the COLE book was more arty, whereas this is straight information, and it fills in for all the books you've been reading about the Fitzgeralds for years, and so now you can finally see what they look like and what the houses look like, and the movies that he worked on.
LR: I'm told, though, that no one wants big books like that now—coffee table books. Would you like something to drink?
Maria: Can we have some wine for Mr. Warhol, please?
Alright, fine, thank you.
(LR asks AW to turn the tape off. When it goes on again FH has arrived, wearing a broad pin-striped navy blue jacket, maroon knit tie, cuffless drab corduroy pants, tango-coloured wing-tipped shoes, and bright magenta suspenders.)
(sound of liquid pouring over ice)
FH: Do you have any big regrets, Lee?
LR: Well, my deep regret is that I wasn't brought up or educated to have a metier. I'm mainly interested in the arts, but because of my kind of education, my interests were never channeled in any particular field—until it was too late to make use of them except in a dilettante way. I should have been in the decorative arts, as I'm a very visual person. Unfortunately, I have an eye for immediately spotting the most precious and expensive object wherever I go. I really enjoy creating different atmospheres, which totally transport you from everyday life. The ironical thing is one's talent is under the illusion they're giving you the best possible education and you can be a whiz at getting into any university, but if

you don't have any skills or any passion, all those academic requirements mean nothing in the end. So many young people are given no direction, so they become completely frustrated, knowing their requirements are a total waste of time and energy. In the end you only remember what you're interested in. Why be forced to take higher math when finally all you need to know is how to add, subtract, multiply and, at the most, divide.
I think if you see a spark of interest in a child or young person you should immediately make an effort to expose them as much as possible to that particular field.
I really think that the only thing that gives you any real sense of fulfillment is to accomplish something, no matter how small or insignificant it might be considered. I think so many people can't bear to be alone with themselves.
FH: Do you think that's more true for rich people? The "idle rich"?
LR: I don't think money has as much to do with "happiness" as most people seem to think. Unfortunately, I don't know anyone extremely rich or for that matter, powerful, who is happy. They are nervous-tense-frustrated-scared—they need other people to entertain them constantly, they're easily bored. Their circle is narrow and they don't dare break it. Wives are terrified of their powerful, moody husbands. They are women in bondage whose weeks, months and years are spent in acquisition—shopping becomes a disease, an everyday necessity to keep up with the latest and to fill empty time. I know this because I did the same thing for a while until it made me feel useless and disgusted with myself. Now I realize how precious time is. Life is all we have, and you don't want to look back when it's too late feeling and seeing that you have done nothing but collect junk and over-burdened closets. Hopes don't come easily, but if you have imagination, compassion, and joie de vivre, I think you've got it made.
To me money means freedom and comfort. What more is necessary? However, so few people know how to use what they have to the best of their abilities.
(more pouring)
FH: What kind of person do you admire, Lee?
LR: That's difficult to say, but offhand, I admire people who have self-discipline, determination and compassion.
FH: You've passed through a lot of different stages in your life—do you have an "ultimate ambition"?
LR: To be the owner of Interview. No, seriously, I think I have passed through the stages of ambition and I think the most serene feeling is to know you are being true to yourself. I also think it's rewarding when you're satisfied with something you've accomplished and look forward to something else ahead. Apart from that, to be at peace with yourself, to have largesse and curiousity and see your children happy in what they're involved in, if they're fortunate enough to want to be involved in something of interest.
It all sounds so easy, but we can see that it isn't.
FH: And what's the next step in your career?
LR: Well, one lesson that I did learn from my experience in PHILADELPHIA STORY, as well as in television, is to follow your own intuition. Because the "professionals" always say, "We are here to help you. Be sure to ask our advice before you do anything." So many interesting project possibilities came in, and I knew that I wanted to do at least two of them, and I knew that I should do something in the same field immediately because the people I would have been working with would have

taught me a lot, but this professional man said, "What?? You do a western?? Why, that would be perfectly ridiculous and offensive!"
Well it turned out that Brigitte Bardot and Sean Connery did it. So I could have kicked him for his good advice, which is only one of many examples. And then there was another play that I wanted to do in Phoenix, Arizona which was with Cornelia Otis Skinner and Maureen Stapleton, and I could have learned so much from them, but this man said to me, "It's all wrong for you," and I said, "But it's only going to last six weeks, and I'll learn so much by doing it." But I didn't. And with the television story of LAURA I had the most sadistic director—he loved to humiliate you in front of everybody until finally I was just getting ill and I told him that I'd be no good in it if he carried on this way.
But the one thing I learned from all of this was to always follow my own intuition, yet once more I put intuition aside again with the television interviews for CBS.
When you haven't find you're bound to feel pretty it gets easier and easier a Barbara Walters as a lot than she was originally "Maybe I should go on now go on in five minutes ease just comes with time of people ruining things t simply because they say know how to handle it. Se views were good—many a didn't know me. But the c cutting them up like little of having the con esting conversation with s cial in this field. You ha bread with smoked salmo you, Maria
(They talk about possible ON THE MOON, the mus Philips, directed by Paul N by Andy Warhol and adve had opened on Broadway and closed on the Saturd week. Nothing conclusive LR: I thought Genevieve W bought her album the ne AW: I have the whole pl makes me nostalgic alrea home play.
LR: Did you think EQUUS thought the acting was h beautifully staged. Altho much I would have liked actors had played in it. Albee's play SEASCAPE lizards?
establishment compliment the unions dressing rooms condition of the buildings AW: I think that every tim Broadway theater. that it to remodel one dressing LR: What else has he do AW: He's very big. He w the "Mom 'n' Papas" three times and he has a each wife—MacKenzie movie star, and now h coming along who is a beauty Philips with Genevieve Michelle with Warren all so happy
(FH walks over to the lunch table)
LR: I've just got to move over by the fire (AW follows, sounds of the fire crackling)
LR: Do you approve of the color of Fred's

shoes, Andy?
AW: Oh yes, they're funny.
FH: Philip Johnson approves.
LR: He does? I'm just not sure about it. Can't decide. They should go with tweed. Can't you dress properly when you come to see me, Fred?
FH: What's your favorite way for men to dress?
LR: Well of course it depends on the man, but my favorite suit for a man is Prince de Galles tweed. But that looks better on older men
AW: Or very young kids.
LR: But that makes them look old.
AW: Yes, so it really makes them look younger.
FH: That's right. You told me about going to a dance for Jackie and throwing the dress that you were supposed to wear into the closet and pulling out a cheap strapless number because you thought it would make you look older. Kids sixteen trying to look twenty-five come out looking fourteen.

BY RON STEPHENSON

EDITH HEAD
She Dresses Elephants Too

LR: The Impressionist show there is drawing the crowds. I went last Tuesday evening because I usually do go every Tuesday evening, and it was a nightmare.
FH: Tuesday nights at the museum it used to be empty. But they tell me that Diana Vree-
to the Metropolitan Museum.

2–3

"more professional." Bob and I had already made the magazine more professional, increasing its circulation about 7,000 percent. *Interview* was new, lively, and on the verge of success, but I saw what was happening. Rosemary Kent was told she was my boss. I figured it out in about a day, and I was on my way. I'd be back, but Bob was right. I "wouldn't or couldn't defer to authority." I was right too, but my presentation needed a little work.

Rosemary Kent didn't work out so well. She was abrasive, alienating staff and writers. She made some unfortunate public appearances. And she soon developed her own Scavullo problem that made mine seem like nothing. Andy and Fred fired her over the phone when they were out of town. Soon Bob was back as editor, and he knew exactly what to do. His time selling art for Andy had served him well. By now Bob knew the key players in the burgeoning New York fashion world and how to use *Interview* as a tool to reach the fashionable and the rich. Bob accompanied Andy on his heroic party rounds, and he began chronicling their excursions in a column called "OUT."

"OUT" was a play on the concept of "in," but it was also where Bob and Andy were every night. (In a few years, it would be an announcement made by quite a few people with what Andy called "a problem.") "OUT," a column

"she invented the 20th century woman"
says Diana Vreeland to Maxime de la Falaise McKendry

Hoyningen-Huene

"In the years after World War I, women went to work, took the Metro, dined in restaurants, drank cocktails, rouged their cheeks, and showed their legs. Chanel conveyed this headiness and independence in her clothes. She saw fashionable women going out on their own and thought it would be chic to dress them like working girls. She made simple little dresses of wool jersey. Her clients wore these dresses, straight to the knee with cardigans. They went out in simple beige jersey and kasha suits with easy skirts, or slacks and pullover sweaters. Their heads were small, with short hair like Chanel's herself, and they wore velvet berets and felt cloches. For evening Chanel made gunmetal-black, scarlet-red and beige dresses of paillettes and lace; again, the lines were simple, the look smart and clear.

Only when Chanel had totally pared down her clothes did she proceed to cover them—with emeralds, rubies, sapphires, chains, and pearls. More often than not, the rubies were glass cabochons, the ropes of pearl were fake. Chanel popularized artificial jewelry and taught women to use jewels to convey luxury and dash.

Chanel's concept of clothes, and of wearing clothes, effected a revolution that changed fashion entirely, irrevocably, and with great elan. With one fell swoop, Chanel took everything away except the woman herself and whatever was essential. Chanel institutionalized the clean white shirt, the pullover sweater, the skirt with two pockets placed precisely where hands expected to find pockets, the suits with cardigan jackets—all the clothes we now call basic."

—reprinted from Diana Vreeland's catalogue for "The 10s, the 20s, the 30s" show, courtesy of the Metropolitan Museum of Art

MAXIME: *When did you go from being a client to being a friend of Chanel?*
DIANA: In the 30s, when she had a very beautiful house on the Faubourg St-Honore. It had an enormous garden with fountains, the most beautiful *salons* opening on the garden and she entertained too beautifully. She had something like 54 Coromandel screens shaping these rooms into wonderful *alles* of charm. And the food was extraordinary. And the people were the most interesting in Paris. Musicians, artists—it was a proper society that she had around her and everyone was very fascinated by her. You see, she was a great character and charmer and an extraordinarily *attractive* personality around Paris. Her looks were extraordinary. She was bright, dark gold color—wide-faced with a snorting nose, just like a little bull, and deep Dubonnet red cheeks. She was just extraordinarily good-looking—*frightfully atttractive!*
Didn't she have an apartment over her shop?
Yes, she gave up the Faubourg house and as she owned the whole building at 31, rue Cambon and it goes up six flights she worked, received and had her meals in a perfect apartment above the shop. And then when we became friends she always wanted to fit my things in her own private atelier six flights

up, which used to kill me. When you think that this woman at the end was 89 and still walking it twice a day—up and down for lunch and up and down! Don't forget that in a French house you have beautiful rolling staircases up to the *salon* floor and after *that* you're on a stepladder for five flights—a really steep climb! And that used to kill me. I'd always try and get fitted when I'd heard Coco had gone to Lausanne to see her dentist. But as soon as I'd walk in the door there'd be someone waiting saying, "*Mademoiselle vous attend.*" My *God*, I used to get up there so breathless!"

And then I'd get fitted. And she was a nut on sleeves. That was her thing—sleeves. And she never, ever got a sleeve quite, *quite* perfect. She was always snipping and taking out sleeves before openings. As the people were getting into their chairs she was removing another sleeve, driving the tailors absolutely crazy. And then she'd put pins into me so I'd be contorted, and I'd be like this for an hour and a half because she'd be talking and talking and giving me all sorts of little philosophical observations—like, "Live with rigor and vigor," or, "Grow old like a man," and I'd say, "I think most men grow old like old women, myself," and she'd say, "You're wrong, they've got logic, they've got a reality to them,"—with my arm like this the whole time! Then if she really wanted to talk, she'd get pins in under both arms and I simply couldn't move! But I could never say, "Listen, Coco, I am going to die!" I couldn't say that because I couldn't get a word in, d'you understand?

But you know, the extraordinary thing about her was her great *sense of allure.* The word applies to her as I've never known it to apply to anyone else. She had total and complete allure. I went to a wonderful dinner one year before she died and it was for the Duke and Duchess of Windsor—given in her Rue Cambon apartment. We were only six. And I have never been in the presence of such an attractive woman in my life—never, never, never! The fire was burning and there were her beautiful bronze deer around the fireplace and beautiful bound books and marvelous leather on all the chairs and her long brown suede sofa which she always lay on, *cristal du roches* and roses, furs and the Coromandel screens, as a background to everything, moved in different positions. And everything shone. And the leather books gleaming. It was such an atmosphere of one person. Small gilt tables were all arranged comfortably for drinks, for cigarettes, for all the life that had been her life with men and with friends. D'you understand?

I've never seen anything so beautifully arranged—never, never! There's never been such comfort. There's never been anyone who understood exactly what one would have for lunch, for instance. It wouldn't be all that extraordinary but the *toast* would be so beautiful! You'd start with this marvelous toast. There was always toast on the table—very warm and beautifully arranged. And everything was for your comfort and for your delight. There was no other way. She learned very, very early in life how to be very, *very* attractive. One cannot compare with Chanel—nobody! It is impossible. They haven't got the *chien!* Or the chic. She was French! Don't forget—this is different from other people. She was French—totally French!
Diana, tell me, what happened to her estate?
It's one of the most mysterious things in the world. I'm talking about the most subtle mysteries and I don't really like this sort of ground because it's only what I've heard. But a day after her death there wasn't *one* single jewel to be found—not one! Nothing!
It's so strange.
I can't give you any information. I was merely a friend of hers. And I was totally disinterested. First of all, I never want to get into an argument about people. She was a very French, very, *very* violent woman. I tell you, the nostrils were distended morning, noon and night, like a little bull. She always looked marvelous. And she always looked marvelously fresh. She always *smelled* awfully good. You can say, "Well, she made all that perfume." But then any old lady can wear perfume. But she didn't smell like an old lady. She smelled like a young girl. She was delicious.
I wanted to ask you about the perfume.
When we did "The 10s, the 20s, the 30s" show we used Chanel #5 because, to me, it was the most typical scent of the period. And it was the first dressmaker's scent. I adore it. I love it. I simply love it.
I also meant to ask you about the packaging.
From my point of view, it has the best packaging, since the beginning, of any scent. And it is the most distinguished thing she ever put her seal on. And it has been first-selling scent from 1927 right through to the time of her death when I wrote that encyclopedia piece on her. Another thing I think is very interesting is that she is *in* the encyclopedia. I thought that was extraordinary. And that's why I accepted when they asked me to do it. And I was very flattered that they asked me. And I said that in the annals of scent there has never been anything like Chanel #5. For instance, when the Americans came into Paris and the Germans were still quite near by, the G.I.'s stacked up from the Place de l'Opera right down though the streets, right down to the Rue Cambon. And each G.I. was allowed only one bottle. It was the one thing they could say—"Chanel #5." You see how sensible she was.
It's a very luxurious, glamorous, feminine, positive sort of smell, isn't it?
Ah! Fantastic! But there was *nobody, no* place in the world, like Chanel—never, never, never! A very, very extraordinary woman—but don't forget she was totally responsible for the 20th Century woman! She was the spirit of the 20th Century woman. She was a most important woman. I'm not talking about the pill and abortion and all the things that have helped women *now* that they're free. She freed them. She gave them the momentum and the style.

INTER MAN

Viewgirl

hanel at work

1

2

3–5

Opposite page:

1. *Interview*, September 1976;
   photographs: George Hoyningen-Huene
2. *Interview*, July 1976;
   photographs: Peter Gert and Jeff Nike

This page:

1. *Divine in Zandra Rhodes, Interview*, February 1978;
   photograph: Albert Watson
2. *Interview*, January 1975;
   photographs: Bill Cunningham
3. May 1975
4. September 1976
5. January 1976
6. *Interview*, June 1974; photographs: Bill Cunningham

6

devoted to shameless
social climbing, could
have been ridiculous
except that Bob was
exuberantly shameless.
His maneuvering was
a labor of love, and he
also knew how to make
it work as self-parody.
"OUT" was quite
tongue-in-cheek, though Bob was
always trying to get his tongue in other
people's cheeks. Even if it was regularly
mocked by liberal media like *The Village
Voice,* "OUT"'s unabashed aspirations
were refreshingly honest and sometimes
endearingly tacky, especially when Bob
took to courting deposed monarchs,
pretenders, dictators, and their progeny.
Andy was a Democrat, and the more
to the Right that Bob flirted, the more
Andy would make fun of him.

Bob introduced a regular feature
that would last for years, although the
titles "Interman" and "Viewgirl" were
dropped after a while. I always though
"Interman" sounded scary, but the idea
was perfect — full-page pictures of up-
and-coming kids, beautiful kids with
talent, beautiful kids with trust funds.
There were always a lot of them
around, working at *Interview* or sweeping
up at the Factory.

By 1975, on the masthead, under
the words "Andy Warhol's Interview,"
was the legend "The Monthly Glamour
Gazette." The December 1975 issue
featured, among others, Yves Saint

3–7

1

2–6

Laurent, Valentino, Courrèges, Mme Grès, Paco Rabanne, Kenzo, Issey Miyake, Zandra Rhodes, Fernando Sanchez, Steven Burrows, Diane Von Furstenberg, and Iman. By now the magazine's masthead listed an impressive array of established and newly discovered photographers,

2–4

including Scavullo, von Wagenheim, Bill King, Eric Boman, Peter Beard, and Klaus Lucka.

During the seventies, Halston occupied a prominent place in New York, and his studio paralleled the Factory in many ways. It was staffed with young, attractive people, but its denizens rubbed elbows with an even more glamourous uptown crowd. Through Halston and his associates Elsa Peretti and Victor Hugo, the Warhols moved into the center of the emerging disco café society.

"The Monthly Glamour Gazette" worked overtime chronicling the lifestyles of the rich and famous, and it seemed to get more fabulous every month. Of course those were highly fabulous times when everyone made an enormous effort to be fabulous everywhere and at all hours. Bob was out regularly chronicling up a storm, but the magazine never suffered because Bob made some key additions to the staff. Robert Hayes, a young

1. *Interview*, July 1977; photograph: Ara Gallant
2–4. *Interview*, October 1977; photographs: Joshua Greene, Carlos Eduardo de Souza, Allen Lewis Kleinberg, Robin Platzer, and Jade Albert
5. "Out to Lunch with the Valentino Family," *Interview*, November 1977; photographs: Barbara Allen; illustrations: Joe Eula

5

1–6

PHOTO BY ARA GALLANT

1–6. "A Christmas Portfolio by Joe Eula," *Interview*, December 1977
7–8. *Interview*, December 1978; photographs: Scott Heiser

runway: New York by Scott Heiser

7–8

Canadian, was hired as assistant editor, and Marc Balet, a talented young architect and designer, was hired to be art director. Both made an immediate impact on the magazine. Suddenly *Interview* looked as glamorous as it had always wanted to be.

Robert was serious and intelligent with a great eye for photography. Marc was silly and intelligent with a great eye for photography. He also had a very sleek style of design that perfectly reflected the magazine's sensibility and ambitions.

2

Under the direction of Hayes and Balet, *Interview* became an important showcase for innovative photography. Anyone could present a portfolio at *Interview* and be sure that it would be looked at, and the magazine always presented a lineup of photographers to rival any in the history of publishing. Among the regulars in the late seventies and eighties were Bruce Weber, Robert Mapplethorpe, Michael Tighe, Arthur Elgort, Matthew Rolston, Christopher Makos, Erica Lennard, Neil Selkirk, David Seidner, Peter Strongwater, Michael Halsband, Greg Gorman, Moshe Brakha, Skrebneski, Mario Testino, Jean Pagliuso, Sante D'Orazio, David LaChapelle, Albert Watson, and Herb Ritts.

What made *Interview* an amazing visual experience wasn't just the lineup of top photographers and the array of beautiful people that were their subject. *Interview* was also big. It existed in a brief moment when you could actually distribute a publication larger than 8 ½ by 11 inches. At its peak size of 11 by 17 inches, and with most photographs running a full page, *Interview* was truly larger than life.

Interview's covers, paintings made

1

empress of fashion

DIANA VREELAND

by Jonathan Lieberson

A few weeks ago, a journalist of my acquaintance rang me up and told me to meet him as soon as possible in the crush bar of Carnegie Hall, which I did. That the man was verging on hysteria was transparently clear even to a mind as untrained in psychopathology as mine. "It's Diana Vreeland," he said, "You know her. Who is *she*? I've been trying and trying to get a *story*." "Nonsense, man, it's simple," I riposted authoritatively, "she was until 1970-something, the editor of *Vogue* magazine — and before that an editor at *Harper's Bazaar* — and now works as a special consultant to the COSTUME INSTITUTE of the METROPOLITAN MUSEUM OF ART. She's been awarded the Legion d'Honneur and many other — " "No, no, no, no, no, NO! " he bellowed, his trembling hand trying to elevate a second bourbon to his lips, "What is she like? I can't find out anything from her. What are her opinions? I can't even find out where she was born!" "Have you established whether she was, in fact, born?" I queried. When he proceeded to burst into tears, sobbing uncontrollably, I realized that my probing had been just what a doctor would have ordered, a cathartic. "There, there, there," I said, "tears will solve nothing. Chin up. Tell me about it." It transpired that he had gone to interview Mrs. Vreeland and had failed to unearth a single stable fact. History never repeated itself with her. At one interview, from what he could perceive, her birthplace had been somewhere in the Atlas mountains, in a nomad community, accompanied by Berber ululations. Then, sentences later, it would be Nebraska, with Indians dancing around the natal tepee, then the City of Light, then Dusseldorf. Peru had been the site of her education, Arabian satraps had sponsored her wedding, Scottish farmers had told her the facts of life, etc.. The deadline for an article about her was approaching, notebooks filled with contradictory material were piled high on his desk, his electric and gas bills had to be paid. "You must help me!" he cried, his eyes brimming with hot salt tears. Then he sank into an alcoholic coma, allowing me time to think. Yes, here was a problem, a problem as difficult as any the deductive powers of Sherlock Holmes had ever confronted. If only out of loyalty to my unhinged friend, I was determined to get to the bottom of this case and face Mrs. Vreeland with these allegations. To my delight, the opportunity to do so arose that very night, as the two of us were dining out together.

DIANA VREELAND: There is a Who's Who, *you know.*
JONATHAN LIEBERSON: Yes, but what the man was hinting at was, to put it bluntly, that you seem to be . . . self-invented.
DV: But don't we all *invent ourselves? Look here, I was naturally influenced by the literature of my youth and tried to exploit the idea, you know. . . .*
JL: That the personality is a work of art. Oscar Wilde, Pierre Loti, etc.. The idea that every gesture, every utterance, is part of a total design, an economy, just as words are combined in a poem or dabs of oil in a painting.
DV: Yes. But I think that is all very true. I did tell you I fought for a long time to be like other people. Of course, I was always sort of a loner, I suppose. I always had to think out everything for myself . . . I suppose that is what you call a loner. Now where *do you put this screen?* Where *do you put that sofa?* How *do you arrange that dressing-table . . . . But my room never came out like anyone else's. It used to* kill *me!*
JL: So when did you give up the struggle?
DV: Hmmmmmm. You know, many years ago, I mean many, many years ago, I was on the train to Chicago — the 20th Century train — and Frisco was there. Now don't you know who I mean? Oh, but he was marvelous! A black dancer, with a bowler hat and the most exquisite shoes. And he woke up and asked the waiter for ice cream and apple juice. This was breakfast, *you understand. And the waiter said, 'But we don't have it,' and Frisco said, 'Fake it!' That story has always been a big influence on me. Fake it!*
JL: (lamely) So you don't really care for mechanical conformists.
DV: I don't like the jambon tonight either. It's too harsh. I don't like harsh food.

An abrupt exchange, admittedly, but I felt sure that part of the case had been cracked. If I could only break down her resistance further. . . . But then she raised a disturbing thought.

DV: To tell you the truth, should we spend this much time on ourselves? I mean, I've lived all my life working very hard and in the last two of three years, so many people have asked me so many questions — and none of them are interesting to anybody, not even interesting to answer. You can say, that's part of business, okay. But don't you think we should rather be going on *with our lives? Look, nothing I've ever done is extraordinary. Of course, I worked, but there's nothing extraordinary about* that. *Why did I go to work? It was a hell of a long time ago.*
JL: You had your husband Reed and two children. . . .
DV: No, I was married twelve or thirteen years before I went to work. Those were the wonderful years in which I read. You see, I was just an idle woman. I had a nurse. I had a nanny, a luxurious life in London. What small education I ever got I got in those years.
JL: What did you read?
DV: I read everything! I would have read the phone book if you put it in front of me. I just read. Naturally, the whole 19th century. The French, the Russian writers. Stendhal. The typical literature of young girls. I never read Jane Austen, but I will some day. . . . Also, a lot *of books on painters and literary men, a lot of memoirs. . . . But I went to work to make money, not because I was bored. It was money that I wanted. Reed was a very gentle man. He was the youngest of five children, the only one who* got with it. *He had a rich father, but w*
little. Reed looked after everybody —
course he didn't say, 'Go to work
Carmel Snow asked me to work. I me
ed that he should look after me and
JL: I imagine that was hardly the t
century ago.
DV: I daresay, but perhaps they ha
heritage. I always felt that money wa

how far back I go. There was a time when it was considered vulgar and unnecessary to pursue money, but today anyone who doesn't believe in money must be out of their minds! I mean, it's only intelligent to wish to look after yourself properly. It is wonderful to have a lot of it — I was brought up with people like that — but we just weren't that rich. Consequently, I thought about it all *the time. I've never stopped thinking about it* all *my life. But, you know, it's not anything that's terribly* attractive *to have on one's mind all the time. . . . But it's always been on mine. Not that I was in shame or had any reason to be ashamed. I do not want you to get the impression that there was any sort of money grubbing.*
JL: But you have never been really poor. . . .
DV: But I didn't know how to handle money. When I first came here, for example. You've got to believe me, I'm not telling you the monkeyshines! I'd go to lunch and rather than handle money and give the man a tip . . . I had no standard to go by, I'd always had a car and driver in London . . . I'd keep *the taxi until* after *lunch! But your question . . . . Yes, I've had periods in which I literally had nothing. I couldn't afford another cake of soap. NO MORE BILLS! We just had to catch up. Once I got myself into debt. This was a real lesson in life. It had nothing to do with my family, just me. It was quite a lot of money. So I told myself, 'you gotta watch it.' I just didn't spend any money . . . like if you are fat, you just don't eat. And then one day, Reed breezed into my room and he said, 'Well, I've just spoken to the office and gotten the news. You don't owe anybody in the world a cent.'*
JL: What a relief.
DV: Oh, you are wrong. It felt like nothing at all. For three years I had on my back this terrible load. It meant nothing *to me to be rid of it because I had no right to be in debt in the first place. You know, I wonder about prisoners. They're told, 'You are free, you are innocent, you can go anywhere.' I'm sure they usually feel nothing. They don't burst into tears or hysterics or joy or 'I told you so.' It's nothing. To be on the straight path isn't a bloody thing. It's just* ordinary.
JL: In your case, the 'straight path' meant working pretty hard.
DV: No one knows how hard one works. Don't you loathe the word, 'workaholic?' It has nothing to do with an important thing, that you and your secretary are at the office until 6:30. But that's life, kiddo. Twenty-four-hour work doesn't go on in America. Twenty-four hour work is what Italy and Holland did after the war. The lights never went out! Reed and I went to Paris right after the war. When we arrived, there was no bread except from potato flour, no soles except for wooden soles. You could tell the time of day by looking at people going to and from their offices.
JL: Going back to the question of career, it seems to me that many, many people not only want to do something other than what they do, but *are* something else. Let me explain. This ad man is a painter who suppressed his interest in painting because of the pressure of making a living. He isn't someone who secretly wishes to be something else, he *is* a painter, but he extinguishes this creative direction because he has to make money. That telephone operator is a singer, that editor is a writer. . . .
DV: Well, if I hadn't done what I did, I'd have done nothing. Very few people are creative, don't you think? I mean, all people are meant to be creative in a certain way. What way? Perhaps I was cut out to be a wonderful housewife, with a marvelous sense of cooking, being with my friends, running a perfect house. But I am not ambitious towards anything. Life has rolled my way. . . . You know, I've always had such wonderful opportunities, but I never made the effort, haven't put on the pressure. Naturally, I've been offered many jobs — and many years ago — a company of my own in which I'd call the shots. But I never took them. I'd have more money if I had, but I wouldn't have the privileges I have today. I've always remained totally myself, which is to say, without any idea . . . of what to do. Basically, I'm a person who is only interested in the pleasures and enjoyments of life. All the rest is left to the men. I've always remained what you might call 'feminine' about the whole thing.
JL: This is curious. Your actions, your career do not seem as if they were hampered by narrow little conventions about 'femininity' — they were, in today's jargon, the actions of a 'liberated woman.' But your description of yourself, your view of women —
DV: Oh hell, what does 'liberation' mean? About ten years ago, some girls came into my office and told me they had discovered women are free. This is a weakness of the world. Someone thinks they've discovered something for the first time. They want to be authoritative about it. Now these girls said, 'Aren't you ashamed *to be talking about decorativeness, about ornamentation,' blah-blah-blah. Now look, these girls had had the pill for ten years. How free can you get? Isadora Duncan was free. How liberated can you get? I remember my grandmother very well. She was an impossible, extraordinary woman. If* anyone *was liberated, she was. . . . Outside her bedroom she had a big balcony overlooking the garden, and she had all these Italians working for her. Then one day, she said, 'Where is Elsa?' Elsa was a maid and she was not available by bell. Anyway, 'WHERE IS ELSA?' Now it was six in the morning. 'She's gone to Church, Madam.' 'CHURCH? I COME BEFORE GOD!' It was* six *in the morning and I remember her shouting. Of course, I went straight back to sleep. But servants never stayed with my grandmother.*
JL: While we're on the subjects of groups, causes and movements, you don't strike me as identifying with much of anything.
DV: Well, I haven't spent much time looking into other people's lives. There is no question about it: when I was at the mags, I was at the center of the town, and now I'm not. But I've never been part of any group. I've always had my own tea and toast

3

Opposite page:
1. December 1980
2. *Interview*, December 1980
3. *Diana Vreeland and Consuelo Crespi, Interview*, March 1978; photograph: Bob Colacello

This page:
1. *Interview*, March 1978; photographs: Kevin Farley
2. *Interview*, May 1980; photograph: Scott Heiser
3. *Victor Emanuel, Valentino, and Marie Helene de Rothschild in Gstaad, Interview*, 1979; photograph: Bob Colacello

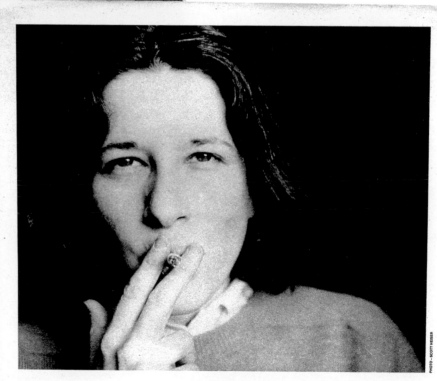

Fran on
FASHION

MARC BALET: *Fran, American fashion is no longer being dictated to the American woman. Do you think that's a plus or a minus?*

FRAN LEBOWITZ: I think it's a minus. Because I'm a great believer in expertise, and I feel that there are some people who know more about certain things than other people. I, for instance, feel that Diana Vreeland knows more about fashion than you. . .and you should listen to her. Magazines like *Vogue* used to tell people what to wear, what to think, what to read. . .now they go into the streets and see what the secretaries are wearing, and take their cue from them. This has resulted in a somewhat less attractive visual landscape.

MB: *And what about punk fashion?*

FL: What about it? I think punk fashion is fine if you're 19-years-old, which you are not. For anyone older I think it exhibits the basest sort of longing. People who are interested in that are people who still believe that being a teenager is glamorous.

MB: *Do you go to the punk places?*

FL: No, I don't. I'm too old. And so are they, most of those people.

MB: *What about jeans? Jeans have been around for a long time, do you think they'll stay around or will they go the way of all. . .flesh?*

FL: I think jeans are in for quite a long run. Normal, reasonable jeans. There was a rumour about a year and a half ago that Levis was going to stop making all-cotton jeans, at which point I stockpiled. So I have enough. If there's a jeans famine, I'm safe.

MB: *And designer jeans?*

FL: To me designer jeans is a concept at odds with itself. It's like educational television, they cancel each other out.

MB: *And that also relates to sports dressing, people running around town in little tennis outfits now, or jogging to the office. Sneakers are everywhere. How do you feel about someone wearing sneakers as opposed to shoes?*

FL: I suppose it depends on what you're going to do. But I think that all these adults wearing sports clothes makes it appear very much like everyone's at camp. You just don't know what period it is. It's the same thing as dressing to look like a rock star. . .people who dress to look like a particular thing are obviously people who

can't make it up themselves.

MB: *Current men's fashion in general—the narrow ties and wide shoulders—do you think that makes men look more attractive?*

FL: I think it makes men look very much like the young Frank Sinatra, which is fine with me. I think that's a good look.

MB: *Do you think that's going to continue?*

FL: No. Nothing continues, Marc. That is the essence of life.

MB: *And what about men wearing makeup?*

FL: It's okay if they don't get it on my sofa.

MB: *And hats, do you think men should wear hats?*

FL: I think men or women should only wear hats if it is part of their uniform that they are compelled by law to wear to work. Policemen can wear hats, firemen can wear hats. Art directors cannot wear hats, particularly fire hats.

MB: *What about fur? Women dressing in fur. . .are you anti-fur?*

FL: I'm very pro-fur. I'm in favor of anything that results in the death of an animal. I also think fur is very flattering. Anyone looks good in sable.

MB: *Are diamonds a girl's best friend?*

FL: I think diamonds are probably a girl's best acquaintance. A girl's best friend are emeralds.

MB: *Are you in favor of the best-dressed list every year, or do you think that it should be outlawed?*

FL: No, I'm very much in favor of the best-dressed list. I'd be more in favor of it if they'd allow me to draw it up. Which I am volunteering for.

MB: *Do you have a favorite outfit that you wear?*

FL: I wear all the same kinds of clothes. I wear all Brooks Brothers' shirts, Levis, and sweaters. To me a spring wardrobe is taking off my sweater. I just get them in various colors.

MB: *Why don't you wear earrings?*

FL: I have no ears.

MB: *You have no ears, Fran?*

FL: That's right—I was kidnapped twice.

Understandably weary of hearing her entire life's work referred to in the singular, i.e. "her book" Fran will absent herself from this page for a number of months, during which time she will make every effort to finish her last book, *Social Studies*.

FRAN ON FASHION is one of a series of video presentations shown on Manhattan Cable TV, Channel 10. Watch for May's Fashion feature: *The Empress and the Commissioner*, starring Diana Vreeland and Henry Geldzahler, also on Channel 10.

from photographs by Richard Bernstein, were a powerful part of the formula. They mimicked Andy's style in a big, postery way, transforming publicity into Pop art.

Interview didn't cover fashion in the conventional way. A lot of fashion stories accompanied interviews with designers or models or anyone who looked good in clothes. Interview also covered the fashion shows in its own distinctive style. Scott Heiser photographed the action on the runway as action more than fashion, creating great semiabstract shots, sometimes a blur or a shadow, sometimes just a detail — perhaps a hem — but always with an original and aesthetic treatment that was more about art than the rag trade.

The more successful Interview became, the more Andy Warhol wanted to be involved. He started out doing interviews grudgingly, but as the magazine became increasingly popular, Andy was not only doing interviews but also becoming Interview's best promoter, handing out autographed copies on Madison Avenue, schmoozing with

advertisers at Factory lunches, and, much to the dismay of the editors, offering to put many, many people on the cover of the magazine. Andy wasn't "hands on" in the usual sense when it came to the direction of Interview. But he had a way of nudging his editors in the right direction. He would often make a suggestion in such a low-key flattering way that the editor would do

nothing could be finer than
CAROLINA HERRERA
by Andre Leon Talley

DIANA VREELAND once defined style with this axiom: "It helps to get you down the stairs." CAROLINA HERRERA has marched up and down many stairs with a style that seems almost genetic to an elite group of wealthy Latin American-born women. Silver-spoon fed on Paris couture and in her close collaboration with three couturiers in her native Caracas, she has now stamped her style (so aptly called 'le bombe style' by Empress Vreeland) into her first collection of ready-to-wear and couture. The collection is made and sold from her East 57th Street headquarters in Manhattan.

Empress Vreeland's favorite vision of Carolina Herrera is a point of clarification. "I remember about two years ago she came to dinner dressed right out of a Goya painting. She had a dress that was ten to twelve inches from the floor, white stockings and black silk pumps. Her hair was encased in a snood. She's got this superb line, this incredible browline. She has a very strong, noble forehead. And when she says she is going to do something, watch out! She is definite and always follows through. She's really a blonde bombshell. And her attention to perfect detail and exquisite fitting of her first collection is something remarkable. I say RRRRRReeee-Mark-abbble."

This remarkable technique and attention to perfect detail is based on the architectural structure and exaggerated baroque school of Paris couture which Senora Herrera knows inside out. This sultry looking, impeccably groomed and exquisitely mannered lady is simply marketing her passion — high chic.

With a certain Carole Lombard frozen veneer that subterfuges a vibrant personality, she greets one from a half mile away as her personal mix of tuberose and jasmine essences float down the hall from her suite or engulfs an entire dinner table of 24. As in her blown out dresses, her fragrance is an explosion.

I have positioned Carolina like an Infanta in her big pouf ball gowns for page one news, danced with her in what she calls the 'Spanish style' on nightcrawling treks as she whirled about making noble bullring gestures and clipping the air with her profile, and as I sit with Carolina and her husband, REINALDO, sipping iced tea for this conversation, I feel it. I feel the staccato rhythm of this joint quality they possess. They are gifted with a 'ferocity of elegance.'

ANDRE LEON TALLEY: How many pieces?
CAROLINA HERRERA: There are 50.
ALT: I don't mean the pieces in your collection. How many pieces of luggage do you travel with? And what type of luggage is it?
CAROLINA: Do I have to say how many? Ah, it is sometimes twelve, sometimes fifteen. It all depends on the season.
REINALDO HERRERA: My grandmother used to travel with 140 suitcases and trunks.
ALT: Where was she going with such an army of valises?
REINALDO: To Rio, to New York, crossing the Atlantic by boat with tons of trunks of shoes.
CAROLINA: When I come to New York in December and I have my ball gowns, it sometimes takes one suitcase for one, maybe two dresses. It all depends. I have Vuittons which are the very best because they are constructed like little trunks. Then I have old gray Guccis which are unsigned. I don't mind traveling with that much luggage. I don't know if Reinaldo minds. No, he doesn't really. He never complains.

A brief inspection of the private apartment of Carolina and Reinaldo Herrera to see what she travels with that requires so many suitcases. Her bed is laden with those little pillows seen on beds in the very best homes that are big enough for one elbow. They are covered in white linen hand-embroidered with a garden bouquet. On Carolina's dressing table: a set of gold monogrammed brushes and combs with matching mirrors, silver frames with photos of her four daughters, miniatures of

of her in a white Mainbocher dress drawn by the late Rene Bouche 25 years ago. It is a gift to Carolina in honor of her first collection. The card reads: 'In admiration for a new star in the zodiac, for enormous efforts with enormous results.'

CAROLINA: This is the most gorgeous gift. CZ Guest is one of my favorites because she never changes her style. That I love. I also like Bianca Jagger who has created a style that people try hard to emulate. Nan Kempner is always perfectly dressed for an American woman. And Diana Vreeland is extraordinary for everything: her intelligence, her personality, her style, her home, her work. I have admired her since I was a child making clothes for my dolls. I have always loved clothes but I don't think it is necessary to be on top of fashion all the time. I usually have ten ballgowns made for the season — it depends. But I also love wearing a four, five, ten-year-old dress. For very special, sentimental moments, I love a comfortable old dress. I always like purity. Simple lines with extravagant details is how I have always dressed and it's what I do in my collection. I never do giant sleeves and then six bows on the skirt. Look at my Infanta dress in black lace. The line is pure and the sleeve is the decorative detail. I will never show something that has four, five, six tassels hanging from the waist.
ALT: You have this feeling for the exaggerated, bombastic, the super-sleeve for gala-going clothes.
CAROLINA: You know why? I believe when you walk into a room and have a dress with some exciting detail only in the skirt, everybody notices that upon your entrance: Boom! Then the room becomes packed and you have to swim through the crowd with no notice whatsoever. With important sleeve details always executed with perfection, you have a frame for your face. Then you don't disappear throughout the evening. It is very important to keep the focus upon your face which is the nucleus of a woman's allure.
ALT: Do you decide at the last moment which ball gown to wear for an event or is it thought out days in advance?
CAROLINA: Sometimes I decide and never change. Often at the last moment I have an alternative and I change.
ALT: Your lingerie? Is this all imported from France?
CAROLINA: Most of it is made at home in Caracas. Everything in Caracas is couture, my dressmaker, my hatmaker, my shoemaker. The people learn the craft from their mothers, their grandmothers. We simply did not grow up with pret-a-porter. I mostly have old-fashioned satin and lace lingerie. My sheets are sometimes Porthault, sometimes from Italy. I love linen sheets. And at our house, they are pressed directly on the bed everyday. I have linen sheets from Paris that are hand-embroidered. They are not all white, some sets are pale peach, some blue. The pale peachy, apricot tones are becoming to one's face upon waking. I'm not very pink without makeup. I can go a little green.
REINALDO: You're pink after Janet Sartin.
ALT: What is the secret of your flawless complexion? And who does your hair?
CAROLINA: I use a lot of Janet Sartin. And I don't drink at all. I usually don't smoke. Now I am smoking because I was nervous and working very hard. NEVER COCA COLA OR TAB! I drink orange juice. Not too many desserts. But when I do, I can eat a whole box of chocolates. I can manage an entire half of a chocolate cake once in a while.
ALT: Five days a week, when in New York, is Janet Sartin before noon. Even if she has just slipped from some gay buck's arms at 5 a.m. after doing her nightly gymnastics of mad fandangos. Do you go everyday?
CAROLINA: No, but I understand why she would. It is so relaxing and you come out with the glow of a 15-year-old. I go maybe six times a year. As for my hair, Rene at the Plaza has been doing it for 12 years. And in Caracas, I have been at Bassi for 20 years. When I like something and the detail is perfect, I don't change.
ALT: What are your favorite colors?

keeps all her vintage Balenciagas, Dior, Fath, Patou, Balmain dresses in one large room. And they are preserved in plastic with date tags, the matching accessories lined up underneath each dress. I hear she also had special pine trunks made in Caracas in the grand old days just to crate evening gowns across the Atlantic or to come up to New York for the social season.
REINALDO: She [...] museums.

brocade, not typical dressmaking fabric.
ALT: Since when did you buy couture and how has your personal style evolved?
CAROLINA: Always, always, I have loved clothes. And designing is something I have wanted to do for years. I just never had the time what with the children, my husband, the house and all. My first important dress when I went to Paris at 15 [...] couture. It was white point d'esprit and I bought one [...] 15, I was allowed just one couture dress.
[...] ke larger additions to your teen-age wardrobe.
[...] net Balenciaga at fourteen. I was taken by my grand-
ER OWN DESIGN. PHOTOGRAPH BY CRIS ALEXANDER.
HAIR & MAKEUP–RENE HOTEL PIERRE; JEWELRY–CAROLINA HERRERA.

A large gray pig [...]

1–2

Allure: the quintessential vicomtesse

Jacqueline de Ribes
by
Reinaldo Herrera

A remembrance of things pa

what Andy wanted and think it was his own idea. "Gee, that typeface was so great. Maybe you should use it for everything." In some ways, Andy was a sort of nutty professor, because without ever being overly intrusive he was able to train his "kids" to anticipate his taste and sensibility.

Andy's own interviews set a style that has been imitated around the world by dozens of mag-

azines. It hasn't ever been duplicated, really, because who else could carry it off? Andy's pose, as a kind of idiot-savant conversationalist, was ideal. It was all in the details, the ironies and ambiguities. Andy perfected the chitchat small-talk style of interview: the parts other magazines would edit out became the essence of the thing.

Brigid Berlin, Andy's best friend and collaborator of longest standing, and Pat Hackett, Andy's secretary and diary collaborator, helped perfect the Andy Warhol interview style with their casual but flawless editing, their way of condensing something too hot for publication into a few cryptic words, fast-forwarding with telltale words

2–4

5

6 7

Calvin Klein
by
Bianca Jagger & Andy Warhol

1. *Interview*, December 1982; photograph: Bruce Weber
2. December 1982
3. February 1984
4. February 1987
5. *Tina Chow*, *Interview*, January/February 1983; photograph: Christopher Makos
6. *Christie Brinkley*, *Interview*, November 1983; photograph: Christopher Makos
7. *Interview*, September 1981; photographs and design: Philippe Morillon
This page:
1–2. *Interview*, December 1982; photographs: Bruce Weber
3. *Interview*, February 1981; photographs: Cecil Beaton and Helmut Newton

FRIDAY, OCTOBER 8, 1982, 12:30 P.M. Andy Warhol and Calvin Klein, whose fashion empire is fast approaching the billion-dollar-a-year mark, are lunching in a private tatami room at Kitcho, a Japanese restaurant on West 46th Street, not far from Calvin's Seventh Avenue headquarters. While waiting for co-Interviewer Bianca Jagger, AW begins to dish last night's opening of "Cats" with the Golden Boy of American Fashion.

CALVIN KLEIN: Bianca will be here any minute.

ANDY WARHOL: I'm going to stand around you all the time at any party. It's the best. All those people just come over and it's like 18 deep.

CK: Last night I had a very important experience, seeing for the first time my daughter become a young woman. She was so sensitive, self-confident and charming. I talked to her mother this morning and I said I think that she's done the greatest job bringing Marci up.

AW: Last week she was this short, this week she's as tall as you are. I didn't know who she was. I thought she was a movie star [when I saw her] with Tim Hutton. Girls can really change their looks.

CK: She doesn't look at all like she did when she was eleven years old—the photographers were crazed. Bianca and I and Tim and Marci came together. Whenever I'm with Bianca I just want to hold her and protect her. Marci felt very comfortable being with Tim and at one point she even turned to him and said, "It must be awful for you being followed by this constant barrage of photographers," and he said it was. But I think Marci was a little suspect because she said to me later that there was a little smile on his face.

AW: Bianca wore the best dress last night; I saw it in your fashion show.

CK: I think Bianca looked so incredible last night. Marci kept going on and on about how she fell in love with Bianca and she fell in love with you. She loved everyone.

AW: I love all your commercials. Who does them?

CK: Well, I've worked on commercials with Dick Avedon.

AW: Oh really? Which ones did he do?

CK: All of the ones we did with Brooke. In those commercials Brooke was performing as an actress, different roles: the liberated woman, the teenager, the housewife, and I think people misunderstood that whole concept. They just saw it as provocative. To me it was very sensual and beautiful. People very rarely remember lines of a commercial. "What comes between me and my Calvins? Nothing." That made media history. So I was accustomed to working in a studio. Suddenly, we went out to California because we wanted to try something different; we wanted to do commercials about active wear, for people who care about their bodies. We went on location, and I must say it was like doing a major film. I insisted that we start at sunrise every day, so that meant getting up at two or three o'clock in the morning to prepare clothes in order that we could be on location an hour before the sun came up. I was totally twisted around preparing to work before the sun came up. We worked from sun up to sun down for ten days.

CALVIN KLEIN AT HOME. PHOTOGRAPH BY BRUCE WEBER.
GROOMING—THOM PRIANO FOR GARREN, N.Y.
CAMERA—PENTAX

(Bianca Jagger arrives.)

AW: Gee, you look pretty.

CK: You look gorgeous. Just to sum it up, I envisioned those commercials as something very classic and surreal; having divers with incredible bodies just dive into water that was very still, having people run and sweat, having Andy McDowell, who looks like Elizabeth Taylor as a child, with the curly hair, just stretching her body.

BIANCA JAGGER: Oh, you're wearing a pocket watch. I was going to get you one when I saw that you did not have one yesterday.

AW: Is it a pocket watch?

CK: Yes, of course. It's on the longest chain, I feel like it's a yo-yo.

AW: Last night was like the old days. I couldn't believe it. I was happy I was next to Calvin because all the pretty people came over and they were all fighting over everybody.

CK: That's because I was with Bianca. Marci said it was just the most incredible experience to meet some of my friends. She said it was one of the best evenings she's ever had. She's always been my child and suddenly she was a young woman. It's so gratifying. If you think of all that that kid has gone through in her life. To see her happy and feeling good about herself, natural around people when it would have been so easy for her to feel intimidated. I'm so over-protective, but at the same time it's her life and there comes a time when she has to decide. I feel she's not quite at the age when she can make every decision for herself.

AW: Does she study acting?

CK: No, she's not interested in acting, she wants to be a journalist which frightens me like crazy.

BJ: Why? She could be a wonderful journalist.

CK: That would be the ideal. How many wonderful journalists are there out there?

BJ: Since we're talking about Marci, tell me if you do or don't want to talk about the kidnapping of your daughter. A lot of people imagine that famous and successful people don't have a normal life; they see them in photographs and they think they live in a fantasy world. They don't realize that often they are born into a normal family, they have kids and have to go through everything that everybody goes through, except they are in the public eye.

CK: But you see Bianca, our children don't have normal lives.

BJ: Well, my daughter does to a certain extent. I try to make her life as normal as possible.

CK: But we make a conscious effort. Don't you think I try to do the same thing?

BJ: I know you do.

CK: You said I don't have to speak about the kidnapping; but it was a traumatizing experience. It was not something that any of us can get over or that I can even put into words.

BJ: Children can forget easier than we can.

CK: Not to drag this out, but no matter how much we try to give them a normal life, children of celebrated parents, as much as we try, don't have a normal life. They just simply don't. And children of divorced parents don't have a normal life, even though it's becoming more common. It's still a very traumatic experience for a child to go through.

AW: I was always jealous of kids who had more mothers and fathers than me. I wish my mother and father had gotten divorced.

CK: Oh, A...

AW: Think... and father...

BJ: On the... grow with... not work.

CK: I think... give their... and balanc... ficult for u... and we exp... securities a... or upset th... but sometim... to a degree... just border...

BJ: Can w... is and whe...

CK: Why?

AW: Yes. A... you're so f...

CK: In 19... Newsweek... cover of T... your peak, on the way...

BJ: On the...

CK: I thin... late. They... already pe... thought I p...

BJ: Were you right?

CK: Absolutely wrong. One never peaks... God, if yo... you believ... in living,... life, you c... better and...

AW: Tha... great bec... productio... York is al...

BJ: Big is...

CK: Big i... I'm talkin...

AW: I d... and I just... noon.

CK: Ever... think ab... my fathe... was mak... she was... pair of s...

BJ: How...

CK: My...

AW: No...

BJ: Wh... child?

AW: W... shoes...

CK: Th... She alw... perfect as it could be. She loved clothes and my grandmother was a dressmaker. The fashion aspect was always, in a sense, present in my family and yet it wasn't. My mother loved neutral colors. I spent the first ten years of my life designing beige, cream, white, brown, because those were all the colors that she loved. She would line her jackets in fur, she would d... consider... would c... the Bro...

BJ: Wa...

35

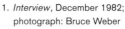

1–2

the greatness of GRÈS
by Thierry Ardisson & Jean Luc Maître

3

through the duller spots. In retrospect, the loaded neutrality of Andy Warhol's celebrity interviews seemed to mirror precisely his portrait-painting technique. He drew his subjects out, vacuumed content, and let them reveal themselves, then manipulated their images subtly with color and a choice of telling specifics.

In early 1983 Bob Colacello left *Interview* after Andy refused to give him a piece of the action. He was capably succeeded by Robert Hayes, who died of AIDS in 1984. Hayes's successor was Gael Malkenson Love, who had worked her way up from receptionist. *Interview* was the kind of place where you could do that. Gael was an excellent editor — smart, ambitious, and tough as an Hermès saddle. Under her editorship, the magazine reached a new height of success — it actually began to turn a profit. There were so many ad pages that the magazine went to perfect binding to accommodate them all.

Andy Warhol died on February 22, 1987. Shortly thereafter, Gael was let go by Fred Hughes. Fred had long thought that she was difficult and abrasive. She was. She was also very good at her job. Fred had a different idea for *Interview*. He thought it could be more intellectual, so he hired his brainy pal Shelly Wanger to replace Gael. *Interview* became more intellectual but less fun. It had its moments, but it was missing something. It was missing its shamelessness, its self-indulgence, its flamboyance, its arch anthropological oomph. Mainly it was missing Andy.

Finally, the Warhol Foundation, required to divest itself of any profit-making or would-be profit-making operations, sold *Interview* to Brant Publications, more or less ending its era.

JEAN-PAUL GAULTIER PHOTOGRAPHED BY MATTHEW ROLSTON.
CLOTHING—JEAN-PAUL GAULTIER...LOCATION—JEAN-PAUL GAULTIER'S SHOWROOM, PARIS...CAMERA—HASSELBLAD.

The French collection: his is hers

Jean-Paul Gaultier by John Duka

Jean-Paul Gaultier has one of those wonderful French faces that, in the space of seconds, can be deadly serious, wrinkle into clownishness, then smooth out into something bordering on handsome. The clothes he designs have that same mercurial quality. At 31, he has been designing independently for seven years and has pushed fashion design to its limits, using the techniques of the couture to create clothes that are at once iconoclastic and funny. He is famous for the lace evening skirts he designed to be worn with sweatshirts. Famous, too, for his sexy double-trench dresses.

Last year, he gained universal recognition with a collection which borrowed freely from Arab culture, and almost single-handedly revived Orientalism, paisley and the fez. This year, he followed that with two revolutionary collections: one that combined the King's Road with the style of American blacks, resulting in a raunchy, dandified street style; the other, a collection in which men and women wore roughly the same clothes, including sarongs and skirts.

With a wink, and an impish smile, Gaultier says that fashion is not to be taken seriously. Beneath that, though, beats a heart longing for new rules and aiming, at the same time, for immortality.

JOHN DUKA: When did you start designing?
JEAN-PAUL GAULTIER: I started a long time ago, when I was a child. I was living in Paris with my grandmother when I was about twelve years old. She was kind of a healer. She made face masks for clients and she taught people how to apply makeup. And she was a fortune teller, all at the same time. I would see her clientele, and I'd watch them before and after. She gave them advice, like "You should do that, you should wear that." So I made the connection between their clothes, their appearance,

and what happens in one's private life. I saw all of this at the age of twelve. After that, I made shampoo for my grandmother, for her white hair. After that she had confidence in me. I was also looking at the TV programs. I saw all the great actresses. And after that I started to read women's magazines, Elle, Marie Claire. I taught myself fashion that way. I read things like, "Yves Saint Laurent presented a very beautiful collection, it was very Parisian." I would look at the photographs and think, "Oh, so this is Parisian," and I drew my own conclusions.
JD: So you taught yourself from magazines?
J-PG: I looked at the magazines and at the photos from the haute couture shows. Those were the only ones I saw. I didn't know about ready-to-wear. Or I saw these things in Francoise or Le Figaro like "Today there was a show of Christian Dior" or in Elle one time it was written, "Eugenia Sheppard, the bible of fashion" and I would look at the photos. At the age of fifteen, I was familiar with all of those people. At that time I loved Saint Laurent and Courreges and Cardin because they were more extreme. This from about 1966 to '70.
JD: Courreges has changed a lot since then, he's not as extreme now. I saw some of his clothes in his new New York store. It's interesting—he has 3,500 square feet on the ground floor of this enormous skyscraper and his clothes don't seem to work today.
J-PG: Maybe because the moment is different. I think the moment now is very mixed and confused, and yet in other ways it's not confused. It's a mixture of different cultures and sociology. For example, Steven Sprouse makes a type of fashion that has some reminiscence of the '60s look—like Courreges—but it's today. The fabrics have changed, the spirit has changed. My clothes are sometimes inspired by some '70s style, or '50s or '60s, but it's translated through my eye.
JD: Your clothes mix a lot of influences. I see a London influence and I see a black

78

This page:
1. *Ann Magnuson*, Interview, September 1983; photograph: Christopher Makos
2. *Interview*, February 1985; photographs: Matthew Rolston
Opposite page:
1. *PJ's, Tranny Bar, Miami Beach*, Interview, September 1986; photograph: David LaChapelle
2. *Emmanuel Xuereb, NYC*, Interview, November 1986; photograph: David LaChapelle
3. *Student Fashion One*, Studio Berçot Series, Interview, January 1986; photograph: Matthew Rolston
4. *Aly Claw Hand*, The Surreal Thing Series, Interview, November 1987; photograph: Matthew Rolston

MODEL TERI TOYE WEARING JEAN-PAUL GAULTIER PHOTOGRAPHED BY MATTHEW ROLSTON.
HAIR—JULIEN d'IS, PARIS…CLOTHING—JEAN-PAUL GAULTIER'S, "MODE MASCULIN"—SPRING '85 COLLECTION…LOCATION—LE BALAJO CLUB,
PARIS/COURTESY—ALBERT AND SERGE…TERI TOYE/CONTACT: CLICK MODELS, N.Y., CITY MODELS, PARIS.

American influence. Why did you mix all that together? When I saw your show last time, I was amazed at how black and how English it was. But also, how French it was and how it's a lot of your whimsy. Why all that mixture?
J-PG: I think a lot of people feel that mixture because people travel and are shocked by what they see in other countries, and they have a reaction from that. So I, for example, feel closer to the streets of London than the streets of Paris, because I hate the poorness of Paris streets. By "poor" I mean not rich in imagination. Everybody wants to be like the other one; it's very conservative and bourgeoise. It's not even chic or interesting; they want to be anonymous. In London, I don't really get my inspiration, I get my energy. I get depressed in Paris today because the chic Parisienne of today isn't the chic Parisienne of yesterday.
JD: What is the chic of Paris today?
J-PG: For me, chic can be like fashion: one day it can be one thing and the next it can be another. It's nothing. It's what you want it to be. So it's everything, because it's relative and subjective. For me it's more attitude than clothes. For example, the most beautiful clothes worn by people not ch[...]
JD: But your clothes have a lot of attitu[...] is that even without someone wearing [...] combinations, the colors, the accessor[...]
J-PG: Yes, they have an attitude. But [...] without the accessories, it looks more— it looks more classical. Basically I wan[...] or abstract things.
JD: Now what does "real" mean? Whe[...] up, and those cutaway velvet coats, ho[...]

J-PG: It's real in the sense that it's something that you can make yourself; it's something very simple in conception. You can wrap the jacket around, you can make it yourself. It's movement. You have a scarf and a jacket and you do different things with them. It's all movement. You have all the different prints together.
JD: The prints are such a wonderful statement.
J-PG: The prints were a reaction against the moroseness of the moment. Before the prints I saw so many polyester dresses on old women, and they were so ugly with those flowers, and things like that, so vulgar. I had a reaction against that, and so for about five years after, I was making only plain black or plain classical colors. Now I need something else and I think people need something else, too. It's never only my own reaction. It's what I feel people would like. I try to observe them and see by their attitude what they would like.
JD: Did you go to fashion school or college?
J-PG: I didn't go to fashion school. I went to college, but not for classical schooling. On the day of my 18th birthday, I started at Pierre Cardin [...]

253

I don't think *Interview* was the first artist-owned magazine. Elaine de Kooning had a very amusing little magazine in the late fifties and early sixties. Les Levine started a small art-gossip magazine called *Culture Hero* about the same time as Andy started *Interview*. But

(ABOVE) JON, 1987 (BELOW) JON, 1983

2   *Interview* was more than an artist's magazine. It was art. Sometimes it could be corny, annoying, or pretentious. But generally it was the fulfillment of Andy Warhol's idea of Business Art. *Interview* was an extraordinary artistic document of its times and a crucial influence on all manner of media.

I remember that in the early seventies, when Time-Life launched *People* magazine, *People* contributing editor Patrick O'Higgins (of *Auntie Mame* fame) told us that the gossipy weekly was inspired by *Interview*. It seemed kind of silly at the time. *Interview* was tiny.

Sunday afternoons, the Bowery presents a curious spectacle. Instead of disheveled, disused and displaced winos, one confronts teeming clusters of the young and restless. Resplendent in inevitable leather jackets and combat boots, hair fashioned into spikes or shorn completely, the kids have fled their suburban blight for CBGB's Hardcore Matinee. Having an afternoon of hardcore music may sound like conducting a black mass at noon—but remember, hardcore kids have to go to school like everybody else.

The hardcore kids differ from their derelict neighbors in *choosing* their alienation; they proudly wear their anomie on their leather sleeves. Learn the names of the groups the kids venerate—emblazoned on the nearest leather jacket—and you have what sounds like pop groups from the anti-matter universe. Agnostic Front, Jodie Foster's Army, Chappaquiddick Plus Five, the Dicks, the Crucifixes, Toxic Shock, Jerry's Kids and the Cro-Mags bear names that, by antithesis, constitute a course in

Western Civ.

Hardcore has retained punk's flair for negation, rage, mind-splitting volume, fiercely fast rhythms and a kind of industrial frenzy. While groups that were formerly punk, like the Damned and the Stranglers, have been housebroken and seem hellbent on producing this generation's "MacArthur Park," hardcore has kept the sound and the fury. Now, as "new age" music threatens to ensnare the world in its ether, hardcore begins to look—and sound—pretty attractive.

Drew Carolan began photographing the CBGB Sunday afternoon crowd in 1983, after convincing them that he was neither a marine nor a cop. Now, four years later, Drew has rounded up some of his subjects for a second look. The critic Harold Bloom claims that "doing the opposite" is just another form of imitation. If so, we can look at the hardcore kids—before and after—and in their antifashion glimpse a fashionable heart of darkness.

—*Fayette Hickox*

Style: post punk

After a Fashion

photographs by Drew Carolan

(ABOVE) FEE, 1983 (BELOW) FEE, 1987. ALL PHOTOGRAPHS FROM A SERIES CALLED "MATINEE."
1983 LOCATION, CBGB'S, N.Y. RESEARCH ASSISTANT—LYNZ.

Opposite page:
1. *Interview*, November 1988; photographs: Karen Kuehn
2. *Ungaro, Interview*, May 1986; photograph: David Seidner
3. *Interview*, May 1987; photographs: Drew Carolan
This page:
1. *Chanel, Interview*, June 1985; photograph: David Seidner
2. *Jean Patou, Interview*, May 1986; photograph: David Seidner

1–2

Interview was an original and almost conceptually pure idea. It challenged written journalism and its excesses with pure vernacular and its excesses. An *Interview* interview was like being there. *Interview*'s interviewers weren't professionals with axes to grind; they were celebrities, insiders, characters. They didn't follow the public-relations

program — they manifested their own personalities. The *Interview* interview was the perfect fly-on-a-very-glamorous-wall experience. It presented what being famous was like from the inside. It defined the new fashion sensibility, for better or worse. It was a new kind of fashion magazine. It wasn't out to sell garments or makeup or fragrance, although it would do all of that. It was out to sell itself. And that is pretty much what fashion is all about.

PENN ON PA

photographs by
BRADFORD BRANSON
art direction and
collage by FRITZ KOK
styling by
KIM BOWEN

Fantasy, danger, glamour, and a sense of the absurd—together they represent an important aspect of fashion in the *fin de siècle* '80s, a time that recalls the '50s but with an edge.

This confluence couldn't have happened at a more propitious time, as 200 million Americans have just yawned their way to

Andy Warhol

ER

1–2

Opposite page:
1. *Interview*, November 1988; photographs: Bradford Branson; art direction and collage: Fritz Kok
2. Photograph by Francis Ing from an article on Warhol by Daniela Morera for *Italian Vogue*, 1982
3. February 1989
4–5. *A Bikini Story*, *Interview*, June 1991; photographs: Ellen von Unwerth

This page:
1. *Michael Monroe, Lead Singer for Jerusalem Slim*, *Interview*, July 1992, photograph: Steven Meisel
2. *Joe Leste, Lead Singer for Bang Tango*, *Interview*, July 1992; photograph: Steven Meisel
3. *Helena Christensen and Michael Hutchence*, *Interview*, March 1994; photograph: Sante D'Orazio

3

1

drew

ess

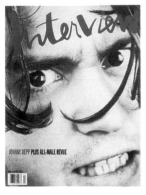

2–3

4–7

ust

darling

8–9

roses

destiny

green, gr

breakfast

courage

drew

1–2

Opposite page:

3

Fashion Victims
The Legacy of Andy Warhol

Thomas Sokolowski

THE WORLD OF FASHION was Andy Warhol's perfect world. He filled it, like some grand terrarium, with everything that nature had denied him, rearranging it into another style to suit a different moment.

Fashion was the mirror into which he gazed to see his own physical reality and, in so doing, crafted a strategy to make the world see him as something more than his own reflection. Beast became beauty. Fashion allowed Warhol to become a new man, to mold a new world, and to alter his surroundings at will. However, as many times as he shaped a new format, he remained smack-dab at the center, omnipresent and unwavering. In fashion, outsider became insider. This was what it was all about. Changing the costumes, adapting the text, walking the walk, turning the mirrors against the wall. Warhol was now on the other side of the looking glass. Major magic was done, and black magic at that! In fashion, Warhol saw the world as he wished to see it. Creating *Interview* magazine, he fashioned a stage on which the world would see him as he saw himself. It featured no standard fashion shoot.

Not surprisingly, portraiture was the true center of his art, and with it he could paint image after image after image that looked more true than real. Nowhere was this truer than among his self-portraits. There he was the true master, the real fashion artist.

If portraiture forms the cloth into which is woven Warhol's artistry, self-portraiture provides the defining pattern of the weave. As the truly traditional artist that, at base, he was, self-imaging was a necessary evil in which he frequently luxuriated and through which he fashioned an ever-changing simulacrum of aspirant, sensate beauty. From an early 1942 pencil drawing of a somewhat geeky collegiate Andrew Warhola to the almost horrific, seemingly decapitated, heads done just six months before his untimely death in February 1987, Warhol's chronicling of his own visage clearly records his ongoing discomfort with his physiognomy.

Uncommonly harrowing, those last 1986 portraits serve as a collective synecdoche of Warhol's thoughts and desires. Standing clearly apart from all of his other portrait work, these head-on levitating masks, radiating spikes of artificial hair, recall ancient descriptions of the gorgon Medusa. The tale of this infamous demiurge, whose power to fascinate drew in equal parts upon beauty and horror, was certainly known to Warhol. Despite the fact that her tresses were writhing, snaky locks, ancient sources tell us that Medusa's extreme beauty had the power to compel and then petrify all who gazed upon her; even her mirror reflection could prove deadly. Once the legendary hero Perseus had slain her, the goddess Athena placed Medusa's visage on her aegis, and from then on all who looked upon the shield were turned to stone. That this mythological allegory appealed to Warhol with its implications of Narcissine adoration is further enticing. Perchance he saw its exhortation against vanity as reproach to his own obsession with his appearance and, therefore, chose to make his ultimate self-portraits into chilly reliquaries of hubris, intensely powerful, yet almost impossible to behold. "See what happens to those who spend too much time standing in front of the mirror!" they seem to chide. While reveling in their collective resplendence, Warhol himself must have had second thoughts about setting out these works before a guileless public unaware of their inherent vice. Subsequently, he covered his Medusan faces with camouflage veils that reveal the recognizable topography of the face but protect the uninitiated from the vile, fatal power of the exposed mask. In choosing camouflage for his protective covering,

Andy Warhol, *Self-Portrait*, 1986

Warhol acknowledged the patterned disguise (first called "dazzle painting" by the British in 1917) as the proper artistic conveyance for creating a misleading impression, much like the fashion world's use of make-up. Given Warhol's chosen mode of monosyllabic response to almost any query posed by any questioner, his decision to obscure his portrait image should come as no surprise. Therefore, like Medusa, Warhol in these final portraits would maintain his hegemony over the art and artists who were to follow in his wake, leaving these archetypal icons as mordant oxymorons expressing the fatal beauty of some fashion victim.

Warhol, who bore both physical and emotional scars from the 1968 attack by Valerie Solanas, chose a visual metaphor that bespoke the fatal conjunction of physical beauty and the tragic consequences it often engenders. It is, therefore, not surprising that many of the key icons of the Warhol pantheon of female beauty, such as Marilyn Monroe and Judy Garland, were only painted after their early and tragic deaths; even Edie Sedgwick, the *Poor Little Rich Girl* of 1964–65, was surrounded by an aura of tragedy that only added to her scintillation. In the world of glamour, it is always better to have passed on than to be merely passé; *vide* the peripatetic corpse of Eva Peron. Only some mode of necrophilic magic or cosmetic artistry could make beauty survive, but at what price? Eschewing the Madonna/whore binary that is so favored by cultural apologists of the postmodern era, Warhol rather found the hero/martyr parallelism much more to his liking, for each side of that equation demands a purity of type that is enduring and unhindered by the quotidian. In fact, once a hero/beauty goddess has been created, there is no place for him/her to go but down, and down in a big way — that is, to become a victim at the hands of the imperfect! No wonder that he became entranced with the Kennedy assassination, which conveniently transformed the fairy-tale princess Jacqueline Bouvier Kennedy into the tragic Madonna persona. Not uninterestingly, Andy chose not to emblazon her later manifestation as the calculatingly jaded — and no longer young — Jackie O! (One wonders what Andy would have made of Wayne Koestenbaum's recent valentine-encomium *Jackie?*) The fifteen-minute mantra requires a terminus post quem after all! The tabloid persona of Mrs. Onassis becomes the fulcrum of the fashion turn that these late portraits take and which help form the visual legacy that survives him. Certainly the predatory figure of the infamous paparazzo Ron Gallela, who dogged Jackie in her later years, making her private life into an unexpurgated public hell, must have appeared to Warhol as a *doppelgänger* of his own nemesis, Valerie Solanas. Even Warhol himself fell in line with these image assassins, using his beloved, antiquated Polaroid camera to repeatedly "point and shoot," to capture all of his famous portrait sitters. Each and every one of his subjects participated in the lineup, were sized up and then immortalized as visages of mute, ineluctable, and chilly perfection.

One paramount legatee to the Warholian tragico-glamour ethos is JonBenet Ramsey, the "Little Miss Fun Bubble" from Boulder, Colorado, who was found murdered in her parents' home on Christmas Day 1996. Ardent Catholic that Warhol was, he would have appreciated the almost sacral placement of her dead body under the family Christmas tree after its discovery. The Sygma Studio publicity shots of the

261

Fashion feature photographed at The Andy Warhol Museum, *Vogue Italia*, September 1996

reigning JonBenet bear close resemblance to later Warhol portraits of Dolly Parton, Marisa Berenson, and Cornelia Guest. The beauty statement imposed on JonBenet was decidedly retro, like the ones Andy had chosen for each of his sitters, decidedly off-center and just a tad unflattering, but always attention-getting.

Andy and JonBenet's handlers knew, as the French do, that makeup is both a cosmetic and a form of deception. As Richard Goldstein has commented in a recent issue of *The Village Voice*, her makeover into a tiny blonde bombshell gave America the martyr/icon poster girl in the public campaign against child abuse for whom it long had been waiting. As he adroitly points out: "But being blonde is not necessarily its own reward. The color of angel hair is also the sign of the sex kitten, and of little girls in suntan lotion ads with their pert bottoms bared. The precious child comes perilously close to being an object of allure." Thus, a fashion plate is transformed into a fashion victim, a move that the child Andy must have recalled with painful clarity. In addition, Andy himself was not inured to the appeal of kiddie starlets. His first star crush was Shirley Temple, the epitome of Depression-era *jeunesse dorée*, whose autographed publicity stills filled the pages of "her biggest fan's" earliest photo album. And it was to her golden-child, Kewpie-doll appearance that Warhol turned as a source for his portrait of the child star after the adult Shirley Temple Black's own death from cancer. Like JonBenet, Warhol would proverbially lay Little Mary Sunshine to rest in her pageant tiara and ballgown at what the ancient Greeks would have deemed her *akme*. While the fashion fabulist in Warhol would have loved the glamorous mimicry of this late-millennial tragedy, his more quiet moralist streak would have declared "*Sic semper divae*"; fame purchased at the altar of fashion must ultimately claim its sacrificial victim. And how much better if the fashion victim, hustling his/her beauty, were young and guileless, how much better and deeper the grief.

It is all too easy to trace Andy Warhol's own vic-

timization at the hands of second-rate imitators and poseurs in the worlds of art and fashion in the decade following his death. On the other hand, first-rank designers such as Stephen Sprouse, Gianni Versace, Vivienne Tam, and others have produced some startling homages to the King of Pop and did so even in collections shown during his lifetime. Their knowing tributes to the Warholian contribution to American culture and the pantheon of national icons that he created are chic costumes that they have designed to be worn by yet another generation of arriviste super-stars who gain credibility, publicity, and, perhaps, eventual ascendancy by wearing Warhol footnotes on their luscious chests and rumps! It is, however, those Warholian quotations pullulating across the photo-graphic fashion spreads of *Vogue, Mademoiselle, Marie Claire*, and *Vanity Fair* that both boggle the mind and stimulate the now-omnipresent vogue for hapless-adolescent, laid-back lust. While the tight visual quotes are numerous and easy to spot, it is the more generic, even atmospheric morass of Generation-X gamines and androgynous studs languorously sprawled out in disreputable environs that truly evoke the ineffable Warhol Look. The still photography and films of Larry Clark have trafficked in this louche ethos for the past ten years, as have the recent Allure perfume advertisements. However, the aesthetic climaxed in the notorious ad campaign for Calvin Klein underwear that caused a fracas reaching all the way to the corridors of power on Capitol Hill. The "Warhol look" imbues this entire campaign. Its artistic aggregate derives from a clear knowledge of Warhol's film oeuvre (especially *My Hustler, Lonesome Cowboys*, and *Chelsea Girls*), com-plete with banal dialogue and straight-on camera angles as well as the willowy insouciance of those fifties' line drawings of boys produced during his first decade resident in New York City. Hardly buff examples of current, late-nineties body culture, the actor/models chosen for this ad series become just the latest generation of fashion victims, even though their bruises are merely cosmetic and their slight physiques

self-imposed. While the body type is contradictory, the attitude of the teen models directly corresponds to the somnambulant, non-acting "style" of Joe Dallesandro without any of the latter's "I don't give a fuck" erotic sweetness. These latter-day studlets are all ice princesses. Whereas Warhol's Factory superstars ran the gamut from Social Register progeny to the lesser coronets of Europe, the current crop appear decidedly working class, if not actual street hustlers, pulled directly from their beats along Times Square and other urban skid-row locales. Where Joe Dallesandro would sell his favors for a smoke or a toke, or even for the blissful hell of it, his successors seem to be forced into this faux prostitution by faux desperation. "I'm a fashion victim, dude," they seem to say. Thus, their stylized victimization adroitly choreographed by fashion queens for retail magnates becomes all the more polemical. (These photographic retail docudramas might even contain some revisionist parody of Hiram Powers's *Bound Slave,* the nineteenth-century American neoclassicist's famous sculpture whose blatant nudity was tolerated by Victorians since she was "forced into it" by demonic heathen forces.) That is, "The designer made me do it!!"

If Andy Warhol's legacy to the world of style and glamour is to be defined in any clear way, it must comprehend Warhol's almost religious adherence to the dogma of the mercurial transience of fashion along

Corinne Day, *Rose, Brewer St, London, The Face,* 1993

with his uncanny ability to almost magically ascertain in just which direction the wind was blowing, always getting it right while countless others would find themselves mired in the muck of a forgotten couture cul-de-sac. His grail was beauty, a beauty that he

Steven Meisel, *L'Uomo Vogue,* 1995

frequently found and heaped around his Factory like the spoils of a big-game hunter, be they objets d'art or pieces of flesh. Like some twentieth-century *marchand-mercier,* he consistently crafted the look, doctored the taste, and then sold the world on it not by words, not even by actions, but simply by being there, by being Warhol. Thus this consummate outsider born far from the right side of the tracks became the arbiter of cool. Simultaneously, then, he would play both parts against each other, fashion victim and fashion power broker. And though his influence continues to be felt strongly even a decade after his death, his artistic whole remains a figment, the very word that he once remarked should be his epitaph. Yet, a figment so strong, so palpable, that like Medusa's glance it can still turn dissemblers to stone. "See," Andy appears to say, "Beauty carries with it a tremendous responsibility, and levies a horrible price. As a lure to the unknowing, it is magical, but once the unsuspecting are reeled in, they are your victims. And once beauty begins to fade, you too become its victim." Ultimately, Warhol, like Beauty, draws us in, compelling us to look closer and closer, spinning us around his ever-brilliant flame, making us his victims, or maybe his slaves, acknowledging always the uncompromising power of fashion that only allows any of us, even Andy, a short time in the sun. *Sic transit gloria mundi.*

263

This page: 1. Andy Warhol, *D. D. Ryan*, c. 1980–82 2. Andy Warhol, *Bianca Jagger*, c. 1976 3. Patrick McMullan, *John Samuels IV, Calvin Klein, and Andy Warhol at Studio 54*, 1980 4. Patrick McMullan, *Andy Warhol and Baby Jane Holzer Outside Linda Stein's House*, 1986 5. Andy Warhol, *Liza Minnelli*, 1979 6. Andy Warhol, *André Leon Talley*, 1982 7. Christopher Makos, *Elizabeth Taylor and Andy Warhol*, 1981 8. Andy Warhol, *Halston*, c. 1977 9. Andy Warhol, *Valentino Fashion Show*, c. 1982 10. Debbie Harry in *Andy Warhol's Fifteen Minutes*, 1986 11. *Fashion: Kansai in New York*, 1980 12. Andy Warhol, *Valentino Fashion Show*, c. 1982

Opposite page: 1. Patrick McMullan, *Kenny Scharf, Andy Warhol, and Keith Haring*, 1986 2. Patrick McMullan, *Andy Warhol and Cornelia Guest*, 1985 3. Andy Warhol, *Diana Vreeland*, c. 1979 4. Andy Warhol, *John Sex*, 1984 5. Amina Warsuma in *Fashion: Models and Photographers*, 1979 6. Bob Colacello, *Bianca and Mick Jagger*, c. 1977 7. Andy Warhol, *Jellybean Benitez and Madonna*, c. 1983 8. Roxanne Lowit, *Andy Warhol at the Ritz*, 1982 9. Andy Warhol, *Giorgio Armani*, 1981 10. Andy Warhol, *Sid Vicious*, c. 1978

Uptown/Downtown Style

THE NEW YORK NIGHTCLUB SCENE became white-hot in the late 1970s and 1980s at Studio 54, Area, the Mudd Club, Palladium, and other discothèques. Andy Warhol was seen at these nightspots with a various but always interesting entourage. Like his 1960s Silver Factory, the clubs were populated by the period's trend-setters and were a locus for the mingling of uptown and downtown, establishment and avant-garde, artists and fashionable society. This mix, always inspiring to Warhol, now infused his life and work.

In his social life, as well as in his studio, Warhol participated in the worlds of glamour, style, and fashion perhaps more actively than ever before. If the fashion icon Diana Vreeland was the artist's guide to the mysteries of high fashion and high society, the tatty-chic Jean-Michel Basquiat was his main line to

Uptown is for people who have already done something. Downtown is where they're doing something now. I live uptown but I love downtown.

Andy Warhol with Bob Colacello, *Andy Warhol's Exposures*, 1979, p. 232

the downtown world of artists and performers, who were indebted to the freedoms Warhol pioneered. Fred Hughes, the artist's closest associate, was never far from his side, and though Hughes seemed to prefer the uptown world, he was able to pilot the pair uptown and downtown with an always debonair look and manner.

The new disco scene began with Studio 54, and Warhol, who enjoyed watching the celebrities packing the dance floor and banquettes, frequented the club with friends Halston, Liza Minnelli, and Bianca Jagger. The artist regularly attended Halston's fashion shows in his Olympic Tower atelier and was also seen at shows of Valentino, Versace, Gaultier, and other designers. During this period, Warhol acquired a wide array of designer clothing, from Givenchy to Fiorucci, to wear and add to his collections. For the 1975 exhibition "Fashion as Fantasy" at the Rizzoli Gallery in New York, he deconstructed and then reassembled designer clothing by sewing together mixed pieces cut from various designers' clothes.

At downtown clubs like Area and Palladium, those making the scene mingled in and around installations by artists including Warhol, Basquiat, and Kenny Scharf. Keith Haring, who had a close relationship with Warhol, was perhaps inspired by him when he created his Pop Shop, which sold clothing and other items decorated with Haring's work. Haring, in turn, may have inspired Warhol to create T-shirts, sneakers, and scarves emblazoned with his own images, something he had not done with clothing since the 1960s. In the mid-1980s, Warhol also collaborated with the young designer Stephen Sprouse to create a line of clothing based on his *Camouflage* paintings.

Opposite page: 1. Roxanne Lowit, *Andy Warhol at the Met,* 1983 2. Andy Warhol, *Fashion Model,* c. 1982 3. Christopher Makos, *Liza Minnelli and Andy Warhol,* 1978 4. Andy Warhol, *Carolina Herrera,* 1979 5. Patrick McMullan, *Thierry Mugler and Andy Warhol,* 1986 6. Christopher Makos, *Gang of Four* (Liza Minnelli, Andy Warhol, Bianca Jagger, and Halston at Studio 54 on Liza Minnelli's birthday), 1978
This page: 1. Roxanne Lowit, *Sonia Rykiel and Andy Warhol at the Rainbow Room,* 1981 2. Russell Todd in *Fashion: Male Models,* 1979 3. Issey Miyake in *Andy Warhol's T.V.,* 1983 4. Tina Chow in *Andy Warhol's T.V.,* 1981 5. Andy Warhol, c. 1980 6. Cris Alexander, *Bob Colacello, Fred Hughes, and Andy Warhol at the Office,* c. 1979 7. Roxanne Lowit, *Halston Model and Andy Warhol,* 1982 8. Paige Powell, *André Leon Talley and Andy Warhol at Christophe de Menil's Dinner Party,* 1986

Warhol's portrait paintings, photographs, and video work provide a vivid picture of the worlds in which he moved during the 1970s and 1980s. Yves Saint Laurent, Halston, Versace, Helene Rochas, Tina Chow, Basquiat, and Sprouse are among the fashionable subjects of the artist's many portraits. Warhol incessantly photographed the scene, just as he himself was frequently photographed, and many of his images mark him as an accomplished fashion photographer, revealing the look of the moment or the movement of clothing as a model moves down the runway. For features in French *Vogue* and the Italian magazine *Donna*, the artist used Polaroid photographs to depict New York City life and fashion. As he became increasingly involved in video production, Warhol's innovative cable television series *Fashion*, *Andy Warhol's T.V.*, and *Andy Warhol's Fifteen Minutes* covered everything from haute couture to punk. The programs' interviews and runway footage focused on male models, Diana Vreeland, Debbie Harry, Giorgio Armani, and many others.

In what might appear the ultimate seduction of the fashion world, Warhol himself became a model in advertisements, fashion features, and runway shows. The artist's last public appearance, only a few days before his death in February 1987, was as a model for a show of Kohshin Satoh's fashions at the Tunnel club in downtown Manhattan. Throughout this period, Warhol served as a constant conduit of ideas between the diverse worlds he inhabited.

— MF/MK

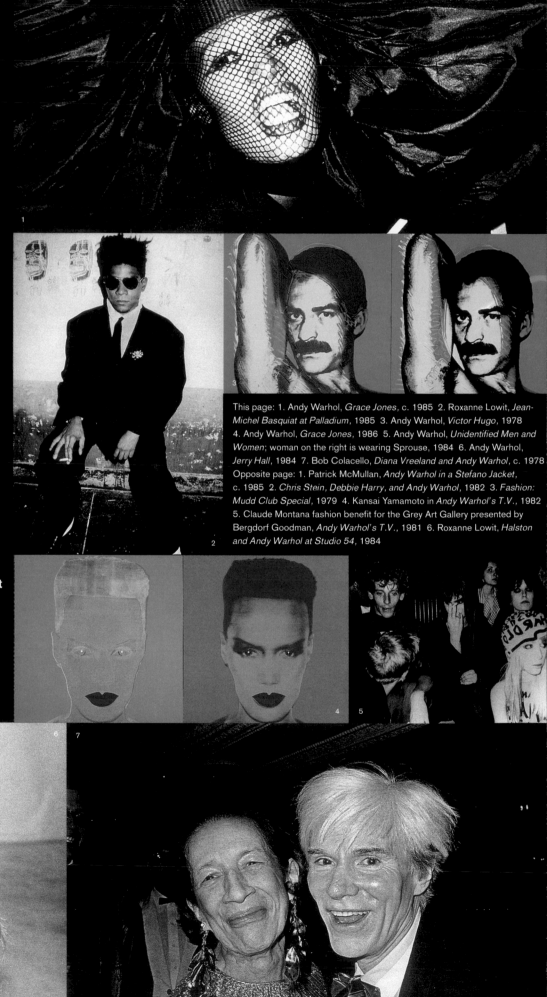

This page: 1. Andy Warhol, *Grace Jones*, c. 1985 2. Roxanne Lowit, *Jean-Michel Basquiat at Palladium*, 1985 3. Andy Warhol, *Victor Hugo*, 1978 4. Andy Warhol, *Grace Jones*, 1986 5. Andy Warhol, *Unidentified Men and Women*; woman on the right is wearing Sprouse, 1984 6. Andy Warhol, *Jerry Hall*, 1984 7. Bob Colacello, *Diana Vreeland and Andy Warhol*, c. 1978
Opposite page: 1. Patrick McMullan, *Andy Warhol in a Stefano Jacket*, c. 1985 2. *Chris Stein, Debbie Harry, and Andy Warhol*, 1982 3. *Fashion: Mudd Club Special*, 1979 4. Kansai Yamamoto in *Andy Warhol's T.V.*, 1982 5. Claude Montana fashion benefit for the Grey Art Gallery presented by Bergdorf Goodman, *Andy Warhol's T.V.*, 1981 6. Roxanne Lowit, *Halston and Andy Warhol at Studio 54*, 1984

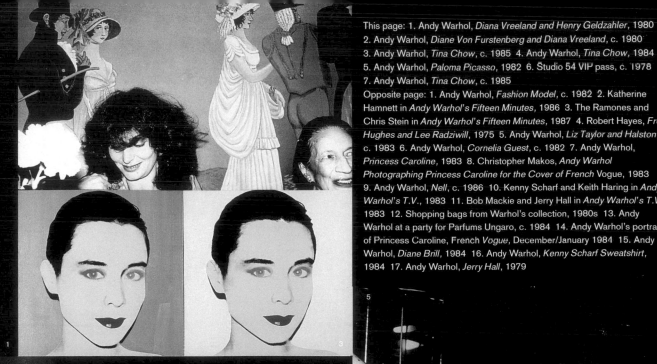

This page: 1. Andy Warhol, *Diana Vreeland and Henry Geldzahler*, 1980
2. Andy Warhol, *Diane Von Furstenberg and Diana Vreeland*, c. 1980
3. Andy Warhol, *Tina Chow*, c. 1985 4. Andy Warhol, *Tina Chow*, 1984
5. Andy Warhol, *Paloma Picasso*, 1982 6. Studio 54 VIP pass, c. 1978
7. Andy Warhol, *Tina Chow*, c. 1985
Opposite page: 1. Andy Warhol, *Fashion Model*, c. 1982 2. Katherine
Hamnett in *Andy Warhol's Fifteen Minutes*, 1986 3. The Ramones and
Chris Stein in *Andy Warhol's Fifteen Minutes*, 1987 4. Robert Hayes, *Fred
Hughes and Lee Radziwill*, 1975 5. Andy Warhol, *Liz Taylor and Halston*,
c. 1983 6. Andy Warhol, *Cornelia Guest*, c. 1982 7. Andy Warhol,
Princess Caroline, 1983 8. Christopher Makos, *Andy Warhol
Photographing Princess Caroline for the Cover of French* Vogue, 1983
9. Andy Warhol, *Nell*, c. 1986 10. Kenny Scharf and Keith Haring in *Andy
Warhol's T.V.*, 1983 11. Bob Mackie and Jerry Hall in *Andy Warhol's T.V.*,
1983 12. Shopping bags from Warhol's collection, 1980s 13. Andy
Warhol at a party for Parfums Ungaro, c. 1984 14. Andy Warhol's portrait
of Princess Caroline, French *Vogue*, December/January 1984 15. Andy
Warhol, *Diane Brill*, 1984 16. Andy Warhol, *Kenny Scharf Sweatshirt*,
1984 17. Andy Warhol, *Jerry Hall*, 1979

**The key to the success of
Studio 54 is that it's a
dictatorship at the door and
a democracy on the floor.**

Andy Warhol with Bob Colacello,
Andy Warhol's Exposures, 1979

CHANEL

31, RUE CAMBON · PARIS

He said, "Diana, it gets more like pagan Rome every night."
Diana answered, "I should hope so."

Andy Warhol with Bob Colacello, *Andy Warhol's Exposures*, 1979

Andy Warhol in conversation with Diana Vreeland and Fred Hughes, March 20, 1976*

D.V.: Would you like a little drop? You and I are the only vodka drinkers I know.

A.W.: Oh, okay, I'll have a little drop.

D.V.: Wasn't it the most marvelous, gorgeous – Divine models – I'm totally exhausted.

A.W.: You're wearing your family jewels from David Webb. Is that a David Webb?

D.V.: He knows everything, this man. Do you think it looks a bit démodé? I put it on with certain sort of feeling.

A.W.: No, it's the prettiest one I've ever seen. I've been trying to buy one like that.

D.V.: I think it's so beautiful. I've got an enormous one like that that someone copied.

A.W.: There's a big sale going on of David Webb, I think Monday or Tuesday.

D.V.: Is there really?

A.W.: At Parke Bernet.

D.V.: I think it is the prettiest thing he ever made.

A.W.: I think that's the most beautiful one.

D.V.: But I always felt it's a little démodé. I had the first you know. He sort of made it for me and I mean he gave it to me. He was divine to me. He gave me these ear-rings, I think they're so chic.

A.W.: They are.

D.V.: These I don't think are démodé at all but I worry about this...

F.H.: No, but it's amusing...

D.V.: It's amusing, it's got life. I agree with you. And I sent him so many customers after this. I sent him Charlie Engelhard. My God, he bought enamel animals and diamonds as if there were no tomorrow. Charlie said to me one night, "Where can I do my Christmas shopping? I don't know what to get for anybody..." I said, "Why don't you go to Maximillian? You might like some of the furs." This is the first time he ever went there and he walked in and he bought nine mink coats, *nine*.

A.W.: Gee, we don't meet people like that anymore. Where are they?

D.V.: Well, there's only one Charlie Engelhard.

A.W.: Send him down to the office. Is he still around?

D.V.: No, he died. He was so sweet and kind. He was sort of big time. He was sort of like Louis XIV. At the end he walked with a cane because he was crippled with arthritis. He was fifty, which was no age at all. He walked like the pictures you know of Louis XIV – with a stick – where he looked very high and looked from side to side. I saw him coming out of 21 with all these little girls one night. It was the most beautiful sight, totally Louis XIV, just before Christmas he was giving out, I suppose, hundred-dollar bills to every single solitary waiter.

A.W.: Did Fred tell you we went to the leather bars last night.

F.H.: No, because I didn't go I forgot to tell Diana.

D.V.: He never tells me things like that.

A.W.: It's a whole new world. I took Phillip Niarchos and John Richardson took me. It was fun reading about you on the plane because Fred bought the *Glass of Fashion*.

D.V.: That was written a long time ago, wasn't it?

A.W.: No. In the fifties...

D.V.: It was nice, though. One appreciates things...

A.W.: I read it once before. But why doesn't anybody mention that lady – the, er, the Chilean lady...

D.V.: You know, I had a lot to do with that book. I have to tell you something. I say it to you too because I know you both so well and I know you'll never repeat it but it will sound as if I'm bragging. But I brought all those people like Rita Lideck, Madame Arasoise who's Arturo's aunt...

A.W.: Oh, is that who that was? You mean Arturo Lopez's aunt?

F.H.: By marriage. His wife Patricia was her niece.

D.V.: Well, all I can tell you is that in 1911 she had a completely white room with mattresses in gray satin and the walls were covered in Picassos.

A.W.: The book kept saying that she invented Jean Michel Frank.

D.V.: Oh, I think so. Oh, but everybody followed her, but everybody.

F.H.: The book says that he adored her...

A.W.: And he picked up ideas from her.

F.H.: No, that he was a kind of a protégé of hers.

A.W.: How come nobody ever mentions her? It's the first time I ever heard of her...

D.V.: But when I mentioned her to Cecil who's his generation... Now for instance when she brought that little swatch of shocking pink to Elsa – it's really the pink of Peru. She's Chilean, you see. And she said, "I make this the most chichi color!"

A.W.: The book didn't even say that. She brought the shocking pink...

D.V.: Nobody really knows that, but really nobody. I didn't even tell that to Cecil this time because Elsa was alive. You know, this was twenty years ago.

A.W.: Oh, so she brought shocking pink then. How great.

D.V.: I have one thing left in shocking pink and it's the interior of a dressing gown that was made for me about 1930. It's in beautiful condition. I never wear it because I never wear dressing gowns – I just wear a sort of peignoir. I'm either in bed or I'm up dressed.

A.W.: Edie Beale came down to see us yesterday.

D.V.: Who did?

A.W.: Edie Beale.

D.V.: Oh no. How marvelous. God, I thought she was attractive. She has such style and when she dances with the flag, you know... I mean, she's really wonderful.

A.W.: She wore the piece of fabric around her.

F.H.: Like in the movie.

D.V.: She has no clothes, I take it.

A.W.: No.

F.H.: It's sort of a great invention, because, like the pin comes right here... Look, Diana, so her leg is shown right up to here. It's really kind of great. She just does it to show that look.

D.V.: That's adorable. I'm so glad I saw that movie.... And somehow I didn't want to see it, because I've seen all that tawdry side of the Hamptons. I've seen all those ghastly people with their bosoms falling below their stomachs – you know that look? You know what I'm talking about, don't you? That absolutely deadbeat salt water spray stuff. And the mother is beautiful. Something so touching.

A.W.: I think they're really great.

D.V.: And then of course the great thing that people say is that their privacy was invaded. Listen, they were having the time of their lives.....

A.W.: Do you take hormones?

D.V.: Oh, yes.

A.W.: What are they?

D.V.: They're marvelous. I'll tell you what they do.

A.W.: You mean all girls take them?

D.V.: Everybody takes them and after a certain period in your life, I don't mean you start out with them...

A.W.: What's it for?

D.V.: It's the balance of hormones in your system.

A.W.: But some people don't take them.

D.V.: Well, if they don't the chances are that they're erratic. They're old, their skin goes, their bodies go. When the hormones give out... You see, this is one of the great things of modern science.

A.W.: You mean most girls take hormone shots?

D.V.: I used to take shots. I haven't taken shots in years. But I take one hormone every night before I go to bed.

A.W.: Is it a pill?

D.V.: It's a pill.

A.W.: What does it do for you?

D.V.: You see, if you really visualize the world the way it really was, the average woman at forty was an old woman. I don't mean to say she was middle-aged. She was through. Her skin was through, her mouth was like a knife, she had no lips – she had nothing. Her skin was dry, her...

A.W.: So hormones actually...

D.V.: It takes over when your natural hormones leave off.

A.W.: But wouldn't that be like amphetamines?

D.V.: It's got nothing to do with anything, except basic nourishment. Hormones sound awfully sexy and everything, and they are sexy. They give you... everybody takes them – everybody, everybody. It's the greatest gift of modern science to women. I mean, you sit next to women of all ages at dinner – why? Because they are totally nourished with something that didn't exist thirty years ago. Look at a woman like darling Elsie. She's the most marvelous woman. Her mentality is so great.

A.W.: Does she take hormone treatments?

D.V.: I'm sure she's never had one. Do you know why? Because her skin is totally stretched. It's white as stone.

A.W.: Why is that?

D.V.: Because the hormones gave out years ago and nothing ever took its place. Oh, no – never run down hormones. If I were you, if you ever go to a – whatever a man gynecologist is called – what do you call them?

A.W.: There aren't any.

D.V.: There are but I don't know what they're called. You should go. They don't give you all the sexiness – I'm not talking sexiness, I'm talking skin, I'm talking...

A.W.: But I know what the transvestites do, like Candy. Their beard would stop growing and their breasts would develop. You could actually see it happen. It was incredible. And their skin would get really nice. It was weird. I thought only that kind of person took them. I didn't know everybody took them.

D.V.: But everybody – I mean, everybody. A person like myself takes...

A.W.: But why isn't amphetamine the same thing? It gives you a little zip.

D.V.: It isn't zip. It goes into your system...

A.W.: But so does amphetamine.

Previously unpublished manuscript from The Andy Warhol Museum archives.

Andy Warhol interviewed by K. H.*

Andy Warhol
Height: Medium
Weight: 114–117
Birthdate: Boys don't have to tell their age any more!
Birthplace: McKeesport, Pennsylvania

K.H.: Everyone knows about Andy Warhol the artist and social celebrity.
A.W.: Well, I've only been doing it for about three weeks, and I've had around twelve jobs…
K.H.: How did you get involved in modeling?
A.W.: Marc Balet, art director of *Interview*, asked if I wanted to be with Zoli, and I said, Yeah, but then Larocca called me and asked if they could buy my hands. I then thought that would have been easier, and I was sorry that Zoli didn't decide that hands were better than faces.
K.H.: What was your first job?
A.W.: My first job. It's funny, first jobs and first doing jobs are different things. The first job I was asked to do was a job for Barneys. The first job I actually shot was the Andrea Blanch beauty shot for *Vogue*.
K.H.: It looked wonderful. How did you feel in front of the camera?
A.W.: It was sort of easy for me, because the poor girl I shot with had to come in at about eight in the morning, and had to have her hair teased for, like, ten hours. But I wish I'd been there, because you make more money. They just called me when I had to be there and then shoved me in the picture, and it was over with.
K.H.: That can be a problem for male models. They normally book the girls all day and call men in for an hour.
A.W.: I like sitting around. I mean, that's the most fun. You can use the telephone, and write a novel — do something.
K.H.: How did you feel when Andrea Blanch started shooting?
A.W.: Well, I was a little disappointed, because I had to bring my own clothes. I really wasn't selling anything, so it didn't seem like a regular job. But the Barneys ad was great. I was in Paris last week and I went to this great men's shop. I think it was Daniel Hechter's.
K.H.: The one on St. Germain des Prés?
A.W.: Yeah. I was just wandering in and this salesman just kept staring at me. I assumed he thought that I was the artist, or Andy Warhol or something like that, but he didn't. He just came up and said, "Gee, aren't you the model that was in the Barneys ad in *GQ*?" God! That made my day, my week. It made my year.
K.H.: In the *Vogue* shot, you were the man behind the beautiful woman.
A.W.: Oh, yeah. The girl is so beautiful. I just met her again the other night at Diane Von Furstenberg's. They really spent a lot of time doing her hair up.
K.H.: Then on the whole you have not been intimidated by the camera?
A.W.: Well, no. My first nervous job was yesterday, when I did the Van Lac runway job. It was my first runway, and today's my second. I don't think it's a runway today, I think it's just mixing and mingling with a Bill Blass suit on. But yesterday was my first, going out in public as a model. Well the kids — the girls — were just so sweet. Actually, I want to be a girl model. I think models should become skinny again. I weigh 114 to 117, and

the good thing about it is, I can wear — I can't stand woolen pants so I can wear double pairs of pants on top of my blue jeans, so it fills me out and I look like I'm wearing a thirty-inch waist. It's worked out, I don't have to take my pants off — but the shocking thing is to take my shirt off and everybody sees my scars, and everybody looks away. Anyhow, they had five dressers back there, cute fat ladies — they were so adorable, so sweet. I always wanted to be backstage. And they were great. They had the next shirt ready and I just put it on.
K.H.: How many outfits did you model?
A.W.: I had five shirts.
K.H.: Were you the only male model?
A.W.: No, there were two other guys. It was sort of a good show because it was so small.
K.H.: Preparation for bigger things?
A.W.: Yeah.
K.H.: What do you feel that you as a personality or as an image do to sell a product?
A.W.: I want to be a comedian. And I decided this is a good stepping-stone. Because I just get so nervous, I can't do live TV, and I'm pretty bad at that, but I think I could be a comedian and I thought this is sort of a way to ease into it.
K.H.: I saw you in an ad for Sony. When someone looks at that ad and they see you behind the Sony Betamax…
A.W.: Well, I believe in Sony. And that's the reason I did it, and the Betamax is great, because I've been taping all the movies. I had a Betamax before I even did the ad.
K.H.: Men today, especially young men, are more conscious of the way they look. What do you think?
A.W.: Our magazine tried to make that happen. *Interview* tried to make people dress up again. I hate boys with long hair. I hate the idea that all these sports stars have long hair — I just can't believe it; they seem so old-fashioned. Every one of them looks great. McEnroe just cut his hair, and he looks great. Don't you think he looks great?
K.H.: No. I prefer him with long hair.
A.W.: I disagree. I think he looks great. I like the new glued-down hairdo on men. I was thinking about it and all the old movie stars of the thirties. I'm interested in old photographs. I look at them, and everybody's retouched, even people like Gary Cooper, and all the girls, like Hedy Lamarr. Today people actually look like those movie stars. They're not retouchable. It's amazing. In this country right now, since there's no war — I mean, we've been traveling to colleges and doing tours and stuff, and when everybody's a beauty, it's really scary. God! They're here because they're not in an army. The looks change so fast — last year, it was the exotic look, now it's the all-American look. That's sort of strange.
K.H.: Maybe next we'll have the Andy Warhol look?
A.W.: No. (shyly) I wonder what the next look will be. I can't imagine.
K.H.: What effect do you think the male models are having on the general public?
A.W.: Well, everybody's becoming a fashion victim. I mean, if you walk down Trendy Avenue, you see all these trendy kids wearing different jeans. You're wearing a headband. I mean, are you a model?
K.H.: No. I wore a headband before they became fashionable.
A.W.: Oh, but everybody says that. Every model I've ever known tells me they've invented the hairband. I think Joe Dallesandro did in *Trash*. But then it was actually the hippie thing that brought it about.

K.H.: Well, fashion repeats itself in different forms.
A.W.: *Everything* repeats itself. It's amazing that everybody thinks everything is new, but it's all repeat. That's what makes it sort of interesting. I thought drag queens were finished with years ago, and now you go to a party and there's a new drag queen and it's as if he invented it. It's like a whole new thing. They don't know that drag queens existed before them. When I first met a drag queen, I thought it was something so unusual, and now I go back to seeing old pictures of Weegee's and — well, there were drag queens then. I saw some old photographs of artists in the Village in the forties. They look like the punk parties of the eighties. It looked like the picture was taken yesterday — nothing's changed. It has something to do with time, and I don't know what time is. I wish I knew what it was. It just goes by.
K.H.: How do you dress?
A.W.: I always wear the same old things. Levi's blue jeans and Luchese cowboy boots. Finally I found a pair of boots where every style fits me, my size, 8D. And they really fit so comfortably. I only wear Luchese boots now. They have a waterproof pair that is so terrific. I have a couple of pairs of boots, and I just wear them everywhere. But since I started modeling, I have to wear my black pair — black goes with everything. And then Brooks Brothers shirts are my favorite, but I'm changing now to Van Lacs because they're just so beautiful, but then I like Paul Stuart clothes, because everything is cotton, and Brooks disappoints me a little now; they put polyester in their things. I think if you wear the classics, you're safe. They go on forever. But I love the way Halston dresses, because he dresses only in black, and he has such a great look.
K.H.: What jackets do you wear?
A.W.: Mostly Eddie Bauer and L. L. Bean. I have this great L. L. Bean jacket, fisherman's coat, for my birthday, and I'll wear that. It's a classic. I think they've been doing it for fifty years or something.
K.H.: Do you have any Calvin Klein jeans?
A.W.: Well, I have one pair. I collect jeans. I have a Calvin Klein, a Jordache, a Studio 54. I don't wear them, I just collect them. The fun thing is to walk down the street and see if you can pick out whose jeans someone is wearing by the design on the back.
K.H.: When you go on a job, does someone style you?
A.W.: No, but I want them to. They're all afraid to do anything.
K.H.: What do you think of the money?
A.W.: Oh, I just work for anything.
K.H.: Is your rate $150 an hour?
A.W.: Sometimes. It varies. It's funny to have these checks dribbling in. I can't wait to do my $2,000-a-day job. I want to be in the L. L. Bean or Brooks Brothers catalog.
K.H.: How do your friends react to your new career?
A.W.: They just don't want to believe it.

Previously unpublished manuscript from The Andy Warhol Museum archives. Identity of the interviewer is unknown.

Opposite page: 1. Henry Geldzahler and Diana Vreeland in *Fashion: The Empress and the Commissioner*, 1980 2. Diana Vreeland in *Fashion: The Empress and the Commissioner*, 1980

I'm jealous of what happened to Halston after Ultrasuede. Norton Simon bought his business for millions. He moved to the Olympic Tower. He has an empire. And I have a Factory.

Andy Warhol with Bob Colacello, *Andy Warhol's Exposures*, 1979, p. 39

275

1. Robert Mapplethorpe, *Andy Warhol*, 1986 2, 3, 4. Andy
Warhol, *Pat Cleveland*, c. 1977 5. Andy Warhol's Montauk
scrapbook with photographs of Lee Radziwill, Bianca
Jagger, Dick Cavett, Joe Dallesandro, Andy Warhol, and
Mick Jagger, 1972–78 6. Andy Warhol's Montauk scrap-
book with a photograph of shoe designer Manolo Blahnik
and a drawing by Blahnik, 1972–78 7. Andy Warhol, *Diana
Vreeland Rampant (After Jacques-Louis David,* Napoleon
at St. Bernard*)*, 1984 8. Gregory Kitchen, *Veruschka,
Appolonia, Ara Galant, Andy Warhol and Fred Hughes
at dinner*, 1975 9. Andy Warhol, *Fred Hughes and Diana
Vreeland*, c. 1978 10. Francesco Scavullo, *Iman and
Brigid Berlin*, 1975 11. Grace Jones in *Andy Warhol's
Fifteen Minutes*, 1987 12. Zandra Rhodes in *Andy
Warhol's T.V.*, 1980 13. Marc Jacob's Freudian slip in
Andy Warhol's Fifteen Minutes, 1987

1. Andy Warhol, *André Leon Talley and Diane Brill*, 1984 2. Andy Warhol, *Larissa*, 1984 3. Andy Warhol, *André Leon Talley*, 1984 4. Andy Warhol, *Unidentified Man and Woman*, 1980 5. Article on high society with a photograph of Andy Warhol, *New York*, December 29, 1980/January 5, 1981 6. Andy Warhol, *Terry Toy and Keith Haring*, 1984 7. Andy Warhol, *Bill Cunningham*, 1984 8. Andy Warhol, *Model*, 1982 9. Andy Warhol, *Grace Jones and Keith Haring*, c. 1986

This page: 1. *Fred Hughes*, c. 1975 2. *Fred Hughes and Bianca Jagger*, c. 1978 3. Nicholas Vreeland, *Fred Hughes and Diana Vreeland*, c. 1975 4. *Fred Hughes*, c. 1975 5. George Dubose, *Fred Hughes*, 1985 6. *Fred Hughes and unidentified woman*, c. 1978 7. *Fred Hughes*, c. 1977 8. *Fred Hughes in drag*, c. 1980 9. Jill Krementz, *Fred Hughes and Jerry Hall*, 1987 10. Elizabeth McCullough, *Fred Hughes*, 1985 11. Robert Hayes, *Fred Hughes and Diana Vreeland*, c. 1975 12. David Bailey, *Cecil and Fred Hughes*, 1973 13. *Unidentified man and Fred Hughes*, c. 1983

Opposite page: 1. *Mick Jagger, Jerry Hall, Fred Hughes, and unidentified woman*, c. 1987 2. *Fred Hughes and Elsa Peretti*, 1981 3. *Jane Forth, Donna Jordan, and Fred Hughes*, c. 1971 4. *Fred Hughes*, c. 1972 5. David Bailey, *Fred Hughes*, 1973 6. P. Heurtault, *Paloma Picasso, Fred Hughes, and unidentified woman*, c. 1978 7. *Paul Morrissey, Andy Warhol, Ultra Violet, and Fred Hughes*, c. 1968 8. *Fred Hughes, Jerry Hall, Mick Jagger, and others*, c. 1980 9. *Fred Hughes*, c. 1985 10. Andy Warhol, *Fred Hughes*, c. 1980 11. Alice Springs, *Fred Hughes*, 1988.

I started to work at Interview magazine in 1980; *Interview* headquarters then were in Andy Warhol's Union Square "Factory." The figure who stood out most at the Factory to me wasn't the very famous Andy Warhol, however, it was his friend, right hand man and in-house dealer, Fred Hughes. Fred was Andy's "face man." All the looks, poise, and worldliness that Andy lacked, Fred had in spades. He was Edward VIII and Cary Grant wrapped together into one glove-tight, double breasted, bespoke pin-striped suit. I think of the king not only because of the extraordinary personal style that Fred possessed in common with him, but because I specifically remember Fred reciting Edward's abdication speech word-for-word while standing on a table at the Odeon late one night. And Fred brings the actor to mind because his magnetic smile – his upper lip pushed up across the top of his teeth – could very well have come from watching Grant flash his on the movie screen. (Perhaps it's no coincidence that Cary Grant was an Englishman who re-fashioned himself as an upper-class American, while Fred Hughes, of Houston, Texas, can often seem more the aristocratic Englishman than the English.)

When the young editorial staff brought in their raw material, it was Fred's commentary, much more than Andy's, that refined it, gave it elegance, and often a sense of history and depth. It was Fred as well who pushed for art and architecture articles to be included in the magazine alongside Andy's hilarious celebrity interviews; it was Fred who insisted on articulateness as a counterbalance to all the chatter and naked flesh that starred in Interview's pages every month. Not too long ago Fred gave me a copy of Harold Acton's autobiography, *Memoirs of an Aesthete*. He wrote with a magic marker (the way Andy used to sign things), "for Becker, I loves ya, Fred." I loves ya too Fred.

Robert Becker, former Senior Editor of *Interview*, author of *Nancy Lancaster, Her Life, Her World, Her Art*, New York, 1996.

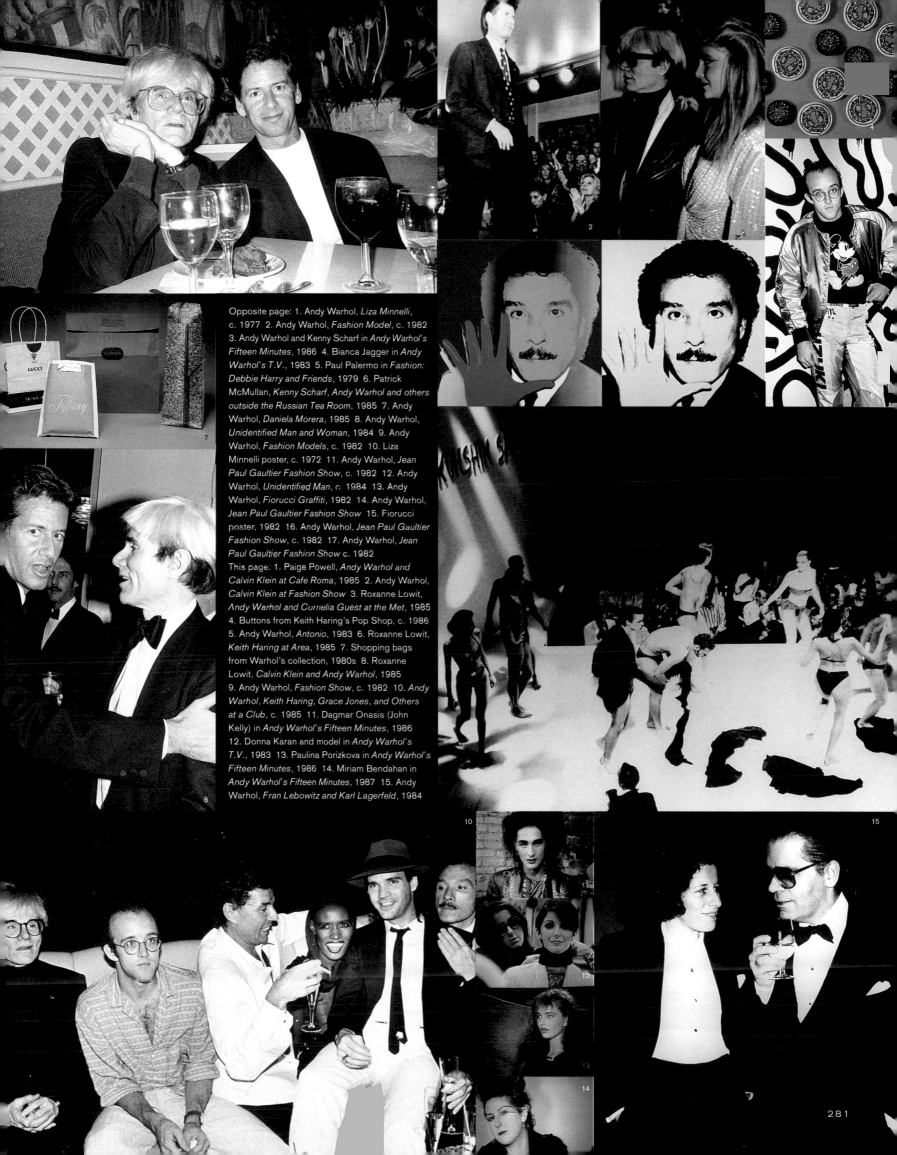

Opposite page: 1. Andy Warhol, *Liza Minnelli*, c. 1977 2. Andy Warhol, *Fashion Model*, c. 1982 3. Andy Warhol and Kenny Scharf in *Andy Warhol's Fifteen Minutes*, 1986 4. Bianca Jagger in *Andy Warhol's T.V.*, 1983 5. Paul Palermo in *Fashion: Debbie Harry and Friends*, 1979 6. Patrick McMullan, *Kenny Scharf, Andy Warhol and others outside the Russian Tea Room*, 1985 7. Andy Warhol, *Daniela Morera*, 1985 8. Andy Warhol, *Unidentified Man and Woman*, 1984 9. Andy Warhol, *Fashion Models*, c. 1982 10. Liza Minnelli poster, c. 1972 11. Andy Warhol, *Jean Paul Gaultier Fashion Show*, c. 1982 12. Andy Warhol, *Unidentified Man*, c. 1984 13. Andy Warhol, *Fiorucci Graffiti*, 1982 14. Andy Warhol, *Jean Paul Gaultier Fashion Show* 15. Fiorucci poster, 1982 16. Andy Warhol, *Jean Paul Gaultier Fashion Show*, c. 1982 17. Andy Warhol, *Jean Paul Gaultier Fashion Show* c. 1982

This page: 1. Paige Powell, *Andy Warhol and Calvin Klein at Cafe Roma*, 1985 2. Andy Warhol, *Calvin Klein at Fashion Show* 3. Roxanne Lowit, *Andy Warhol and Cornelia Guest at the Met*, 1985 4. Buttons from Keith Haring's Pop Shop, c. 1986 5. Andy Warhol, *Antonio*, 1983 6. Roxanne Lowit, *Keith Haring at Area*, 1985 7. Shopping bags from Warhol's collection, 1980s 8. Roxanne Lowit, *Calvin Klein and Andy Warhol*, 1985 9. Andy Warhol, *Fashion Show*, c. 1982 10. *Andy Warhol, Keith Haring, Grace Jones, and Others at a Club*, c. 1985 11. Dagmar Onasis (John Kelly) in *Andy Warhol's Fifteen Minutes*, 1986 12. Donna Karan and model in *Andy Warhol's T.V.*, 1983 13. Paulina Porizkova in *Andy Warhol's Fifteen Minutes*, 1986 14. Miriam Bendahan in *Andy Warhol's Fifteen Minutes*, 1987 15. Andy Warhol, *Fran Lebowitz and Karl Lagerfeld*, 1984

1. Andy Warhol, *Gianni Versace after a Fashion Show*, c. 1984 2. Andy Warhol, *Gianni Versace*, 1984
3. Andy Warhol's portrait of Gianni Versace, *Men's Harper's Bazaar Italia*, c. 1980 4. Andy Warhol, *Gianni Versace*, 1980 5. Andy Warhol, *Paloma Picasso, Gianni Versace, and Candice Bergen*, 1984
6. Fred McDarrah, *Barbara Allen de Kwiatkowski, Andy Warhol, Victor Hugo, and Fred Hughes*, 1977
7. Andy Warhol, *Levi's*, 1984 8. Andy Warhol, *Yves Saint Laurent*, 1974 9. Andy Warhol, *Helene Rochas*, 1975 10. *Unidentified woman, Benjamin Liu, Andy Warhol, Jean-Michel Basquiat, and Paige Powell*, c. 1985 11. Andy Warhol, *Fashion Model*, c. 1982
12. Yves Saint Laurent poster, 1987 13. Betsey Johnson fashion show, *Fashion: The Betsey Johnson Story*, 1980 14. *Fashion: The Betsey Johnson Story*, 1980 15. Article on New York City nightlife in the 1970s, *New York*, April 1993 16. Andy Warhol, *Fashion Show*, c. 1982

1. Roxanne Lowit, *Andy Warhol, Jacqueline Schnabel, Jean-Michel Basquiat, Julian Schnabel, and Kenny Scharf*, 1984 2. Andy Warhol, *Valentino*, 1974 3. Christopher Makos, *Andy Warhol and Jean-Michel Basquiat*, 1982 4. Patrick McMullan, *Andy Warhol in Stefano Jacket and Taylor Mead*, 1985 5. Patrick McMullan, *Andy Warhol in Stefano Jacket with Basquiat Portrait*, 1985 6. Andy Warhol, *Chanel*, 1985 7. Bob Colacello, *Halston and D. D. Ryan*, c. 1979 8. Johnny Dynell, *Jean-Michel Basquiat DJ'ing at Area*, 1986 9. Andy Warhol, *Jean-Michel Basquiat*, 1984 10. Patrick McMullan, *Andy Warhol with Michael Musto's* Downtown *Book Party at Palladium*, 1986 11. Andy Warhol, *Jean-Michel Basquiat*, c. 1985 12. Andy Warhol, *Fashion*, c. 1983

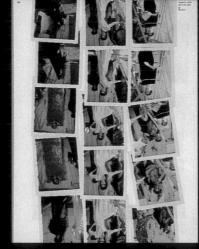

1–13. Fashion feature designed and photographed by Andy Warhol, French *Vogue*, c. 1983: 1–2. with models and Kim Alexis wearing Calvin Klein 3. with models and Kim Alexis wearing Norma Kamali-Omo 4. with Keith Haring and a model wearing Carolina Herrera 5. with Howard E. Rollins, Jr. and a model wearing Halston 6. with Jean-Claude Nedelec and a model wearing Geoffrey Beene 7. with a model wearing Soo Yung Lee 8. with Charles Ludlum and Everett Quinton and Kim Alexis wearing Sylvia Heisel 9. with ▢ A. and Kim Alexis wearing Albert Nipon 10. with James Brown and a model wearing Caumont pour Augustus 11. with Diana Vreeland and Kim Alexis wearing Albert Capraro 12. with New York City Breakers and a model wearing Joan and David 13. with John Sex and a model wearing ▢ Ferrara pour Whiting and Davis 14. Andy Warhol, *Diana Vreeland*, 1983 15. Andy Warhol, *Kim Alexis and John Sex*, 1983 16. Andy Warhol, *Charles Ludlam and Everett Quinton*, 1983 17. Andy Warhol, *Model from* Total Beauty, 1983 18. Andy Warhol, *Kim Alexis, Curtis and Lisa Sliwa, and Guardian Angels*, 1983 19. Andy Warhol, *Models from* Total Beauty, 1983
20. Layout design with Polaroids of Ming Vauze and model in Jackie Rogers, c. 1984 21. Layout design with Polaroids of Guardian Angels and Kim Alexis in Oscar de la Renta, c. 1984 22. Layout design with Polaroids of Stephen Sprouse and Debbie Harry wearing Sprouse, c. 1984
23. Layout design with Polaroids of William Burroughs and model wearing Ann Klein, c. 1984

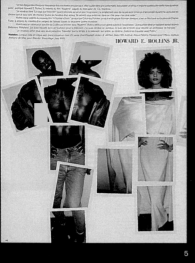

HOWARD E. ROLLINS JR.

JEAN-CLAUDE NEDELEC

CHARLES LUDLAM ET EVERETT QUINTON DE "GALAS"

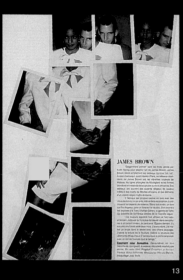

JAMES BROWN

Vogue Avril

PAGE 19
FULL PAGE

Vogue Avril

Vogue Avril

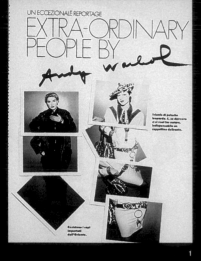

1 2 3 4

1–5. Fashion feature designed and photographed by Andy Warhol, *Donna*, December 1984/January 1985 6. Andy Warhol, *Unidentified Man*, 1984 7. Andy Warhol, *Unidentified Woman*, 1984 8. Andy Warhol, *Victor Hugo*, 1984 9. Andy Warhol, *John Sex*, 1984 10. Andy Warhol, *Jean Paul Gaultier*, c. 1985 11. Andy Warhol, *Diane Brill and Unidentified Man*, 1984 12. Andy Warhol, *Mark Sink and Unidentified Man*, 1984 13. Andy Warhol, *Jean Paul Gaultier and Unidentified Man*, 1984 14. Andy Warhol, *Arian*, 1984

15. Roxanne Lowit, *Andy Warhol Photographing Diane Brill at Jean Paul Gaultier's Party at Area*, 1984 16. Layout design with Polaroids of models and André Leon Talley, 1984 17. Layout design with Polaroids of Jean Paul Gaultier, models, and Francesco Clemente, 1984 18. Layout design with Polaroids of Keith Haring and Juan Dubose, Fred Schneider of the B-52s, Nick Rhodes of Duran Duran, and Victor Hugo, 1984 19. Layout design with Polaroids of Christopher Makos and Jean-Michel Basquiat, 1984

6 7 8 9

10 11 12 13 14

5

15

16

17

18

19

You know, the art of costume designing is basically the art of camouflage rather than fashion design.

Edith Head to Ron Stephenson, *Interview*, January 1975

1. Gregory Kitchen, *Model Wearing Warhol* Composite *Dress*, 1975 2, 3. Federico Suro, *Warhol* Composite *Dress from* Fashion as Fantasy *Exhibition*, 1975
4, 5. Gregory Kitchen, *Model Wearing Warhol* Composite *Dress*, 1975 6, 7. *Raid the Icebox I with Andy Warhol*, 1970 8. Andy Warhol's notes for a perfume idea called "Between," c. 1983 9. John E. Barrett, *Andy Warhol with Jacket Inside-Out*, 1981

1. Fred Hughes dancing with Paige Powell, who is wearing a Sprouse camouflage dress, c. 1987 2,3. Andy Warhol, *Camouflage*, 1986 4. Models wearing Sprouse camouflage clothing, c. 1986 5. Debbie Harry in *Andy Warhol's Fifteen Minutes*, 1987 6. Andy Warhol and Debbie Harry in *Andy Warhol's Fifteen Minutes*, 1986 7. Andy Warhol in *Andy Warhol's Fifteen Minutes*, 1986 8. Fred Hughes dancing with Paige Powell, who is wearing a Sprouse camouflage dress, c. 1987 9. Michael James O'Brien, *Johnny Dynell wearing camouflage pants*, 1996 10. Andy Warhol, *Stephen Sprouse*, c. 1984 11. Todd Tamorrow and Johnny Dynell; Todd is wearing a Sprouse camouflage jacket, 1997 12. Wristwatch sketch by Stephen Sprouse, c. 1985 13, 14. Andy Warhol, *Sneakers*, c. 1984–86 15. Advertisement for Movado watch featuring a watch designed by Andy Warhol, c. 1989 16. Fashion spread with Movado watch designed by Andy Warhol, *Vogue*, c. 1988

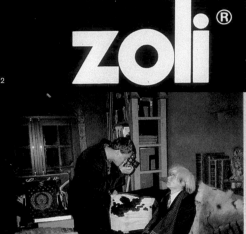

zoli®

146 East 56th Street, New York, N.Y. 1...

LEFT: V. Allen Flusser's field coat. W. French Connection shetland vest. X. Cheveto band-collar shirt for NYC. Y. Giorgio Armani's quilted pants. Z. Walk-Over's suede bucks. RIGHT: AA. Basco's hunting sweater-jacket. BB. Cesarani's cable crew. CC. Crash flannel pants.

Model

Bruce Hainley

Andy Warhol liked fashion. It kept him clothed. It covered his body, which was covered with wounds, some visible, some not, after the .32 bullets "entered the left side of [his] torso," and then "ricocheted through his liver, spleen, pancreas, esophagus, one pulmonary artery, both lungs";[1] covered the corsets, often in floral hues, that held him in place after all that ricocheting, kept him from falling apart — his white skin paler still beneath it all, luminescent with scars and sutures. Looking at Alice Neel's portrait of himself corseted, shirtless, his dugs showing, his eyes closed, he thought it was "gruesome," but at other times he considered the scarred skin he was in "like a Dior dress. It's sort of awful, looking in the mirror and seeing all the scars. But it doesn't look that bad. The scars are really very beautiful; they look pretty in a funny

way."[2] Seeing scars in the mirror was perhaps better and more beautiful than seeing nothing at all. (A repeated fear: "I'm sure I'm going to look in the mirror and see nothing."[3]) Skin is an outfit you can't take off; perhaps identity could be taken off. He said, "Sometimes it's so great to get home and take off my Andy suit."[4]

Andy Warhol liked fashion because of the vocabulary. At various points during his life he wore DeNoyer velveteen jackets, Levi's, boots by Berlutti di Priigi, Brooks Brothers haberdashery, YSL pullovers, Stephen Sprouse driving coats and Lycra turtlenecks, pants by the Leather Man in the West Village, and Jockey underwear. He liked cosmetics, emollients, and astringents, and carried them around in a big bag. *Interview*'s house style always included detailed credits not only for the apparel the models wore but also for makeup, the model and the model's agency, and even for the perfume worn during the shoot. Warhol adored perfumes — the dreamy

This page:
1. Christopher Makos, *Andy Warhol modeling*, 1983
2. Zoli modeling agency promotional poster, c. 1981
3. Paige Powell, *David LaChapelle photographing Andy Warhol for* Cannibal in Manhattan, *a novel by Tama Janowitz*, 1986
4. Advertisement for Barneys New York, c. 1982
Opposite page:
1. Francesco Scavullo, *Warhol with Model (with Whip)*, 1985
2. Advertisement, *Interview*, November 1981
3. Photograph from an article on Andy Warhol, *Amica*, March 1, 1983
4. Andy Warhol with model, *Amica*, c. 1986
5. Advertisement for Paris Planning modeling agency, 1982
6. Christopher Makos, *Andy Warhol*, 1983

BARNEY'S, NEW YORK

names and their dreamy scents, the bottles, the packaging, the advertisements. His favorites were by Chanel and Guerlain; he thought the "right hormones can make Chanel No. 5 smell very butch."[5] When he died, he left behind bottles of Shalimar, Tzigane, and Dans la Nuit.

Andy Warhol liked fashion because of the bodies beneath it. "Whenever somebody came up to the Factory, no matter how straight-looking he was, I'd ask him to take his pants off so I could photograph his cock and balls. It was surprising who'd let me and who wouldn't."[6] He understood that there is no fashion without bodies to wear it. The trajectory of his career is nude and nuder — torsos, sexual parts, oxidation paintings, shadows, skulls — until there was no body left.

Andy Warhol liked fashion because clothes make the man. Fashion assured him that he had a body when too often it wasn't clear that he did. It wasn't as if he could ask someone else. Everybody already thought he was dead after the bullets entered him, a nothing. Even he thought, "I'm really dead. This is what it's like to be dead — you think you're alive but you're dead."[7] His returning again and again to death as a theme was not so much an interest in death as a way of determining what it meant to be alive or not, to have a body or not. His wish to be a machine was a wish to know how a body, particularly the masculine body, is or is not a thing. Fame makes bodies into things, of course, separates the body into persona and person, each having a life of its own — nothing other than the body as a thing and the body not as a thing.

It is not clear that he needed a body to be Andy Warhol. And at first having no body seemed like fun, what he most desired. Truman Capote said that Warhol "would like to have been Edie Sedgwick.... He would like to have been anybody except Andy Warhol."[8] He and Edie did their hair

A face is like a work of art.
It deserves a great frame.

Designers and collectors of limited edition frames for sunglasses and prescription eyewear.
l.a. Eyeworks

1

Andy Warhol gets Picture-Perfect Pictures
with Sony Beta tape.

3

イマ人を刺激する。

6

alike, walked alike, went to the same events together, alike, twins of a sort. But Warhol and Paul Morrissey hired the Factory denizen Allen Midgette, not Edie, when it still seemed like fun for him not to need his own body to be Andy Warhol on tour. "I still thought that Allen made a much better Andy Warhol than I did — he had high, high cheekbones and a full mouth and sharp, arched eyebrows, and he was a raving beauty and fifteen/twenty years younger. Like I always wanted Tab Hunter to play me in a story of my life — people would be so much happier imagining that I was as handsome as Allen and Tab were.... Who wants the truth? That's what show business is for — to prove that it's not what you are that counts, it's what they think you are."[9] It wasn't until he almost wasn't Andy Warhol any longer that all of this became clear: "The whole time I was in the hospital, the 'staff' kept on doing things, so I realized I really did have a kinetic business, because it was going on without me."[10]

What would it mean not to need a body to be someone? What do you do with all the excess flesh? (Does that flesh get lonely?) At first the idea seemed amusing, and then it started to bother him. (Wouldn't it bother you?) It was only by being someone else (he wanted to change his name legally to John Doe; at the end of his life he was admitted to hospital as Bob Robert), having someone else be him (Edie, Allen Midgette) or do things for him (Bob Colacello, sometime editor of *Interview*, and Pat Hackett, Warhol's secretary, partially ghosted some of his books, and various young men — Gerard Malanga, Ronnie Cutrone among them — assisted painting and silk-screening) that he could really begin to figure out who Andy Warhol was and what he did. He started to notice that there might be no end to not having a body. And if there is no body, what exactly is there?

For his first retrospective, at the Institute of Contemporary Art in Philadelphia, all of the art was removed. "[W]e weren't just at the art exhibit — we were the art exhibit, we were the art incarnate…" he remembered.[11] Around the same time, for the Museum of Merchandise at the Arts Council Gallery in Philadelphia, Warhol created a perfume. *Women's Wear Daily* reported: "Andy Warhol — cryptic as always — has switched the name of his creation from 'Eau d'Andy' to 'You're In.'" You're In was a urine yellow "Chanel-type fragrance dispensed in silvered Coke bottles,"

This page:
1. Advertisement for l.a. Eyeworks, 1985
2. *Andy Warhol and model*, c. 1982
3. Advertisement for Sony, 1981
4. Pages from a Zoli modeling agency book, c. 1981
5. Article on Andy Warhol's sponsorship of commecial products, *Forbes*, April 28, 1986
6. Advertisement for TDK, c. 1982
Opposite page:
1. *Andy Warhol and model*, c. 1984
2. Andy Warhol and Grace Jones in an article on New York City nightlife, *Travel & Leisure*, November 1986
3. Andy Warhol modeling in a fashion feature, *Mademoiselle*, August 1982
4. Paige Powell, *Andy Warhol on a modeling shoot*, c. 1986
5. Pages from a Zoli modeling agency book, c. 1981

until Coca-Cola had the perfume removed from the shelves because of trademark infringement. The lingering scent of perfume intensifies presence, even allowing the wearer to remain present after he or she has left the room.

At a time when he was trying to decide how to tell the difference between presence and absence, he designed a perfume that, instead of connoting by its name a dandy's watchful absence, insisted on some kind of presence — if you are in, you are there, somewhere. He knew he might not need his body to be Andy Warhol. This bothered him, perhaps. Urination puts the body in the now. Perfume marked his body's existence in time and space: "If I've been wearing one perfume for three months, I force myself to give it up, even if I still feel like wearing it, so whenever I smell it again it will always remind me of those three months. I never go back to wearing it again; it becomes part of my permanent smell collection."[12] A smell collection might look like nothing but confirmed for Warhol who he was and that he had been.

The perfumed suggestion of being's nothingness haunted him throughout his career. He made two dissimilar pieces called *Invisible Sculpture*. Ronnie Cutrone

has described the earlier, more complicated version: "He may have watched *The Invisible Man* one night on television. So again, we got the Yellow Pages and found burglar alarms, different systems. Some with sound, some with light beams…. We mounted these burglar alarms on brackets all around the perimeter of the big room in the middle of the Factory, which was by then referred to … as Andy Warhol Studios. And we aimed them all at the center of the room where nothing existed. If you walked into the room and you hit this center point, all these alarms would go off. You'd have every

different kind of sound; chirping, booming, buzzing…. But there was nothing there; it was totally invisible. We're again in the great Warhol scheme of things: it was something that was but wasn't."[13] Just as Warhol found himself at times to be.

If the first *Invisible Sculpture* sounded the alarm — not unlike perfume's signaling — of any body's presence, the second was specific to his body, his appearance making nothing happen. On Wednesday, May 8, 1985, he went to a party with artist Jean-Michel Basquiat at Area. They both had work on exhibit. Warhol's piece, his second *Invisible Sculpture*, consisted of "a pedestal, a wall label, and himself displayed in a show-case."[14] Behind a display window, Warhol was his own live mannequin. He had become his art again. It would be difficult to figure out if the sculpture was more invisible when Warhol was present or when he was not. It was in part a memorial for both going to a club and being seen and going to a club and not being seen — being somebody or nobody, something or nothing.

Knowing what went on when his body wasn't there, Warhol started to explore what went on when he was. As much as his exploration was an ontological project, it was even more a fashion crisis. Fashion depends on an individual body being *now*. All of Warhol's work is about whether it is possible to choose to be present or not, and why some feel absent even when present. To find out how and what he was when he was there, Andy Warhol became a model. His modeling had little to do with any sup-posed tentativeness about homosexuality, which for him was natural if not inviolable, but with his difficulty knowing whether he had a body or not and how to be in it if he did. Whatever he was wearing, Warhol modeled the problematics of masculinity, which may not exist.

Being became exteriority in the seventies. Although there were famous models before the seventies — Suzy Parker, Dovima, and China Machado were well known in the fifties, as were Jean Shrimpton, Veruschka, Penelope Tree, Twiggy, and Marisa Berenson in the sixties — modeling became big business in the seventies. Models exem-plified this exteriority. As models, "women could not be replaced by men, and there were no male models."[15] Warhol noticed "There weren't very many young, new-style male models then yet.... In '66 men were

used in photographs still, just to stand there and look butch, to sort of set off the girls and show that the girls were fascinating to them."[16] Male model-ing is one of the few occupations based on a tradition of women's work. Male modeling's rise in the seventies was dependent on the flourishing of the careers of women who modeled and on male homosexuality's entrance into the cultural mainstream. That women models could not be replaced by men would have been questioned by Warhol and his beauties. The Factory superstar Candy Darling teased the model Lauren Hutton about her famous "natural beauty" (and by implication the naturalness of any beauty) when Darling interviewed her for *Interview* in 1973. Candy had her own natural beauty, as did Warhol — an artful presentation of being just what you really are by emphasizing what you really aren't (using wigs, makeup, perfume). Candy wrote: "Lauren Hutton is sitting here, everybody, with about two pounds of make-up on, two pairs of lashes. I mean I could carve my initials in her face and maybe I will."[17]

Warhol pro-ceeded to test this naturalness (of masculinity, of beauty) by becoming a male model fascinat-ed by "the girls," many like Candy, even more fascinated by what occurred when he juxta-posed himself with beautiful boys. Although he had by the mid-seventies appeared in fash-ion spreads for *L'Uomo Vogue* and other magazines modeling Brooks Brothers menswear and blue jeans, Warhol would not start modeling professionally

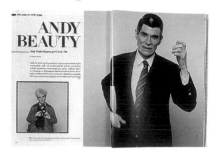

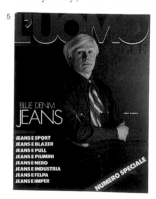

1. Article on Andy Warhol, *Vogue Italia*, February 1982
2. Advertisement for Drexel Burnham, 1986
3. Fashion feature with Andy Warhol, *Männer Vogue*, January 1986
4. Magazine tearsheet featuring Warhol modeling a Stefano jacket, c. 1985
5. *L'Uomo Vogue* cover, June/July 1980
6. Fashion feature with Fred Hughes, Vincent Fremont, Andy Warhol, Ronnie Cutrone, Bob Colacello, and Sean Byrnes modeling Brooks Brothers clothing, *L'Uomo Vogue*, February/March 1974

until the early eighties ("Monday, April 13, 1981: I'm officially a male model now"). Through modeling, Warhol examined male beauty's reliance on passivity, its repeated juxtaposition with and similarity to the freakish and weird, its anonymity. Fellow superstar Jackie Curtis was more pointed than Candy about the supposed naturalness of the natural for women and men: "It's much easier to be a weird girl than a weird guy."[18] Femininity is already considered weird; much of its weirdness is only what masculinity finds weirdly disconcerting within itself and projects onto the feminine.

the reasons he began to model, since male models exist between those two states, even while showing that "it can be exciting to just be your own sex."[20]

In most fashion spreads, Warhol's posing is purposefully stiff — his arms and legs are jointless, his eyes fixed, unblinking. His posed body declares that all models pose, that masculinity is a pose. Next to another model or a group of models, his body highlights their oddness as much as his own. The oddness — theirs, his — allows for the clothing to be seen more clearly than usual. Warhol's modeling shows that bodies are strange and of identical value (bodies are bodies).

Models exist only through repetition; there is no such thing as a model who has only

Absence, monstrosity, and lack are really of masculine provenance. Warhol mused in his *Philosophy*: "Along with having sex, being sexed is also hard work. I wonder whether it's harder for (1) a man to be a man, (2) a man to be a woman, (3) a woman to be a woman, or (4) a woman to be a man. I don't really know the answer…."[19] His interest in investigating the first and second queries — whether it's harder for a man to be a man or to be a woman — was one of

one picture in his book. Representing what someone else is supposed to want or be, the model makes a career of watching, image by image, his own body's decomposition. Warhol's portraits of male beauties operate similarly. Warhol never fetishized singularity. He repeated himself. When he commented on thinking "about all the James Deans and what it means,"[21] he was commenting on the repetition that masculinity, fashion, as well as a model's career necessitate. His portrait of the model Joe Macdonald flattens Macdonald's features, reddens his lips, shadows his eyes with electric blue, doubling the model's head shot as if to show how masculinity

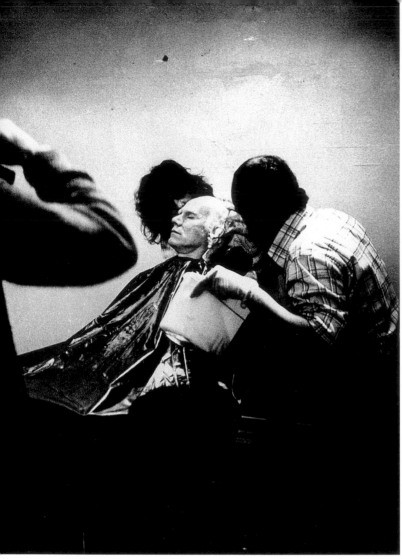

"Jerry Hall came by with a Halston model named Carol, and models just all talk that baby talk, the girls and the boys — you always know when you're talking to a model."[23] He stated that he liked "talkers better than Beauties," but he liked Beauties quite a bit. By becoming a model, Warhol became a man and a beauty; he sexualized his body by

must repeat itself in order to remain what it wishes to appear to be, while demonstrating that appearance to be impossible, made-up masculinity. Warhol's own head shot portrays similar difficulties. On the Zoli head sheet (Warhol began his career as a Zoli model; Zoli Radinsky's agency was the most famous for male models in the late seventies) Warhol's appearance — flat, wigged, blank, sexy — questions whether the Zoli men are and are not the same as he is (beauties), what male beauty is if they are (they are). Weirdly similar, the Zoli men are a male version of Warhol's portrait of Ethel Scull; they are Warhols, the possible result of Warhol's proposal that he sell "his own semen for a limited edition of twenty-five artificially inseminated babies. 'Isn't that a good idea?'"[22]

In *Interview*, on his TV programs, in his diaries, he appreciated the vacuous quality of beauties just being beautiful. Stumbling, fumbling, or looking dazed only made them more beautiful. Warhol wrote in his diary:

repeating the look of the model he was next to. In his interview with Tom Cashin, what is more interesting than the chat between the two male models (Warhol and Cashin) is the fact that Warhol wears the same outfit as Cashin: an Oxford-cloth shirt, a V-neck navy blue pullover. Seeing Warhol juxtaposed with Cashin is a way to begin to understand Warhol's radical ability to manipulate something as seemingly intractable as physical appearance. Either everybody was a beauty or no one was.

Christopher Makos snapped Warhol riding a motorcycle with the Perry Ellis hunk Matt Norklin. Consider not how different they look but how similar. They're just going for a ride, just posing for a picture, just bodies. What do you do with a body? He noted in his diary: "Saw the Christian Dior show and the Valentino show. With the male models, all the really straight-looking models are gay, and all the really gay-looking models are straight. And Christopher and I decided that we should

"Vidal Sassoon Natural Control Hairspray for men—the art of style."

Andy Warhol.
Artist.
New York, N.Y.

start telling people that despite how we look and talk, that we're not gay. Because then they don't know what to do with you."[24] Exactly. Modeling, Warhol embodied — softly, quietly, limply, strangely — what Jean Genet observed looking at a deformed man seated across from him: "Only one man exists and has ever existed in the world. He is, in his entirety, in each of us. Therefore he is ourself. Each is the other and the others." And no one knows what to do with him.

Warhol met many male beauties at Studio 54 and at various bars. (The difference between "hustler" and "model" is often indiscernible: "Chris Makos took us to a bar on 52nd called Cowboys, a hustler bar where Ara and Zoli go to pick up beautiful kids for models."[25]) In 1978, in Paris, Roland Barthes theorized about going to the discotheque Le Palace what Warhol knew by clubbing at Studio 54 (and later at Area): "This means that 'art,' without breaking with past culture (the sculpture of space by laser may indeed recall certain plastic efforts of modernity), extends beyond the constraints of cultural training: a liberation confirmed by a new mode of consumption: we look at the lights, the shadows, the settings, but also we do something else at the same time (we dance, we talk, we look at each other)."[26] Looking at themselves, at the beauty across from them, they moved beyond the idea of "art" as necessarily distinguishable from going out, from fashion, and moved away from the idea of just one boy to the retinal pleasures of boys. Other than Barthes and Warhol, few have provided a way of thinking through such matters and how they intersect with a certain type of masculinity and faggotry. One who might have was Truman Capote, especially in *Answered Prayers*. During the Studio 54 years and after — the portraits, the *Shadows* series, the Polaroids and stitched photographs, the *Party* book — look at everything Warhol did as a way of finishing *Answered Prayers* for Truman Capote who couldn't. Finished, it is as exhilarating and funny as it is sad.

The surface is lonely. The surface is amazing. The surface is nothing special. The surface is deceiving. The surface is all there is. He said: "If you want to know all about Andy Warhol, just look at the surface: of my paintings and films and me, and there I am. There's nothing behind it."[27] By allowing himself to see his own surface, Warhol

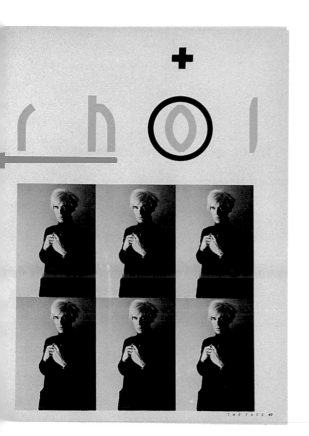

THE FACE 47

was able to see and become the everything and nothing of anybody at all: "Ronnie came with me to Art Kane's studio at 28th and Broadway to pose for a ten-page spread in Italian *Vogue*. There was a Zoli model there who was a stand-in for me, and he had a great body. The spread was that this guy was murdering a girl with black panties over his face. The model was the grandson of Barry Goldwater and we're doing him for *Interview*. Then the panties came off the face and it was actually me who was stabbing the girl in the pictures. So it only took an hour for me to do my part, and it was easy — she put her heel in me and it was really fun."[28] He has a great body and he doesn't. He is the Zoli model, and he isn't. He worried about looking in the mirror for most of his life: "People are always calling me a mirror and if a mirror looks into a mirror, what is there to see?"[29] A lot or nothing. Warhol saw both, endlessly.

Warhol learned to look at himself, to have looks. Described by all that he supposedly wasn't — the sex he didn't have, the seriousness he lacked, and so on — he was the negative example of anything for almost anyone. His body eulogized masculinity. It eulogized living. It eulogized bodies — their disruptions of gender and time; their quotidian movement toward immobility and the regimens used to defer that eventuality. He made something out of nothing, spent years and years learning nothing. He modeled nothing but himself. He believed that

This page:
1, 2. Paige Powell, *Andy Warhol at Tunnel Club Fashion Show*, 1987
3, 4. Christopher Makos, *Miles Davis and Andy Warhol at Tunnel Club Fashion Show*, 1987
Opposite page:
1. Christopher Makos, *Andy Warhol at Tunnel Club Fashion Show*, 1987
2, 3. Paige Powell, *Andy Warhol at Tunnel Club Fashion Show*, 1987

"the thing is to think of nothing…. Look, nothing is exciting, nothing is sexy, nothing is not embarrassing. " "Nothing is perfect — after all… it's the opposite of nothing."[30]

His last self-portraits used camouflage. He came to believe that nothing was more beautiful than he was.

1. David Bourdon, *Warhol* (New York: Abrams, 1989), p. 286.
2. Victor Bockris, *Warhol* (London: Muller, 1989), p. 238.
3. Andy Warhol, *The Philosophy of Andy Warhol: From A to B and Back Again* (New York: Harcourt Brace Jovanovich, 1975), p. 7.
4. Bockris, *Warhol*, p. 328.
5. Warhol, *The Philosophy of Andy Warhol*, p. 150.
6. Andy Warhol and Pat Hackett, *POPism: The Warhol '60s* (New York: Harper & Row, 1983), p. 294.
7. *Ibid*, p. 274.
8. Jean Stein, *Edie, An American Biography* (New York: Knopf, 1982), p. 183.
9. Warhol, *POPism*, p. 183.
10. Warhol, *The Philosophy of Andy Warhol*, p. 92.
11. Warhol, *POPism*, p. 133.
12. Warhol, *The Philosophy of Andy Warhol*, p. 150.
13. John O'Connor and Benjamin Liu, *Unseen Warhol* (New York: Rizzoli, 1996), pp. 65-66.
14. *The Andy Warhol Museum* (New York: Distributed Art Publishers, 1994)
15. James Kaplan, "A Model Life," *New York*, November 8, 1993, p. 30.
16. Warhol, *POPism*, p. 180.
17. *Interview* cover.
18. Warhol, *POPism*, p. 293.
19. Warhol, *The Philosophy of Andy Warhol*, p. 98.
20. Warhol, *The Philosophy of Andy Warhol*, p. 92.
21. Warhol, *The Philosophy of Andy Warhol*, p. 53.
22. Bourdon, *Warhol*, p. 10.
23. Andy Warhol, *The Andy Warhol Diaries* (New York: Warner Books, 1989), p. 393.
24. *Ibid*, p. 369
25. *Ibid*, p. 82
26. Roland Barthes, "At Le Palace Tonight," *Incidents* (Berkeley: University of California Press, 1992), p. 47.
27. Kynaston McShine, ed., *Andy Warhol: A Retrospective* (New York: The Museum of Modern Art, 1990), p. 457.
28. Warhol, *The Andy Warhol Diaries*, p. 381.
29. Warhol, *The Philosophy of Andy Warhol*, p. 7.
30. *Ibid*, p. 9.

List of Illustrations

Compiled by Jesse Kowalski and Lisa Miriello

The following list provides additional information on images reproduced in this publication. Page and illustration numbers are cited in each caption. The abbreviation AWM/AWF signifies The Andy Warhol Museum Founding Collection, The Andy Warhol Foundation for the Visual Arts, Inc.; AWM/Dia signifies The Andy Warhol Museum Founding Collection, Contribution Dia Center for the Arts.

We are grateful to all those who have supplied photographs and for their permission to reproduce them, as well as to Robert Ruschak and Richard Stoner, who photographed most of the art and archival material from the collection of The Andy Warhol Museum.

All photographs and other visual material listed in the *Interview* section originally appeared in issues of *Interview* magazine. Except where noted, ©1997 *Interview* magazine. All rights reserved. Used with permission.

Every effort has been made to determine the existence and ownership of any copyrights in the archival material from the collection of The Andy Warhol Museum that is reproduced in this publication. These archival materials were collected by Andy Warhol, and it has not been possible in every instance to determine the source or origin of the materials from the collection of Andy Warhol or whether any copyright exists in the material. Appropriate copyright credit, where available, has been set forth below. The editors would be grateful for further information. All works by Andy Warhol are © 1997 The Andy Warhol Foundation for the Visual Arts, Inc. – MF/MK

1950s, ink and gouache on paper, 16 1/8 x 15 in. (41 x 38.1 cm.), AWM/AWF

p. 92/2, Andy Warhol, *Scarf*, 1950s, ink and tempera on paper, 12 x 9 5/8 in. (30.5 x 24.4 cm.), AWM/AWF

p. 92/3, Andy Warhol, illustration for *Harper's Bazaar*, 1950s, archives of AWM/AWF, © The Hearst Corporation

p. 92/4, Andy Warhol, *Boot*, 1950s, ink and tempera on paper, 13 1/8 x 11 1/4 in. (33.3 x 28.6 cm.), AWM/AWF

p. 92/5, Andy Warhol, *Boot*, 1950s, ink and wash on paper, 9 1/8 x 10 1/2 in. (23.2 x 26.7 cm.), AWM/AWF

p. 92/6, Andy Warhol, *Fashion Figure*, 1950s, ink and wash on paper, 18 1/4 x 14 5/8 in. (46.4 x 37.1 cm.), AWM/AWF

p. 92/7, Andy Warhol, *Fashion Figure*, 1950s, ink and tempera on paper, 26 7/8 x 15 in. (68.3 x 38.1 cm.), AWM/AWF

p. 93, Page from Warhol's portfolio, 1950s, Archives of AWM/AWF

p. 94/1-8, Andy Warhol, pages from *Fashion 10*, 1950s, collection of Jay Reeg

p. 95/1, Andy Warhol, *Fashion Show Backdrop for "Glamour,"* 1955, tempera and ink on canvas, 106 1/4 x 215 in. (269.9 x 546.1 cm.), collection of Jose Mugrabi, New York

p. 95/2-3, Stephen Bruce, dresses with fabric designed by Andy Warhol, early 1960s, clothing designed by Leila Larmon and Stephen Bruce for Serendipity 3, photograph collection of Stephen Bruce, owner and founder Serendipity 3 restaurant

p. 96-97, Otto Fenn, photographs with butterfly screen projections designed by Andy Warhol, c. 1952, Archives of AWM/AWF

Windows

p. 98-99, Simon Doonan, *Andy Warhol, Compulsive Collector*, Barneys New York window display, 1989, photograph courtesy of Barneys New York

p. 100/1, Andy Warhol working at Horne's department store, Pittsburgh, c. 1947, Archives of AWM/AWF

p. 100/2-3, Andy Warhol and co-workers at Horne's department store, Pittsburgh, 1947, archives of AWM, gift of Larry Vollmer

p. 101, Pat Hackett, *Andy Warhol, Halston, and Victor Hugo in a Halston window display designed by Warhol and Hugo*, 1975, black-and-white photograph, 10 x 8 in. (25.4 x 20.3 cm.), collection of the artist, © Pat Hackett

p. 102, Andy Warhol, Tiffany table setting, c. 1955, Archives of AWM/AWF

p. 103, Andy Warhol, Bonwit Teller window display, 1955, Archives of AWM/AWF

p. 104, Andy Warhol, Bonwit Teller window display, c. 1955, photograph: Virginia Roehl, collection of Gene Moore

p. 105, Andy Warhol, Bonwit Teller window display, c. 1955, photograph: Virginia Roehl, collection of Gene Moore

p. 106, Bonwit Teller window display with three framed drawings by Andy Warhol, c. 1955, photograph: Virginia Roehl, Archives of AWM/AWF

p. 107, Andy Warhol, Bonwit Teller window display, 1957, photograph: Virginia Roehl, collection of Gene Moore

p. 108, Andy Warhol, *Miss Dior*, c. 1955, ballpoint pen and watercolor on paper, 23 5/8 x 17 7/8 in. (60 x 45.4 cm.), AWM/AWF

p. 109, Andy Warhol, Bonwit Teller window display, 1955, collection of The Andy Warhol Foundation for the Visual Arts, Inc.

p. 110, Andy Warhol, *Window Display*, 1970s, gelatin-silver print, 10 x 8 in. (25.4 x 20.3 cm.), collection of The Andy Warhol Foundation for the Visual Arts, Inc.

p. 111/1, Gene Moore, Tiffany window display, March 1, 1956, photograph: Virginia Roehl, Gene Moore Collection, Cooper-Hewitt, National Design Museum, Smithsonian Institution/Art Resource, NY, gift of Gene Moore, 1997, photograph: Matt Flynn

p. 111/2, Gene Moore, Tiffany window display, March 21, 1956, photograph: Virginia Roehl, Gene Moore Collection, Cooper-Hewitt, National Design Museum, Smithsonian Institution/Art Resource, NY, gift of Gene Moore, 1997, photograph: Matt Flynn

p. 111/3, Gene Moore, Tiffany window display, April 20, 1956, photograph: Virginia Roehl, Gene Moore Collection, Cooper-Hewitt, National Design Museum, Smithsonian Institution/Art Resource, NY, gift of Gene Moore, 1997, photograph: Matt Flynn

p. 112/1, Gene Moore, Tiffany window display, March 8, 1957, photograph: Virginia Roehl, Gene Moore Collection, Cooper-Hewitt, National Design Museum, Smithsonian Institution/Art Resource, NY, gift of Gene Moore, 1997, photograph: Matt Flynn

p. 112/2, Gene Moore, Tiffany window display, March 3, 1958, photograph: Virginia Roehl, Gene Moore Collection, Cooper-Hewitt, National Design Museum, Smithsonian Institution/Art Resource, NY, gift of Gene Moore, 1997, photograph: Matt Flynn

p. 113/1, Gene Moore, Tiffany window display, September 24, 1962, Gene Moore Collection, Cooper-Hewitt, National Design Museum, Smithsonian Institution/Art Resource, NY, gift of Gene Moore, 1997, photograph: Matt Flynn

p. 113/2, Gene Moore, Tiffany window display, March 1, 1963, Gene Moore Collection, Cooper-Hewitt, National Design Museum, Smithsonian Institution/Art Resource, NY, gift of Gene Moore, 1997, photograph: Matt Flynn

p. 113/3, Gene Moore, Tiffany window display, April 19, 1965, Gene Moore Collection, Cooper-Hewitt, National Design Museum, Smithsonian Institution/Art Resource, NY, gift of Gene Moore, 1997, photograph: Matt Flynn

p. 113/4, Gene Moore, Tiffany window display, May 4, 1970, Gene Moore Collection, Cooper-Hewitt, National Design Museum, Smithsonian Institution/Art Resource, NY, gift of Gene Moore, 1997, photograph: Matt Flynn

p. 113/5, Gene Moore, Tiffany window display, January 31, 1974, Gene Moore Collection, Cooper-Hewitt, National Design Museum, Smithsonian Institution/Art Resource, NY, photograph: Matt Flynn, gift of Gene Moore, 1997

p. 114/1-4 and

p. 115/1, Matson Jones (Jasper Johns and Robert Rauschenberg), *Recreations in Dimension of 18th-Century Still Lifes*, Tiffany window displays, November 9, 1956, photographs: Virginia Roehl, Gene Moore Collection, Cooper-Hewitt, National Design Museum, Smithsonian Institution/Art Resource, NY, gift of Gene Moore, 1997, photographs: Matt Flynn

p. 114/5-6 and

p. 115/2-4, Matson Jones (Jasper Johns and Robert Rauschenberg), *Landscapes*, Tiffany window displays, July 20, 1957, photographs: Virginia Roehl, Gene Moore Collection, Cooper-Hewitt, National Design Museum, Smithsonian Institution/Art Resource, NY, gift of Gene Moore, 1997, photographs: Matt Flynn

p. 116/1, James Rosenquist, Bonwit Teller window display, 1959, photograph courtesy of the artist

p. 116/2, James Rosenquist, Bonwit Teller window display, c. 1959, photograph courtesy of the artist

p. 117/1, Simon Doonan, *Menswear Window*, Barneys New York window display, fall 1996, photograph courtesy of Barneys New York

p. 117/2, Simon Doonan, *Fashion Week Aftermath*, Barneys New York window display, spring 1997, photograph courtesy of Barneys New York

p. 117/3, Andy Warhol, *Window Display*, 1970s, gelatin-silver print, 8 x 10 in. (20.3 x 25.4 cm.), collection of The Andy Warhol Foundation for the Visual Arts, Inc.

p. 118-19, Andy Warhol, Bonwit Teller window display, 1961, photograph courtesy of Rainer Crone archives, © Rainer Crone

p. 120/1, Mike Bidlo, *Not Warhol, (Advertisement, 1960)*, 1989, synthetic polymer paint on canvas, 72 x 54 in. (183 x 137 cm.), Lent by H. P. Mueller, Switzerland, courtesy Galerie Bruno Bischofberger, Zürich

p. 120/2, Mike Bidlo, *Not Warhol, (Little King, 1961)*, 1989, synthetic polymer paint on canvas, 54 x 40 in. (137.2 x 101.6 cm.), private collection, Switzerland

p. 121/1, Mike Bidlo, *Not Warhol, (Superman, 1960)*, 1989, synthetic polymer paint on canvas, 67 x 52 in. (170 x 132 cm.), private collection, courtesy of Galerie Bruno Bischofberger, Zürich

p. 121/2, Mike Bidlo, *Not Warhol, (Before and After, 1961)*, 1989, synthetic polymer paint on canvas, 72 x 100 in. (183 x 254 cm.), collection of Galerie Bruno Bischofberger, Zürich, photograph: Phillips/Schwab

p. 121/3, Mike Bidlo, *Not Warhol, (Saturday's Popeye, 1960)*, 1989, synthetic polymer paint on canvas, 48 x 40 in. (121.9 x 101.6 cm.), private collection, Switzerland

p. 122/1, Jean-Michel Basquiat in Patricia Field's store window, *Soho Weekly News*, November 15, 1979, photograph: Valerie Herouvis

p. 122/2, Paige Powell, Andy Warhol's *Invisible Sculpture* installation at Area, 1985, black-and-white photograph, 8 x 10 in. (20.3 x 25.4 cm.), collection of the artist, © Paige Powell

p. 123/1, Peter Greenaway, from the exhibition *The Physical Self*, October 27, 1991-January 12, 1992, courtesy Museum Boijmans Van Beuningen, Rotterdam, © Jannes Linders

p. 123/2, Tilda Swinton and Cornelia Parker, *The Maybe*, 1995, installation at the Serpentine Gallery, London, Performance art and mixed media, courtesy of Serpentine Gallery, London, photograph: Hugo Glendinning

Silver Factory Style The 1960s

p. 124-25, Nat Finkelstein, *Edie Sedgwick and Gerard Malanga*, 1965, color photograph, 16 x 20 in. (40.6 x 50.8 cm.), archives of AWM, gift of the artist, © Nat Finkelstein

p. 126/1, Stephen Shore, *Andy Warhol on the fire escape of the Factory*, 1965, gelatin-silver print, 8 x 10 in. (20.3 x 25.4 cm.), Archives of AWM/AWF, © Stephen Shore

p. 126/2, Gerard Malanga, *Nico, Taylor Mead, Ultra Violet, Viva, Ingrid Superstar, Billy Name, Andy Warhol, and others from the Factory*, 1968, gelatin-silver print, 11 x 14 in. (27.9 x 35.6 cm.), Archives of AWM/AWF, © Archives Malanga

p. 126/3, Billy Name, *Andy, Gerard, and Chuck Playing on Couch*, 1965, gelatin-silver print, 14 x 11 in. (35.6 x 27.9 cm.), collection of the artist, © Billy Name

p. 126/4, Billy Name, *Ivy Nicholson*, 1965, gelatin-silver print, 14 x 11 in. (35.6 x 27.9 cm.), collection of the artist, © Billy Name

p. 126/5, David McCabe, *Andy Warhol*, c. 1964, gelatin-silver print, 11 x 14 in. (27.9 x 35.6 cm.), collection of the artist, © David McCabe

p. 127/1, Promotional material for Champion Papers featuring Andy Warhol and Art Kane, 1962, photograph: Art Kane, archives of AWM/AWF

p. 127/2, Billy Name, *Mary Woronov and International Velvet*, 1965, gelatin-silver print, 14 x 11 in. (35.6 x 27.9 cm.), collection of the artist, © Billy Name

p. 127/3, David McCabe, *Andy Warhol against the Factory Wall*, 1964, gelatin-silver print, 14 x 11 in. (35.6 x 27.9 cm.), archives of AWM, gift of the artist, © David McCabe

p. 128/1, Andy Warhol, Paul Morrissey, Baby Jane Holzer, Joe Dallesandro, Holly Woodlawn, and others from the Factory, *L'Uomo Vogue*, April/March 1972, photographs: Oliviero Toscani, Archives of AWM/AWF, © 1972 The Condé Nast Publications, Inc.

p. 128/2, Billy Name, *Andy Warhol at the Factory, Bathroom Series*, 1968, gelatin-silver print, 14 x 11 in. (35.6 x 27.9 cm.), archives of AWM, © Billy Name

p. 128/3, Billy Name, *Factory Magazine Photo Shoot (Andy with Beautiful Girls), Ivy Nicholson, Marisol, and Others*, 1965, gelatin-silver print, 14 x 11 in. (35.6 x 27.9 cm.), archives of AWM, © Billy Name

p. 128/4, Billy Name, *Fred Hughes at the Factory, Bathroom Series*, 1968, C-print, 14 x 11 in. (35.6 x 27.9 cm.), collection of the artist, © Billy Name

p. 128/5, Billy Name, *Andy Warhol at the Factory*, 1964, gelatin-silver print, 11 x 14 in. (27.9 x 35.6 cm.), archives of AWM, © Billy Name

p. 129/1, 2, Andy Warhol, *Self-Portrait*, c. 1963, photobooth photographs, 8 x 1 3/4 in. (20.3 x 4.4 cm.) each, AWM/AWF

p. 129/3-5, Andy Warhol, *Edie Sedgwick*, c. 1965, photobooth photographs, 7 3/4 x 1 1/2 in. (19.7 x 3.8 cm.) each, AWM/AWF

p. 129/6, Andy Warhol, *Gerard Malanga*, c. 1966, photobooth photograph, 7 3/4 x 1 1/2 in. (19.7 x 3.8 cm.), AWM/AWF

p. 129/7, Stephen Shore, *Andy Warhol and Ingrid Superstar*, 1966, gelatin-silver print, 8 x 10 in. (20.3 x 25.4 cm.), Archives of AWM/AWF, © Stephen Shore

p. 129/8, Billy Name, *Jed Johnson at the Factory, Bathroom Series*, 1968, C-print, 14 x 11 in. (35.6 x 27.9 cm.), collection of the artist, © Billy Name

p. 129/9, Billy Name, *Andy Warhol, Brigid Polk (Berlin), Gerard Malanga, and Ingrid Superstar*, 1966, gelatin-silver print, 11 x 14 in. (27.9 x 35.6 cm.), collection of the artist, © Billy Name

p. 129/10, Billy Name, *Paul Morrissey's Apartment*, 1968, C-print, 14 x 11 in. (35.6 x 27.9 cm.), collection of the artist, © Billy Name

p. 129/11, Billy Name, *Viva and Andy Warhol at the Factory*, 1968, C-print, 14 x 11 in. (35.6 x 27.9 cm.), collection of the artist, © Billy Name

p. 129/12, Fred W. McDarrah, *Andy Warhol*, 1966, gelatin-silver print, 20 x 16 in. (50.8 x 40.6 cm.), collection of the artist, © Fred W. McDarrah

pp. 130-31, Nat Finkelstein, *Gerard Malanga*, 1965, color photograph, 16 x 20 in. (40.6 x 50.8 cm.), archives of AWM, gift of the artist, © Nat Finkelstein

p. 132/1, Billy Name, *"Vinyl" with Gerard and Edie*, 1965, gelatin-silver print, 14 x 11 in. (35.6 x 27.9 cm.), collection of the artist, © Billy Name

p. 132/2, David McCabe, *Edie Sedgwick and Gerard Malanga*, 1965, gelatin-silver print, 14 x 11 in. (35.6 x 27.9 cm.), collection of the artist, © David McCabe

p. 132/3, Gerard Malanga in appropriated fashion by Andy Warhol for "Poetry & Fashion" runway show, 1968, black-and-white photograph, 10 x 8 in. (25.4 x 20.3 cm.), collection of Gerard Malanga, © Archives Malanga

p. 132/4, Article on Pop fashion and poetry, *New York Herald Tribune*, January 3, 1965, collection of Gerard Malanga

p. 132/5, Article on Andy Warhol and the Factory, *Pageant*, March 1967, photographs: Bob Adelman, Archives of AWM/AWF, © MacFadden-Bartell Corporation

p. 133/1, Arman, *Gerard Malanga wearing a silkscreened Troy Donahue shirt*, 1963, Polaroid photograph, 5 x 3 1/2 in. (12.7 x 8.9 cm.), collection of Gerard Malanga, © Archives Malanga

p. 133/2, Francesco Scavullo, *Gerard Malanga*, 1969, gelatin-silver print, 20 x 16 in. (50.8 x 40.6 cm.), collection of the artist, © Francesco Scavullo

p. 133/3, Nat Finkelstein, *Gerard Malanga*, 1965, color photograph, 10 x 8 in. (25.4 x 20.3 cm.), archives of AWM, © Nat Finkelstein

p. 134/1, David McCabe, Photo session at David McCabe's studio with an assistant, McCabe, Chuck Wein, Edie Sedgwick, Andy Warhol, and Gerard Malanga, 1965, gelatin-silver print, 11 x 14 in. (27.9 x 35.6 cm.), archives of AWM, gift of the artist, © David McCabe

p. 134/2, David McCabe, *Edie Sedgwick*, 1965, gelatin-silver print, 14 x 11 in. (35.6 x 27.9 cm.), collection of the artist, © David McCabe

p. 134/3, David McCabe, *Gerard Malanga*, 1965, gelatin-silver print, 14 x 11 in. (35.6 x 27.9 cm.), collection of the artist, © David McCabe

p. 134/4, Billy Name, *Ingrid Superstar, Ultra Violet, Paul Morrissey, International Velvet, Viva, Brigid Polk (Berlin), and Tiger Morse*, 1968, C-print, 14 x 11 in. (35.6 x 27.9 cm.), collection of the artist, © Billy Name

p. 134/5-6, Billy Name, *Viva, International Velvet, and Ultra Violet at the Factory*, 1968, C-prints, 14 x 11 in. (35.6 x 27.9 cm.) each, collection of the artist, © Billy Name

p. 134/7, Billy Name, *Ultra Violet, Paul Morrissey, Ingrid Superstar, International Velvet, Viva, Brigid Polk (Berlin), and Tiger Morse*, 1968, C-print, 14 x 11 in. (35.6 x 27.9 cm.), collection of the artist, © Billy Name

p. 135/1, David McCabe, Photo session at David McCabe's studio with Gerard Malanga, Edie Sedgwick, Andy Warhol, McCabe, and an assistant, 1965, gelatin-silver print, 11 x 14 in. (27.9 x 35.6 cm.), collection of the artist, © David McCabe

p. 135/2-4, David McCabe, Photo session at David McCabe's studio with Chuck Wein, Edie Sedgwick, Andy Warhol, and Gerard Malanga, 1965, gelatin-silver prints, 14 x 11 in. (35.6 x 27.9 cm.) each, archives of AWM, gift of the artist, © David McCabe

p. 135/5, Billy Name, *Edie Sedgwick and Gerard Malanga*, 1965, gelatin-silver print, 11 x 14 in. (27.9 x 35.6 cm.), collection of the artist, © Billy Name

p. 135/6, Andy Warhol painting a butterfly on a model's leg, c. 1966, Archives of AWM/AWF

p. 135/7, David McCabe, *Unidentified Man, Chuck Wein, and Andy Warhol*, 1965, gelatin-silver print, 11 x 14 in. (27.9 x 35.6 cm.), collection of the artist, © David McCabe

pp. 136-37, Nat Finkelstein, *Edie Sedgwick*, 1965, color photograph, 16 x 20 in. (40.6 x 50.8 cm.), archives of AWM, gift of the artist, © Nat Finkelstein

p. 138/1, Billy Name, Edie Sedgwick's *Screen Test*, 1965, gelatin-silver print, 14 x 11 in. (35.6 x 27.9 cm.), collection of the artist, © Billy Name

p. 138/2, Andy Warhol, Edie Sedgwick's *Screen Test*, 1965, black-and-white 16mm film, 4 minutes, AWM/AWF

p. 138/3, Billy Name, *Ingrid Superstar, Edie Sedgwick, Bobby Schwartz, Ondine, and Susan Bottomly making Warhol's film "***** (Four Stars)," known originally as "Since,"* 1967, gelatin-silver print, 14 x 11 in. (35.6 x 27.9 cm.), Archives of AWM/AWF, © Billy Name

p. 138/4, Fashion spread with Factory look-alikes, *Harper's Bazaar*, August 1995, photographs: Peter Lindbergh, archives of AWM, © The Hearst Corporation

p. 139/1, David McCabe, *Andy Warhol and Edie Sedgwick*, 1964, gelatin-silver print, 11 x 14 in. (27.9 x 35.6 cm.), archives of AWM, gift of the artist, © David McCabe

p. 139/2, Article featuring Edie Sedgwick, Andy Warhol, and Chuck Wein, *The Sunday Times Magazine*, February 13, 1966, photograph: Burt Glinn, Archives of AWM/AWF

p. 139/3, David McCabe, *Edie Sedgwick and Gerard Malanga*, 1965, gelatin-silver print, 14 x 11 in. (35.6 x 27.9 cm.), archives of AWM, gift of the artist, © David McCabe

p. 139/4, Fashion feature on Edie Sedgwick, *Life*, November 26, 1965, Archives of AWM/AWF, © 1965 Time Inc.

p. 140/1, Nat Finkelstein, *Edie Sedgwick*, 1965, color photograph, 16 x 20 in. (40.6 x 50.8 cm.), archives of AWM, gift of the artist, © Nat Finkelstein

p. 140/2, Article featuring Andy Warhol and Edie Sedgwick, *Elseviers Magazine*, December 24, 1983, Archives of AWM/AWF

p. 140/3, Article featuring Andy Warhol and Edie Sedgwick, *Lo Specchio*, December 1965, Archives of AWM/AWF

p. 140/4, David McCabe, *Edie Sedgwick Dancing at the Factory*, 1965, gelatin-silver print, 11 x 14 in. (27.9 x 35.6 cm.), archives of AWM, gift of the artist, © David McCabe

p. 140/5, Stephen Shore, *Bibie Hansen, Edie Sedgwick, Pat Hartly, and Sandy Kirkland during the filming of* Girls in Prison, 1965, gelatin-silver print, 8 x 10 in. (20.3 x 25.4 cm.), Archives of AWM/AWF, © Stephen Shore

p. 141/1, David McCabe, *Andy Warhol, Edie Sedgwick, and the Empire State Building*, 1965, gelatin-silver print, 14 x 11 in. (35.6 x 27.9 cm.), archives of AWM, gift of the artist, © David McCabe

p. 141/2, Andy Warhol, Edie Sedgwick in *Poor Little Rich Girl*, 1965, black-and-white 16mm film, 66 minutes, AWM/AWF

p. 141/3, Fashion feature on Edie Sedgwick, *Life*, November 26, 1965, Archives of AWM/AWF, © 1965 Time Inc.

p. 141/4, David Bailey, *Andy Warhol and Jane Holzer*, 1973, gelatin-silver print, 11 x 14 in. (27.9 x 35.6 cm.), collection of the artist, © David Bailey

p. 141/5, David McCabe, *Richard Avedon and Andy Warhol at the Museum of Modern Art, New York*, 1964, gelatin-silver print, 11 x 14 in. (27.9 x 35.6 cm.), archives of AWM, gift of the artist, © David McCabe

p. 141/6, David McCabe, *Ultra Violet and Andy Warhol*, 1965, gelatin-silver print, 11 x 14 in. (27.9 x 35.6 cm.), collection of the artist, © David McCabe

p. 141/7, Fred W. McDarrah, *Andy Warhol*, 1963, gelatin-silver print, 20 x 16 in. (50.8 x 40.6 cm.), collection of the artist, © Fred W. McDarrah

p. 142/1-3, David McCabe, *Edie Sedgwick on the set of* Kitchen, 1965, gelatin-silver print, 14 x 11 in. (35.6 x 27.9 cm.), collection of the artist, © David McCabe

p. 143/1-3, David McCabe, *Edie Sedgwick and Co-star Roger Trudeau on the Set of* Kitchen, 1965, gelatin-silver print, 14 x 11 in. (35.6 x 27.9 cm.), archives of AWM, gift of the artist, © David McCabe

p. 143/2, David McCabe, *Edie Sedgwick on the Set of* Kitchen, 1965, gelatin-silver print, 11 x 14 in. (27.9 x 35.6 cm.), collection of the artist, © David McCabe

p. 143/3, David McCabe, *Edie Sedgwick and Co-star Roger Trudeau on the Set of* Kitchen, 1965, gelatin-silver print, 14 x 11 in. (35.6 x 27.9 cm.), archives of AWM, gift of the artist, © David McCabe

p. 144/1, Fashion feature using "Andy Warhol's helium-filled silver pillows," *Vogue*, July 1966, photograph: Penati, Archives of AWM/AWF, © The Condé Nast Publications, Inc.

p. 144/2-3, Nat Finkelstein, *Andy Warhol with Silver Clouds at the Castelli Gallery*, 1966, gelatin-silver print, 8 x 10 in. (20.3 x 25.4 cm.), archives of AWM, © Nat Finkelstein

p. 145/1, Advertisement for cotton, *Seventeen*, September 1966, clothing designer: Rudi Gernreich, Archives of AWM/AWF

p. 145/2, David McCabe, *Andy Warhol and Gerard Malanga*, 1964, gelatin-silver print, 14 x 11 in. (35.6 x 27.9 cm.), archives of AWM, gift of the artist, © David McCabe

p. 146/1, Advertisement for Betsey Johnson's Paraphernalia, *Aspen*, December 1966, Archives of AWM/AWF

p. 146/2, Page from Betsey Johnson's scrapbook, 1960s, collection of Betsey Johnson

p. 146/3, Article on a fashion show by Paraphernalia, *Status & Diplomat*, March 1967, photographs: Jill Krementz, Archives of AWM/AWF, © 1967 Status Magazines, Inc.

p. 146/4, Nat Finkelstein, *Andy Warhol and the Velvet Underground at the Paraphernalia Party*, 1966, gelatin-silver print, 8 x 10 in. (20.3 x 25.4 cm.), collection of the artist, © Nat Finkelstein

p. 147/1, Nat Finkelstein, *Maureen Tucker, Lou Reed, and Others at the Paraphernalia Party*, 1966, gelatin-silver print, 8 x 10 in. (20.3 x 25.4 cm.), collection of the artist, © Nat Finkelstein

p. 147/2, Nat Finkelstein, *Betsey Johnson and Andy Warhol Preparing the Paraphernalia Party*, 1966, gelatin-silver print, 8 x 10 in. (20.3 x 25.4 cm.), collection of the artist, © Nat Finkelstein

p. 148/1, Article on Paraphernalia, *The New York Times*, October 6, 1966, photograph: Edward Hausner, Archives of AWM/AWF, © The New York Times Company

p. 148/2, Nat Finkelstein, *Model at the Paraphernalia Party*, 1966, gelatin-silver print, 10 x 8 in. (25.4 x 20.3 cm.), collection of the artist, © Nat Finkelstein

p. 148/3, Nat Finkelstein, *Edie Sedgwick*, 1966, gelatin-silver print, 8 x 10 in. (20.3 x 25.4 cm.), collection of the artist, © Nat Finkelstein

p. 149/1, Nat Finkelstein, *Andy Warhol and Betsey Johnson at the Paraphernalia Party*, 1966, gelatin-silver print, 8 x 10 in. (20.3 x 25.4 cm.), collection of the artist, © Nat Finkelstein

p. 149/2, Nat Finkelstein, *Betsey Johnson at the Paraphernalia Party*, 1966, gelatin-silver print, 8 x 10 in. (20.3 x 25.4 cm.), collection of the artist, © Nat Finkelstein

p. 150/1, Fashion feature with Nico, c. 1966, Archives of AWM/AWF

p. 150/2, Nat Finkelstein, *Andy Warhol and the Velvet Underground at the Paraphernalia Party*, 1966, gelatin-silver print, 8 x 10 in. (20.3 x 25.4 cm.), collection of the artist, © Nat Finkelstein

p. 150/3, Nat Finkelstein, *John Cale*, 1966, gelatin-silver print, 8 x 10 in. (20.3 x 25.4 cm.), collection of the artist, © Nat Finkelstein

p. 151, Nat Finkelstein, *Unidentified Woman at the Paraphernalia Party*, 1966, gelatin-silver print, 10 x 8 in. (25.4 x 20.3 cm.), collection of the artist, © Nat Finkelstein

p. 152/1, 2, Billy Name, *Lou Reed, Sterling Morrison, Steve Sesnick, and Paul Morrissey on John Cale and Betsey Johnson's Wedding Day*, 1968, C-print, 14 x 11 in. (35.6 x 27.9 cm.), collection of the artist, © Billy Name

p. 152/3, Billy Name, *John Cale and Betsey Johnson on Their Wedding Day*, 1968, C-print, 14 x 11 in. (35.6 x 27.9 cm.), collection of the artist, © Billy Name

p. 152/4, Nat Finkelstein, *Gerard Malanga, John Cale, Nico, Unidentified Man, Danny Williams, Unidentified Woman, Sterling Morrison, Paul Morrissey, Andy Warhol, Lou Reed, and Maureen Tucker*, 1966, gelatin-silver print, 8 x 10 in. (20.3 x 25.4 cm.), archives of AWM, © Nat Finkelstein

p. 152/5, Nat Finkelstein, *Gerard Malanga, Andy Warhol, Mary Woronov, and the Velvet Underground*, 1966, gelatin-silver print, 10 x 8 in. (25.4 x 20.3 cm.), archives of AWM, © Nat Finkelstein

p. 152/6, Nat Finkelstein, *Banner outside the Dom*, 1966, gelatin-silver print, 10 x 8 in. (25.4 x 20.3 cm.), archives of AWM, © Nat Finkelstein

p. 153/1, Billy Name, *Actress, and Viva on John Cale and Betsey Johnson's Wedding Day*, 1968, C-print, 14 x 11 in. (35.6 x 27.9 cm.), collection of the artist, © Billy Name

p. 153/2, Christmas postcard to Andy Warhol from Betsey Johnson and John Cale, c. 1968, Archives of AWM/AWF

p. 153/3, Billy Name, *The Exploding Plastic Inevitable*, 1966, gelatin-silver print, 11 x 14 in. (27.9 x 35.6 cm.), archives of AWM, © Billy Name

p. 153/4, Billy Name, *The Exploding Plastic Inevitable at the Dom*, 1966, gelatin-silver print, 14 x 11 in. (35.6 x 27.9 cm.), archives of AWM, © Billy Name

p. 154/1, The Exploding Plastic Inevitable, *Life*, May 27, 1966, Archives of AWM/AWF, © Time Inc.

p. 154/2, Article on discotheques mentioning the Exploding Plastic Inevitable, *Life*, May 27, 1966, Archives of AWM/AWF, © Time Inc.

p. 154/3, Nat Finkelstein, *Lou Reed and Gerard Malanga*, c. 1966, gelatin-silver print, 8 x 10 in. (20.3 x 25.4 cm.), archives of AWM, © Nat Finkelstein

p. 154/4, Fred W. McDarrah, *Edie Sedgwick, Gerard Malanga, and the Velvet Underground*, 1966, gelatin-silver print, 16 x 20 in. (40.6 x 50.8 cm.), collection of the artist, © Fred W. McDarrah

p. 155/5, The Exploding Plastic Inevitable, *New York Herald Tribune*, April 22, 1966, photograph: Steve Schapiro, Archives of AWM/AWF

p. 156/1, Andy Warhol, Nico in *The Chelsea Girls* reel, *Nico Crying*, 1966, black-and-white and color 16mm film, 204 minutes, AWM/AWF

p. 156/2, Article with Nico and International Velvet, c. 1967, photograph: Jean Distinghin, Archives of AWM/AWF

p. 156/3, Article on the 1960s, with Andy Warhol and Nico, *Esquire*, August 1966, photograph: Frank Bez, Archives of AWM/AWF, © 1966 Esquire, Inc.

p. 156/4, Andy Warhol and Nico in a publicity photograph for Pop Art Theater, 1966, Archives of AWM/AWF

p. 156/5, John Cale, Gerard Malanga, Nico, and Andy Warhol, *Réalités*, 1968, photograph: Hervé Gloaguen, Archives of AWM/AWF

p. 156/6, Billy Name, *Publicity Photograph for* The Chelsea Girls, 1966, gelatin-silver print, 14 x 11 in. (35.6 x 27.9 cm.), Archives of AWM/AWF, © Billy Name

p. 157/1, 2, Andy Warhol, Nico in *The Chelsea Girls* reel, *Nico Crying*, 1966, black-and-white and color 16mm film, 204 minutes, AWM/AWF

p. 157/3, Billy Name, *The Velvet Underground and Nico Posing for Their First Album Cover*, 1966, gelatin-silver print, 11 x 14 in. (27.9 x 35.6 cm.), collection of the artist, © Billy Name

p. 157/4, Guess Jeans ad reminiscent of the Factory, *Interview*, February 1996, photographs: Wayne Maser; art direction: Paul Marciano, archives of AWM, © Guess 1996

pp. 158-59, Nat Finkelstein, *Nico*, 1965, color photograph, 16 x 20 in. (40.6 x 50.8 cm.), archives of AWM, gift of the artist, © Nat Finkelstein

p. 160/1, Fred W. McDarrah, *Nico, Andy Warhol, and Gerard Malanga Printing a* Fragile *Dress*, 1966, gelatin-silver print, 16 x 20 in. (40.6 x 50.8 cm.), collection of the artist, © Fred W. McDarrah

p. 160/2, Advertisement in *The New York Times*, November 8, 1966, Archives of AWM/AWF, © The New York Times Company

p. 160/3, Nico, Andy Warhol, and Gerard Malanga, *Réalités*, 1968, photograph: Hervé Gloaguen, Archives of AWM/AWF

p. 160/4, David McCabe, *Unidentified Woman Wearing* Fragile *Dress, Andy Warhol, and Baby Jane Holzer*, 1965, gelatin-silver print, 11 x 14 in. (27.9 x 35.6 cm.), collection of the artist, © David McCabe

p. 160/5, Andy Warhol, *Fragile*, 1962, synthetic polymer paint and silkscreen on canvas, 24 1/2 x 31 in. (62.2 x 78.7 cm.), private collection, New York

p. 161, Fred W. McDarrah, *Nico*, 1966, gelatin-silver print, 20 x 16 in. (50.8 x 40.6 cm.), collection of the artist, © Fred W. McDarrah

p. 162/1, 2, Billy Name, *Andy Warhol*, 1966, gelatin-silver print, 14 x 11 in. (35.6 x 27.9 cm.), archives of AWM, © Billy Name

p. 162/3, Andy Warhol, Album cover for *The Velvet Underground and Nico*, 1967, Archives of AWM/AWF

p. 162/4, Article on Andy Warhol's *Banana* dress, *The New York Times*, November 8, 1966, Archives of AWM/AWF, © The New York Times Company

p. 162/5, Andy Warhol, *Banana* dress, 1966, collection of Brooklyn Museum of Art, gift of Abraham & Strauss, NY, courtesy of Miss Jane Miller

p. 162/6, Andy Warhol, Detail from *Coca-Cola Bottles*, 1964, synthetic polymer paint on Coca-Cola bottles in wooden crate, 8 x 17 x 12 in. (20.3 x 43.2 x 30.5 cm.), AWM/AWF

p. 162/7, Andy Warhol, *Coca-Cola Bottles*, 1964, synthetic polymer paint on Coca-Cola bottles in wooden crate, 8 x 17 x 12 in. (20.3 x 43.2 x 30.5 cm.), AWM/AWF. The silver-sprayed bottles were made for a Warhol perfume.

p. 163/1 (inset upper right), Andy Warhol, *S & H Green Stamps*, 1965, offset lithograph, 23 x 23 3/4 in. (58.4 x 60.3 cm.), AWM/AWF

p. 163/2 (inset lower left), Eleanor Biddle Lloyd and Samuel Green at the opening of the Andy Warhol exhibition at ICA, Philadelphia, 1965, black-and-white photograph, 8 x 10 in. (20.3 x 25.4 cm.), collection of Institute of Contemporary Art, University of Pennsylvania

p. 163/3 (background), Andy Warhol, *S & H Green Stamps*, 1962, synthetic polymer paint on paper, 24 x 18 in. (61 x 45.7 cm.), AWM/AWF

p. 164/1, Fred W. McDarrah, *Edward Avedisian, Suzanne Moss (wearing* Brillo Box *Dress), Margarette Lampkin, and Andy Warhol at Factory Party*, 1964, gelatin-silver print, 16 x 20 in. (40.6 x 50.8 cm.), collection of the artist, © Fred W. McDarrah

p. 164/2, Article on Pop fashions, *Life*, February 26, 1965, Archives of AWM/AWF, © 1965 Time Inc.

p. 164/3, Andy Warhol and Suzanne Moss (wearing *Brillo Box* dress) at Factory party, 1964, Archives of AWM/AWF

p. 164/4, Article on Pop fashion with designs by Andy Warhol, *TV Guide*, March 5, 1966, photographs: Roger Prigent; model: Barbara Feldon, archives of AWM, gift of Janice Hulme, © 1966 Triangle Publications, Inc.

p. 165/1, Andy Warhol, *Brillo Box*, 1964, synthetic polymer paint and silkscreen on wood, 17 x 17 x 14 in. (43.2 x 43.2 x 35.6 cm.), AWM/AWF

p. 165/2, Billy Name, *Andy Warhol with a* Brillo Box *and Billy Name's Cat*, 1964, gelatin-silver print, 14 x 11 in. (35.6 x 27.9 cm.), archives of AWM, © Billy Name

p. 165/3, David McCabe, *David Whitney*, 1964, gelatin-silver print, 11 x 14 in. (27.9 x 35.6 cm.), archives of AWM, gift of the artist, © David McCabe

p. 166/1, Andy Warhol, *Flowers*, 1964, synthetic polymer paint and silkscreen on canvas, 81 3/8 x 81 3/4 in. (206.7 x 207.6 cm.), AWM/AWF

p. 166/2-3, David McCabe, *Andy Warhol Working on the* Flowers *Series*, 1964, gelatin-silver print, 11 x 14 in. (27.9 x 35.6 cm.), archives of AWM, gift of the artist, © David McCabe

p. 166/4 (background image), Stephen Sprouse, *Halston fashion show*, c. 1972, color super 8mm film, collection of the artist

p. 167/1, Andy Warhol, *Flowers*, 1964, synthetic polymer paint and silkscreen on canvas, 80 7/8 x 81 in. (205.4 x 205.7 cm.), AWM/AWF

p. 167/2, David McCabe, *Andy Warhol Working on the* Flowers *Series*, 1964, gelatin-silver print, 14 x 11 in. (35.6 x 27.9 cm.), archives of AWM, gift of the artist, © David McCabe

p. 167/3 (background image), Stephen Sprouse, *Halston fashion show*, c. 1972, color super 8mm film, collection of the artist

p. 168/1, Howell Conant, Andy Warhol's *Thirteen Most Beautiful Women* projected onto one of the stars of the movie, Ivy Nicholson, 35mm color slide, collection of the artist, © Howell Conant

p. 168/2, Howell Conant, Andy Warhol's *Batman/Dracula* and *Couch* projected onto Baby Jane Holzer, 35mm color slide, collection of the artist, © Howell Conant

p. 168/3, Fashion feature with Andy Warhol's movies projected onto models, *Life*, March 19, 1965, photographs: Howell Conant, collection of Jay Reeg, © 1965 Time Inc.

p. 168/4, Fashion feature with a silver theme, *Mademoiselle*, November 1965, photographs: David McCabe, Archives of AWM/AWF, © 1965 The Condé Nast Publications, Inc.

p. 169/1, Howell Conant, Andy Warhol's *Batman/Dracula* projected onto a model, 1965, 35mm color slide, collection of the artist, © Howell Conant

p. 169/2, Howell Conant, Andy Warhol's *Henry Geldzahler* and *Eat* projected onto models, 1965, 35mm color slide, collection of the artist, © Howell Conant

p. 170/1, Nat Finkelstein, *Andy Warhol Filming Nico's* Screen Test, 1965, gelatin-silver print, 8 x 10 in. (20.3 x 25.4 cm.), Archives of AWM/AWF, © Nat Finkelstein

p. 170/2, Nat Finkelstein, Donyale Luna's *Screen Test*, 1965, gelatin-silver print, 10 x 8 in. (25.4 x 20.3 cm.), collection of the artist, © Nat Finkelstein

p. 170/3, David McCabe, Film screening at the Factory, 1965, gelatin-silver print, 11 x 14 in. (27.9 x 35.6 cm.), archives of AWM, gift of the artist, © David McCabe

p. 170/4, Billy Name, Ivy Nicholson's *Screen Test*, 1966, gelatin-silver print, 14 x 11 in. (35.6 x 27.9 cm.), archives of AWM, © Billy Name

p. 170/5, David McCabe, *Andy Warhol behind the Camera*, c. 1964, gelatin-silver print, 14 x 11 in. (35.6 x 27.9 cm.), archives of AWM, gift of the artist, © David McCabe

p. 171/1, Andy Warhol, Dennis Hopper's *Screen Test*, 1964, black-and-white 16mm film, 4 minutes, AWM/AWF

p. 171/2, Andy Warhol, Suzanne Janis's *Screen Test*, 1964, black-and-white 16mm film, 4 minutes, AWM/AWF

p. 171/3, Andy Warhol, Francesco Scavullo's *Screen Test*, 1966, black-and-white 16mm film, 4 minutes, AWM/AWF

p. 171/4, Andy Warhol, Beverly Grant's *Screen Test*, 1964, black-and-white 16mm film, 4 minutes, AWM/AWF

p. 171/5, Andy Warhol, Gerard Malanga's *Screen Test*, 1964, black-and-white 16mm film, 4 minutes, AWM/AWF

p. 171/6, Andy Warhol, Edie Sedgwick's *Screen Test*, 1965, black-and-white 16mm film, 4 minutes, AWM/AWF

p. 171/7, Andy Warhol, John Giorno's *Screen Test*, 1963, black-and-white 16mm film, 4 minutes, AWM/AWF

p. 171/8, Andy Warhol, Lou Reed's *Screen Test*, 1965, black-and-white 16mm film, 4 minutes, AWM/AWF

p. 171/9, Andy Warhol, Ivy Nicholson's *Screen Test*, 1965, black-and-white 16mm film, 4 minutes, AWM/AWF

p. 171/10, Andy Warhol, Brooke Hayward's *Screen Test*, 1964, black-and-white 16mm film, 4 minutes, AWM/AWF

p. 171/11, Andy Warhol, Ann Buchanan's *Screen Test*, 1964, black-and-white 16mm film, 4 minutes, AWM/AWF

p. 171/12, Andy Warhol, Imu's *Screen Test*, 1964, black-and-white 16mm film, 4 minutes, AWM/AWF

p. 171/13, Andy Warhol, Baby Jane Holzer's *Screen Test*, 1964, black-and-white 16mm film, 4 minutes, AWM/AWF

p. 171/14, Andy Warhol, Paul Morrissey's *Screen Test*, 1965, black-and-white 16mm film, 4 minutes, AWM/AWF

p. 171/15, Andy Warhol, Billy Name's (Billy Linich) *Screen Test*, 1964, black-and-white 16mm film, 4 minutes, AWM/AWF

p. 172/1, Andy Warhol, *Blow Job*, 1963, black-and-white 16mm film, 41 minutes, AWM/AWF

p. 172/2, Movie poster, c. 1970, 33 1/4 x 23 1/4 in. (84.5 x 59.1 cm.), AWM/AWF

p. 172/3, Andy Warhol, *Bike Boy*, 1967-68, color 16mm film, 109 minutes, AWM/AWF

p. 172/4, Paul Morrissey poster, c. 1967, 25 x 18 in. (63.5 x 45.7 cm.), collection of The Andy Warhol Foundation for the Visual Arts, Inc.

p. 172/5, Andy Warhol, Album cover for *Sticky Fingers* by the Rolling Stones, 1971, Archives of AWM/AWF

p. 172/6, Joe Dallesandro modeling, c. 1969, photographs: Bill King; jewelry: Robert Mapplethorpe, Archives of AWM/AWF

p. 173/1, Billy Name, *Joe Dallesandro at the Factory*, 1968, C-print, 14 x 11 in. (35.6 x 27.9 cm.) each, collection of the artist, © Billy Name

p. 173/2, Francesco Scavullo, *Joe Dallesandro and baby*, 1968, gelatin-silver print, 20 x 16 in. (50.8 x 40.6 cm.), collection of the artist, © Francesco Scavullo

p. 173/3, Advertisement for Calvin Klein Jeans with Joe Dallesandro, *Details*, December 1995, collection of Michael Ferguson, © Calvin Klein Jeans

p. 173/4, Advertisement for Calvin Klein Jeans with Joe Dallesandro and Kate Moss, *Spin*, December 1995, collection of Michael Ferguson, © Calvin Klein Jeans

p. 174/1, Nat Finkelstein, *Andy Warhol and Baby Jane Holzer*, 1965, color photograph, 16 x 20 in. (40.6 x 50.8 cm.), archives of AWM, gift of the artist, © Nat Finkelstein

p. 174/2, Article on Baby Jane Holzer, *Life*, March 19, 1965, photograph: Howell Conant, collection of Jay Reeg, © 1965 Time Inc.

p. 174/3, Article on Andy Warhol and his society friends, *Town & Country*, May 1973, photograph: Arnold Newman, Archives of AWM/AWF, © The Hearst Corporation

p. 174/4, Article featuring Jane Forth, *Life*, July 4, 1970, photograph: Jack Mitchell, Archives of AWM/AWF, © Time Inc.

p. 174/5, Fashion feature with Jane Forth, *Queen*, c. 1970, photographs: Bill King, Archives of AWM/AWF

p. 174/6, Billy Name, *Publicity Still of International Velvet for* The Chelsea Girls, 1966, gelatin-silver print, 14 x 11 in. (35.6 x 27.9 cm.), collection of the artist, © Billy Name

p. 174/7, Publicity photograph of Nico, Mary Woronov, Andy Warhol, and International Velvet, c. 1966, Archives of AWM/AWF

p. 174/8, Billy Name, *Castelli Gallery* Flowers *Show with Baby Jane Holzer, Andy Warhol, and Gerard Malanga*, 1964, gelatin-silver print, 11 x 14 in. (27.9 x 35.6 cm.), collection of the artist, © Billy Name

p. 175/1, Billy Name, *International Velvet Performing in Andy Warhol's Film "***** (Four Stars),"* 1966, gelatin-silver print, 14 x 11 in. (35.6 x 27.9 cm.), collection of the artist, © Billy Name

p. 175/2, Article featuring Andy Warhol and women of the Factory, *Avant-Garde*, May 1968, photographs: Lee Kraft, Archives of AWM/AWF, © 1968 Avant-Garde Media, Inc.

p. 175/3, Brigid Polk (Berlin) being interviewed by Andy Warhol, c. 1968, Archives of AWM/AWF

p. 175/4, Billy Name, *Andy Warhol, Brigid Polk (Berlin), and Rodney Kitzmiller at the Factory, Bathroom Series*, 1968, C-print, 14 x 11 in. (35.6 x 27.9 cm.), collection of the artist, © Billy Name

p. 175/5, Lee Kraft, *Andy Warhol and Viva*, 1968, gelatin-silver print, 10 x 8 in. (25.4 x 20.3 cm.), Archives of AWM/AWF, © Lee Kraft

p. 176/1, Fred W. McDarrah, *Jed and Jay Johnson and Andy Warhol*, 1969, gelatin-silver print, 16 x 20 in. (40.6 x 50.8 cm.), collection of the artist, © Fred W. McDarrah

p. 176/2, Jack Mitchell, *Jay and Jed Johnson*, 1970, gelatin-silver print with selenium toning, 20 x 16 in. (50.8 x 40.6 cm.), collection of the artist, © Jack Mitchell

p. 176/3, Cecil Beaton, *Andy Warhol and Jed and Jay Johnson*, 1969, gelatin-silver print, 20 x 16 in. (50.8 x 40.6 cm.), courtesy of Sotheby's London, © Cecil Beaton

p. 176/4, Andy Warhol, *Jed Johnson*, c. 1974, Polaroid photograph, 4 1/4 x 3 3/8 in. (10.8 x 8.6 cm.), AWM/AWF

p. 176/5, David McCabe, *Andy Warhol at Philip Johnson's Glass House, Connecticut*, 1964, gelatin-silver print, 14 x 11 in. (35.6 x 27.9 cm.), archives of AWM, gift of the artist, © David McCabe

p. 176/6, Article on Andy Warhol with Ingrid Superstar, Jed Johnson, Gerard Malanga, Geraldine Smith, Warhol, Candy Darling, and Brigid Polk (Berlin), *Esquire*, December 1969, photograph: Claude Picasso, Archives of AWM/AWF

p. 176/7, Philippe Halsman, *Factory Crowd*, 1968, gelatin-silver print, 11 x 14 in. (27.9 x 35.6 cm.), Archives of AWM/AWF, © Time Inc.

p. 176/8, Fashion feature with Factory look-alikes, *Elle*, June 18, 1990, photographs: Jean-Baptiste Mondino, Archives of AWM/AWF, © Hachette Filipacchi, Inc.

p. 177/1, Raeanne Rubenstein, *Factory Crowd and Cecil Beaton*, 1969, gelatin-silver print, 11 x 14 in. (27.9 x 35.6 cm.), collection of the artist, © Raeanne Rubenstein

p. 177/2, Cecil Beaton, *Ultra Violet, Andy Warhol, Brigid Polk (Berlin), Candy Darling, and Unidentified Woman*, 1969, gelatin-silver print, 20 x 16 in. (50.8 x 40.6 cm.), courtesy of Sotheby's London, © Cecil Beaton

p. 177/3, Raeanne Rubenstein, *Andy Warhol and Cecil Beaton*, 1969, gelatin-silver print, 14 x 11 in. (35.6 x 27.9 cm.), collection of the artist, © Raeanne Rubenstein

p. 177/4, Cecil Beaton, *Cecil Beaton and Viva*, 1969, gelatin-silver print, 16 x 20 in. (40.6 x 50.8 cm.), Cecil Beaton courtesy of Sotheby's London, © Cecil Beaton

p. 177/5, Calvin Klein advertisement reminiscent of Richard Avedon's photograph of the Factory crowd, 1994, archives of AWM, © 1994 Calvin Klein Cosmetics Corporation

pp. 178-79, Richard Avedon, *Andy Warhol and members of The Factory*, left to right: Paul Morrissey, director; Joe Dallesandro, actor; Candy Darling, actor; Eric Emerson, actor; Jay Johnson, actor; Tom Hompertz, actor; Gerard Malanga, poet; Viva, actress; Paul Morrissey; Taylor Mead, actor; Brigid Polk, actress; Joe Dallesandro; Andy Warhol, New York City, October 30, 1969, gelatin-silver print, 120 x 420 in. (304.8 x 1066.8 cm.), collection of the artist, © 1975 Richard Avedon. All rights reserved.

p. 180, Richard Avedon, *Andy Warhol*, New York City, August 20, 1969, gelatin-silver print, 60 3/4 x 48 3/4 in. (154.3 x 123.8 cm.), collection of the artist, © 1975 Richard Avedon. All rights reserved.

p. 181, Richard Avedon, *Viva, actress*, New York City, January 14, 1971, gelatin-silver print, 24 x 20 in. (61 x 50.8 cm.), collection of the artist, © 1993 Richard Avedon. All rights reserved.

Drag and Transformation

p. 180, Andy Warhol, *Untitled (Manicure Station)*, 1982, gelatin-silver print, 10 x 8 in. (25.4 x 20.3 cm.), collection of The Andy Warhol Foundation for the Visual Arts, Inc.

p. 181, Andy Warhol, *Untitled (Pedicure)*, 1982, gelatin-silver print, 10 x 8 in. (25.4 x 20.3 cm.), collection of The Andy Warhol Foundation for the Visual Arts, Inc.

p. 184/1, Warhol's wig, 1970s , Archives of AWM/AWF

p. 184/2, Andy Warhol, *Framed Wig*, 1987, Andy Warhol's wig and Plexiglass frame, 16 1/4 x 12 1/4 x 1 3/8 in. (41.3 x 31.1 x 3.5 cm.), AWM/AWF

p. 185, Warhol's dyed surgical corsets, c. 1985-87, Archives of AWM/AWF

p. 186/1, Toiletries and cosmetics used by Warhol, c. 1950s-1980s, Archives of AWM/AWF

p. 186/2, *Michael Salem Says*, transvestite boutique catalogue, 1973, Archives of AWM/AWF

p. 187, Jack Mitchell, *Andy Warhol and Jane Forth at Lamston's*, 1970, gelatin-silver print with selenium toning, 20 x 16 in. (50.8 x 40.6 cm.), collection of the artist, © Jack Mitchell

p. 188, Andy Warhol, *Female Movie Star Composite*, c. 1962, ink, photographs, and tape on paper, 23 x 14 5/8 in. (58.4 x 37.1 cm.), AWM/AWF

p. 189/1, Andy Warhol, *Female Movie Star Composite* mechanical, c. 1962, Archives of AWM/AWF

p. 189/2, Andy Warhol, *Female Movie Star Composite* photostat, c. 1962, Archives of AWM/AWF

p. 190/1, Andy Warhol, *Make Him Want You*, 1960, synthetic polymer paint and crayon on canvas, 33 x 35 3/4 in. (83.8 x 90.8 cm.), AWM/Dia

p. 190/2, Andy Warhol, *Wigs*, 1960, synthetic polymer paint and crayon on canvas, 70 1/8 x 40 in. (178.1 x 101.6 cm.), AWM/Dia

p. 191/1, Andy Warhol, *Before and After 3*, 1962, synthetic polymer paint and pencil on canvas, 72 x 99 5/8 in. (182.9 x 253 cm.), collection of Whitney Museum of American Art, New York; Purchase, with funds from Charles Simon, photograph © 1997 Whitney Museum of American Art

p. 191/2, Source for *Before and After* series, *National Enquirer*, Archives of AWM/AWF

p. 192/1, Otto Fenn, Self-portrait in drag, c. 1952-54, Archives of AWM/AWF

p. 192/2, Otto Fenn, Contact sheet, self-portraits in drag, c. 1952-54, Archives of AWM/AWF

p. 192/3, Andy Warhol, *Otto Fenn*, 1950s, ink on paper, 11 x 8 1/2 in. (27.9 x 21.6 cm.), AWM/AWF

p. 192/4, Andy Warhol, *Man with Earring*, 1950s, ink on paper, 11 x 8 1/2 in. (27.9 x 21.6 cm.), AWM/AWF

p. 192/5, Otto Fenn, Contact sheet, self-portraits in drag, c. 1952-54, Archives of AWM/AWF

p. 193/1, Cecil Beaton, *Andy Warhol and Candy Darling*, 1969, gelatin-silver print, 16 x 20 in. (40.6 x 50.8 cm.), courtesy of Sotheby's London, © Cecil Beaton, photograph

p. 193/2, Otto Fenn, *Andy Warhol with altered nose*, c. 1952, Archives of AWM/AWF

p. 193/3, Melton-Pippin, *Portrait of Andy Warhol*, c. 1952, Archives of AWM/AWF

p. 193/4, Candy Darling, photobooth photographs with alterations, c. 1954, collection of Jeremiah Newton

p. 194, Francesco Scavullo, *Candy Darling and Michael J. Pollard*, 1969, Cibachrome, 16 x 20 in. (40.6 x 50.8 cm.), collection of the artist, © Francesco Scavullo

p. 195/1-3, Fred Hughes, *Candy Darling*, c. 1969, details from contact sheet, 8 1/2 x 11 in. (21.6 x 27.9 cm.), collection of the artist, © Fred Hughes

p. 195/4, David Bailey, *Candy Darling*, 1973, gelatin-silver print, 11 x 14 in. (27.9 x 35.6 cm.), collection of the artist, © David Bailey

p. 195/5, Francesco Scavullo, *Candy Darling*, 1973, Cibachrome, 20 x 16 in. (50.8 x 40.6 cm.), collection of the artist, © Francesco Scavullo

p. 196/1, George Haimsohn, *Portrait of Candy Darling*, 1972, gelatin-silver print, 14 x 11 in. (35.6 x 27.9 cm.), collection of the artist, © George Haimsohn

p. 196/2, Richard Bernstein, *Candy Darling*, silkscreened poster, c. 1971, 23 1/2 x 32 1/2 in. (59.7 x 82.6 cm.), collection of The Andy Warhol Foundation for the Visual Arts, Inc.

p. 196/3, Publicity photograph of Candy Darling inscribed to photographer George Haimsohn, c. 1972, gelatin-silver print, 10 x 8 in. (25.4 x 20.3 cm.), collection of George Haimsohn

p. 196/4, Andy Warhol, Candy Darling on a David Bailey photo shoot, *Factory Diaries*, 1972, black-and-white and color 1/2-inch reel-to-reel videotape, varying lengths, conceived by Andy Warhol, AWM/AWF

p. 196/5, Francesco Scavullo, mock-up design for *Cosmopolitan* with Candy Darling as covergirl, November 1972, mixed media, 10 x 8 in. (25.4 x 20.3 cm.), collection of Jeremiah Newton, © Francesco Scavullo

p. 196/6, Kenn Duncan, Publicity still for *Some of My Best Friends Are....*, 1971, gelatin-silver print, 10 x 8 in. (25.4 x 20.3 cm.), collection of Jeremiah Newton, © American International Pictures

p. 196/7, Fred W. McDarrah, *Candy Darling*, 1970, gelatin-silver print, 20 x 16 in. (50.8 x 40.6 cm.), collection of the artist, © Fred W. McDarrah

p. 197, Bill King, Candy Darling and male model, 1970, contact sheet, 10 x 8 in. (25.4 x 20.3 cm.), collection of Janet McClelland, © Bill King Photographs, Inc.

p. 197 inset, Candy Darling and male model in *Queen*, 1970, photograph: Bill King, Archives of AWM/AWF

p. 198/1, Candy Darling, Holly Woodlawn, and Jackie Curtis, *Vogue*, June 1972, photograph: Richard Avedon, Archives of AWM/AWF, © Condé Nast Publications, Inc.

p. 198/2, Advertisement for *Women in Revolt!*, *The Village Voice*, February 24, 1972, Archives of AWM/AWF, © 1972 The Village Voice, Inc.

p. 198/3, Poster for *Women in Revolt!*, 1972, 41 x 27 in. (104.1 x 68.6 cm.), Archives of AWM/AWF

p. 198/4-7, Publicity photographs for *Women in Revolt!*, 1972, Archives of AWM/AWF

p. 199/1, Francesco Scavullo, *Holly Woodlawn*, 1969, Cibachrome, 16 x 20 in. (40.6 x 50.8 cm.), collection of the artist, © Francesco Scavullo

p. 199/2, Holly Woodlawn poster, inscribed "Andy, Holly Woodlawn 10 Years Later, Love Holly", 22 x 17 in. (55.9 x 43.2 cm.), photograph: Frank Kolleogy, collection of The Andy Warhol Foundation for the Visual Arts, Inc.

p. 200/1, Richard Bernstein, Poster for *Cabaret in the Sky*, 1974, 35 x 23 in. (88.9 x 58.4 cm.), photograph: Bill King, collection of The Andy Warhol Foundation for the Visual Arts, Inc.

p. 200/2, Bill King, Source photograph for *Cabaret in the Sky* poster, 1974, gelatin-silver print, 14 x 11 in. (35.6 x 27.9 cm.), collection of Janet McClelland, © Bill King Photographs, Inc.

p. 200/3, Letter from Holly Woodlawn to Andy Warhol, 1975, Archives of AWM/AWF

p. 200/4-6, Photographs from Jackie Curtis' wedding, July 22, 1969, Archives of AWM/AWF

p. 201/1, Jackie Curtis, c. 1969, Archives of AWM/AWF

p. 201/2, Article on Jackie Curtis, *Esquire*, May 1971, photographs: Bud Lee, Archives of AWM/AWF, © 1971 Esquire, Inc.

p. 201/3, Jackie Curtis, c. 1975, Archives of AWM/AWF

p. 201/4, Billy Name, *Mario Montez*, 1965, gelatin-silver print, 14 x 11 in. (35.6 x 27.9 cm.), collection of the artist, © Billy Name

p. 201/5, Fred W. McDarrah, *Jackie Curtis*, 1974, gelatin-silver print, 20 x 16 in. (50.8 x 40.6 cm.), collection of the artist, © Fred W. McDarrah

p. 201/6-8, Andy Warhol, Divine, *Andy Warhol's T.V.*, 1981, color 3/4-inch videotape, 30 minutes, conceived by Andy Warhol, directed by Don Munroe, produced by Vincent Fremont, AWM/AWF

p. 202/1, Andy Warhol, *Shoes*, 1980, synthetic polymer paint, silkscreen, and diamond dust on canvas, 70 x 90 in. (177.8 x 228.6 cm.), AWM/AWF

p. 202/2, Source for *Shoes* series, Archives of AWM/AWF

p. 203, Andy Warhol, *Shoes*, 1980, synthetic polymer paint, silkscreen, and diamond dust on canvas, 90 x 70 in. (228.6 x 177.8 cm.), AWM/AWF

p. 204-5, Andy Warhol, *Ladies and Gentlemen*, 1975, synthetic polymer paint and silkscreen on canvas, 50 x 42 in. (127 x 106.7 cm.) each, AWM/AWF

p. 206, Andy Warhol, *Ladies and Gentlemen*, 1975, synthetic polymer paint and silkscreen on canvas, 40 x 50 in. (101.6 x 127 cm.) each, collection of Jose Mugrabi, New York

p. 207, Andy Warhol, *Ladies and Gentlemen*, 1975, synthetic polymer paint and silkscreen on canvas, 120 x 80 2/3 in. (305 x 205 cm.), private collection

pp. 208-9, Andy Warhol, *Lips* book, c. 1975, bound book with marbleized paper cover, silkscreen and tape on paper, 8 x 8 3/4 in. (20.3 x 22.2 cm.), AWM/AWF

p. 210, Andy Warhol, *Mick Jagger*, 1975, screenprint on paper, 1 from a portfolio of 10, 43 1/2 x 29 in. (110.5 x 73.7 cm.), AWM/AWF

p. 211/1, Andy Warhol, *Mick Jagger*, 1972, Polaroid photograph, 4 1/4 x 3 3/8 in. (10.8 x 8.6 cm.), AWM/AWF

p. 211/2, Andy Warhol, *Mick Jagger*, 1975, screenprint on paper, 1 from a portfolio of 10, 43 1/2 x 29 in. (110.5 x 73.7 cm.), AWM/AWF

p. 213, Andy Warhol, *Candy Darling*, 1969, Polaroid photograph, 4 1/4 x 3 3/8 in. (10.8 x 8.6 cm.), AWM/AWF

p. 215/1, Andy Warhol, *Jane Fonda and Candy Darling*, 1969, Polaroid photograph, 4 1/4 x 3 3/8 in. (10.8 x 8.6 cm.), AWM/AWF

p. 215/2, Andy Warhol, *Candy Darling*, 1969, Polaroid photograph, 4 1/4 x 3 3/8 in. (10.8 x 8.6 cm.), AWM/AWF

p. 215/3, Andy Warhol, *Jackie Curtis*, 1969, Polaroid photograph, 4 1/4 x 3 3/8 in. (10.8 x 8.6 cm.), AWM/AWF

p. 217/1, Andy Warhol, *Candy Darling and Gerard Malanga*, 1969, Polaroid photograph, 4 1/4 x 3 3/8 in. (10.8 x 8.6 cm.), AWM/AWF

p. 217/2, Andy Warhol, *Divine*, 1974, Polaroid photograph, 4 1/4 x 3 3/8 in. (10.8 x 8.6 cm.), AWM/AWF

p. 218/1-4, Andy Warhol, *Factory Diary*, 1981, color 3/4-inch videotape, one hour, conceived by Andy Warhol, AWM/AWF

p. 219/1, Christopher Makos, *Altered Image*, 1981, gelatin-silver print, 16 x 20 in. (40.6 x 50.8 cm.), collection of the artist, © Christopher Makos

p. 219/2-3, Andy Warhol, *Factory Diary*, 1981, color 3/4-inch videotape, one hour, conceived by Andy Warhol, AWM/AWF

p. 220/1-4, Andy Warhol, *Self-Portrait*, 1981, Polaroid photographs, 4 1/4 x 3 3/8 in. (10.8 x 8.6 cm.) each, AWM/AWF

p. 221, Christopher Makos, *Altered Image*, 1981, gelatin-silver print, 16 x 20 in. (40.6 x 50.8 cm.), collection of the artist, © Christopher Makos

p. 222-24, Andy Warhol, *Self-Portrait*, 1981, Polaroid photographs, 4 1/4 x 3 3/8 in. (10.8 x 8.6 cm.) each, AWM/AWF

p. 225, Christopher Makos, *Altered Image*, 1981, gelatin-silver print, 20 x 16 in. (50.8 x 40.6 cm.), collection of the artist, © Christopher Makos

Interview

p. 226-27, Bianca Jagger cover, *Interview*, no. 29, January 1973, photograph: Francesco Scavullo; artwork: Richard Bernstein, Archives of AWM/AWF

p. 228/1, *Interview*, no. 27, November 1972, photographs: Paul Morrissey and Francesco Scavullo, Archives of AWM/AWF

p. 228/2, *Interview*, no. 31, April 1973, Archives of AWM/AWF

p. 228/3, *Interview*, vol. 4, no. 4, April 1974, photographs: Horst, archives of AWM/AWF

p. 229/1, Peter Beard, *Naomi Sims Astride a Crocodile*, 1973, gelatin-silver print, 13 x 19 in. (33 x 48.3 cm.), collection of the artist, courtesy of Time is Always Now Gallery

p. 229/2, Joe Dallesandro back cover, *inter/VIEW*, vol. 1, no. 11, August 1970, Archives of AWM/AWF

p. 229/3, Rita Hayworth cover, *inter/VIEW*, vol. 1, no. 11, August 1970, Archives of AWM/AWF

p. 230/1, *Interview*, vol. 2, no. 5, May 1972, illustrations: Joe Eula, Archives of AWM/AWF

p. 230/2, Elizabeth Taylor in Iran, *Interview*, vol. 6, no. 7, July 1976, photograph: Firooz Zahedi, archives of AWM/AWF

p. 230/3, Donna Jordan cover, *Interview*, vol. 2, no. 5, May 1972, photograph: Chris von Waggenheim; artwork: Richard Bernstein, archives of AWM/AWF

p. 231/1, Charles James, *Interview*, no. 27, November 1972, photograph: Cecil Beaton

p. 231/2, Diana Ross, *Interview*, no. 28, December 1972, photographs: Bill King; artwork: Richard Bernstein, Archives of AWM/AWF

p. 232/1, *Interview*, no. 29, January 1973, photograph: Francesco Scavullo, Archives of AWM/AWF

p. 232/2, *Interview*, no. 31, March 1973, Archives of AWM/AWF

p. 232/3, Andy Warhol and Naomi Sims cover, *Interview*, no. 28, December 1972, photograph: Berry Berenson; artwork: Richard Bernstein, Archives of AWM/AWF

p. 232/4, Subscription form featuring Geri Miller, *Interview*, no. 29, January 1973 photograph: Ronnie Cutrone, Archives of AWM/AWF

p. 233/1, *Interview*, vol. 5, no. 4, April 1975, Archives of AWM/AWF

p. 233/2, Rudolph Nureyev, John Lennon, and Yoko Ono cover, *Interview*, vol. 2, no. 6, June 1972, photographs: Andy Warhol; artwork: Richard Bernstein, Archives of AWM/AWF

p. 234/1, *Interview*, vol. 4, no. 11, November 1974, photographs: Alejandro Reino, Archives of AWM/AWF

p. 234/2, Salvador Dali cover, *Interview*, no. 32, May 1973, photograph: Francesco Scavullo; artwork: Richard Bernstein, Archives of AWM/AWF

p. 234/3, *Interview*, no. 32, May 1973, photographs: Francesco Scavullo, Archives of AWM/AWF

p. 235/1, 2, Francesco Scavullo, *Bianca Jagger*, 1973, gelatin-silver prints, 20 x 16 in. (50.8 x 40.6 cm.) each, collection of the artist, © Francesco Scavullo

p. 235/3, Patti D'Arbanville cover, *Interview*, no. 31, April 1973, photograph: Francesco Scavullo; artwork: Richard Bernstein, Archives of AWM/AWF

p. 235/4, Anjelica Huston and Jack Nicholson cover, *Interview*, vol. 4, no. 4, April 1974, photograph: Klaus Lucka, Archives of AWM/AWF

p. 236/1, Lauren Hutton cover, *Interview*, no. 37, October 1973, photograph: Francesco Scavullo; artwork: Richard Bernstein, Archives of AWM/AWF

p. 236/2, Francesco Scavullo, *Lauren Hutton*, 1973, gelatin-silver print, 14 x 14 in. (35.6 x 35.6 cm.), collection of the artist, © Francesco Scavullo

p. 236/3, *Interview*, no. 32, May 1973, photographs: Anton Perich, Archives of AWM/AWF

p. 237/1-3, *Interview*, no. 30, March 1973, illustration: David Croland; photographs: Andy Warhol, Francesco Scavullo, and Catherine Milinaire, Archives of AWM/AWF

p. 238/1, *Interview*, vol. 5, no. 3, March 1975, photographs: Bill King, Archives of AWM/AWF

p. 238/2, Lee Radziwill cover, *Interview*, vol. 5, no. 3, March 1975, photograph: Bill King; artwork: Richard Bernstein, Archives of AWM/AWF

p. 238/3, Francesco Scavullo, *Juan Ramos, Jerry Hall, and Antonio*, 1975, gelatin-silver print, 20 x 16 in. (50.8 x 40.6 cm.), collection of the artist, © Francesco Scavullo

p. 238/4, Antonio, *Paris Cafe Society – Club Sept*, 1975, ink on paper, 27 x 19 in. (68.6 x 48.3 cm.), courtesy of Galerie Bartsch & Chariau

p. 239/1, *Interview*, vol. 4, no. 1, January 1974, Archives of AWM/AWF

p. 239/2, Antonio, *Paris Cafe Society – Marie France, Stella, and Galia*, 1975, black-and-white Instamatic photographs, 17 1/2 x 13 in. (44.5 x 33 cm.), courtesy of Galerie Bartsch & Chariau

p. 239/3, Antonio, *Paris Cafe Society – Pascal, Jean Paul, Jean Eudes*, 1975, black-and-white Instamatic photographs, 17 1/2 x 13 in. (44.5 x 33 cm.), courtesy of Galerie Bartsch & Chariau

p. 240/1, *Interview*, vol. 6, no. 9, September 1976, photographs: George Hoyningen-Huene, archives of AWM/AWF

p. 240/2, *Interview*, vol. 6, no. 7, July 1976, photographs: Peter Gert and Jeff Nike, Archives of AWM/AWF

p. 241/1, Albert Watson, *Divine in Zandra Rhodes*, 1978, gelatin-silver print, 20 x 15 1/2 in. (50.8 x 38.1 cm.), collection of the artist, © Albert Watson

p. 241/2, *Interview*, vol. 4, no. 6, June 1974, photographs: Bill Cunningham, Archives of AWM/AWF

p. 241/3, Mr. and Mrs. Kenneth Jay Lane cover, *Interview*, vol. 5, no. 5, May 1975 photograph: Bill King; artwork: Richard Bernstein, Archives of AWM/AWF

p. 241/4, Bianca Jagger cover, *Interview*, vol. 6, no. 9, September 1976, photograph: Chris von Waggenheim; artwork: Richard Bernstein, Archives of AWM/AWF

p. 241/5, Marisa Berenson cover, *Interview*, vol. 6, no. 1, January 1976, photograph: Ara Gallant; artwork: Richard Bernstein, Archives of AWM/AWF

p. 241/6, *Interview*, vol. 5, no. 1, January 1975, photograph: Bill Cunningham, Archives of AWM/AWF

p. 242/1, Raeanne Rubenstein, *Bob Colacello and Andy Warhol at work on* Interview, 1976, gelatin-silver print, 11 x 14 in. (27.9 x 35.6 cm.), collection of the artist, © Raeanne Rubenstein

p. 242/2, Models photographed with Andy Warhol's *Shadows* paintings at Heiner Friedrich Gallery, *Interview*, vol. 9, no. 4, April 1979, photographs: Bob Kiss, Archives of AWM/AWF

p. 242/3, Lally Weymouth cover, *Interview*, vol. 6, no. 5, May 1976, photograph: Ara Gallant; artwork: Richard Bernstein, Archives of AWM/AWF

p. 242/4, Lisa Taylor, Dustin Hoffman, and Beverly Johnson cover, *Interview*, vol. 6, no. 6, June 1976 , photograph: Ara Gallant; artwork: Richard Bernstein, Archives of AWM/AWF

p. 242/5, C. Z. Guest cover, *Interview*, vol. 6, no. 8, August 1976, artwork: Richard Bernstein, Archives of AWM/AWF

p. 242/6, Diane Von Furstenberg cover, *Interview*, vol. 7, no. 3, March 1977, photograph: Ara Gallant; artwork: Richard Bernstein, Archives of AWM/AWF

p. 242/7, Barbara Allen cover, *Interview*, vol. 7, no. 7, July 1977, photograph: Klaus Lucka; artwork: Richard Bernstein, Archives of AWM/AWF

p. 243/1, *Interview* subscription form from *Flash Art*, no. 101, January/February 1981, Archives of AWM/AWF

p. 243/2, Isabella Rossellini cover, *Interview*, vol. 8, no. 1, January 1978, photograph: Peter Strongwater; artwork: Richard Bernstein, Archives of AWM/AWF

p. 243/3, Peter Beard cover, *Interview*, vol. 8, no. 2, February 1978, photograph: Bob Kiss; artwork: Richard Bernstein, Archives of AWM/AWF

p. 243/4, Mariel Hemingway cover, *Interview*, vol. 8, no. 5, May 1978, photograph: Patrick Demarchelier; artwork: Richard Bernstein, Archives of AWM/AWF

p. 243/5, Paloma Picasso and Rafael Lopez-Sanchez cover, *Interview*, vol. 8, no. 6, June 1978, photograph: Eric Boman; artwork: Richard Bernstein, Archives of AWM/AWF

p. 243/6, Jerry Hall cover, *Interview*, vol. 8, no. 7, July 1978, photograph: Peter Strongwater; artwork: Richard Bernstein, Archives of AWM/AWF

p. 244/1, *Interview*, vol. 7, no. 7, July 1977, photograph: Ara Gallant, Archives of AWM/AWF

p. 244/2-4, *Interview*, vol. 7, no. 10, October 1977, photographs: Joshua Greene, Carlos Eduardo de Souza, Allen Lewis Kleinberg, Robin Platzer, Jade Albert, Archives of AWM/AWF

p. 244/5, "Out to Lunch with the Valentino Family," *Interview*, vol. 7, no. 11, November 1977, photographs: Barbara Allen; illustrations: Joe Eula, Archives of AWM/AWF

p. 245/1-6, "A Christmas Portfolio by Joe Eula," *Interview*, vol. 7, no. 12, December 1977, illustrations: Joe Eula, Archives of AWM/AWF

p. 245/7-8, *Interview*, vol. 8, no. 12, December 1978, photographs: Scott Heiser, Archives of AWM/AWF

p. 246/1, Portrait of Diana Vreeland painted in John Singer Sargent's studio, London, mid-1930s, *Interview*, vol 10, no. 12, December 1980, photograph: Ned Murray, Archives of AWM/AWF

p. 246/2, Diana Vreeland cover, *Interview*, vol. 10, no. 12, December 1980, photograph: Cris Alexander; artwork: Richard Bernstein, Archives of AWM/AWF

p. 246/3, Bob Colacello, *Diana Vreeland and Consuelo Crespi*, 1978, gelatin-silver print, 8 x 10 in. (20.3 x 25.4 cm.), collection of the artist, © Bob Colacello

p. 247/1, *Interview*, vol. 8, no. 3, March 1978, photographs: Kevin Farley, Archives of AWM/AWF

p. 247/2, *Interview*, vol. 10, no. 5, May 1980, photograph: Scott Heiser, Archives of AWM/AWF

p. 247/3, Bob Colacello, *Victor Emanuel, Valentino, and Marie-Helene de Rothschild in Gstaad*, 1979, gelatin-silver print, 8 x 10 in. (20.3 x 25.4 cm.), collection of the artist, © Bob Colacello

p. 248/1, *Interview*, vol. 11, no. 6/7, June/July 1981, photograph: Cris Alexander, Archives of AWM/AWF

p. 248/2, Bianca Jagger cover, *Interview*, vol. 8, no. 12, December 1978, photograph: Barry McKinley; artwork: Richard Bernstein, Archives of AWM/AWF

p. 248/3, Liza Minnelli cover, *Interview*, vol. 9, no. 9, September 1979, photograph: Clive Arrowsmith; artwork: Richard Bernstein, Archives of AWM/AWF

p. 248/4, Deborah Harry cover, *Interview*, vol. 9, no. 6, June 1979, photograph: Barry McKinley; artwork: Richard Bernstein, Archives of AWM/AWF

p. 248/5, Georgina Brandolini cover, *Interview*, vol. 9, no. 3, March 1981, photograph: Bob Kiss; artwork: Richard Bernstein, Archives of AWM/AWF

p. 248/6, Maura Moynihan cover, *Interview*, vol. 11, no. 6/7, June/July 1981, photograph: Peter Strongwater; artwork: Richard Bernstein, Archives of AWM/AWF

p. 248/7, Diana Ross cover, *Interview*, vol. 12, no. 1, October 1981, photograph: Peter Strongwater; artwork: Richard Bernstein, Archives of AWM/AWF

p. 248/8, *Interview*, vol. 10, no. 12, December 1980, Archives of AWM/AWF

p. 249/1, 2, *Interview*, vol. 12, no. 9, September 1982, Archives of AWM/AWF

p. 250/1, *Interview*, vol. 12, no. 12, December 1982, photograph: Bruce Weber

p. 250/2, Calvin Klein cover, *Interview*, vol. 12, no. 12, December 1982, photograph: Bruce Weber; artwork: Richard Bernstein, Archives of AWM/AWF

p. 250/3, Mick Jagger cover, *Interview*, vol. 14, no. 2, February 1984, photograph: Albert Watson; artwork: Richard Bernstein, Archives of AWM/AWF

p. 250/4, Diane Lane cover, *Interview*, vol. 11, no. 2, February 1981, photograph: Ara Gallant; artwork: Richard Bernstein, Archives of AWM/AWF

p. 250/5, Christopher Makos, *Tina Chow*, 1983, gelatin-silver print, 8 x 10 in. (20.3 x 25.4 cm.), collection of the artist, © Christopher Makos

p. 250/6, Christopher Makos, *Christie Brinkley*, 1983, gelatin-silver print, 8 x 10 in. (20.3 x 25.4 cm.), collection of the artist, © Christopher Makos

p. 250/7, *Interview*, vol. 11, no. 9, September 1981, photographs and design: Philippe Morillon, Archives of AWM/AWF

p. 251/1, 2, *Interview*, vol. 12, no. 12, December 1982, photographs: Bruce Weber, Archives of AWM/AWF

p. 251/3, *Interview*, vol. 11, no. 2, February 1981, photographs: Cecil Beaton and Helmut Newton, Archives of AWM/AWF

p. 252/1, Christopher Makos, *Ann Magnuson*, 1983, gelatin-silver print, 20 x 16 in. (50.8 x 40.6 cm.), collection of the artist, © Christopher Makos

p. 252/2, *Interview*, vol. 15, no. 2, February 1985, photographs: Matthew Rolston, Archives of AWM/AWF

p. 253/1, David LaChapelle, *PJ's, Tranny Bar, Miami Beach*, 1986, gelatin-silver print, 20 x 24 in. (50.8 x 40.6 cm.), collection of the artist, courtesy of Staley-Wise Gallery, New York, © David LaChapelle

p. 253/2, David LaChapelle, *Emmanuel Xuereb, NYC*, 1986, 20 x 24 in. (50.8 x 40.6 cm.), collection of the artist, courtesy Staley-Wise Gallery, New York, © David LaChapelle

p. 253/3, Matthew Rolston, *Student Fashion One*, Studio Berçot Series, 1986, gelatin-silver print , 20 x 16 in. (50.8 x 40.6 cm.), collection of the artist, courtesy of Fahey/Klein Gallery, Los Angeles, © Matthew Rolston

p. 253/4, Matthew Rolston, *Aly Claw Hand*, The Surreal Thing Series, 1987, gelatin-silver print, 20 x 16 in. (50.8 x 40.6 cm.), collection of the artist, courtesy Fahey/Klein Gallery, Los Angeles, © Matthew Rolston

p. 254/1, *Interview*, vol. 18, no. 11, November 1988, photographs: Karen Kuehn, Archives of AWM/AWF

p. 254/2, *Interview*, vol. 17, no. 5, May 1987, photographs: Drew Carolan, Archives of AWM/AWF

p. 254/3, David Seidner, *Anh Duong in Ungaro*, 1986, black-and-white-toned silver print, 24 x 20 in. (61 x 50.8 cm.), collection of the artist, © David Seidner

p. 255/1, David Seidner, *Betty Lago in Chanel*, 1985, black-and-white-toned silver print, 24 x 20 in. (61 x 50.8 cm.), collection of the artist, © David Seidner

p. 255/2, David Seidner, *Anh Duong in Christian Lacroix for Jean Patou*, 1986, black-and-white-toned silver print, 24 x 20 in. (61 x 50.8 cm.), collection of the artist, © David Seidner

p. 256/1, *Interview*, vol. 18, no. 11, November 1988, photographs: Bradford Branson; art direction and collage: Fritz Kok, Archives of AWM/AWF

p. 256/2, *Vogue Italia*, no. 356, March 1982, photograph: Francis Ing, © Vogue Italia, Archives of AWM/AWF

p. 256/3, Andy Warhol cover, *Interview*, vol. 10, no. 2, February 1980, photograph: Andy Warhol, Archives of AWM/AWF

p. 256/4-5, Ellen von Unwerth, *A Bikini Story*, 1991, stylist: Joe McKenna; clothes: Azzedine Alaia, gelatin-silver prints, 20 x 16 in. (50.8 x 40.6 cm.) each, collection of the artist, © Ellen von Unwerth

p. 257/1, Steven Meisel, *Michael Monroe, Lead Singer for Jerusalem Slim*, 1990, gelatin-silver print, 20 x 16 in. (50.8 x 40.6 cm.), collection of the artist, © Steven Meisel

p. 257/2, Steven Meisel, *Joe Leste, Lead Singer for Bang Tango*, 1990, gelatin-silver print, 20 x 16 in. (50.8 x 40.6 cm.), collection of the artist

p. 257/3, Sante D'Orazio, *Helena Christensen and Michael Hutchence*, 1994, stylist: Donatella Versace; clothes: Gianni Versace, Iris print, 16 x 20 in. (40.6 x 50.8 cm.), collection of the artist, © Sante D'Orazio

p. 258/1, James Walters and Drew Barrymore, *Interview*, vol. 22, no. 7, July 1992, photograph: Bruce Weber, Archives of AWM/AWF

p. 258/2, Bruce Weber, *Bobby Pumbel and Something from His Barbra Streisand Record Collection*, 1995, gelatin-silver print, 14 x 11 in. (35.6 x 27.9 cm.), collection of the artist, © Bruce Weber

p. 258/3, Bruce Weber, *Surf Couple*, 1995, gelatin-silver print, 14 x 11 in. (35.6 x 27.9 cm.), collection of the artist, © Bruce Weber

p. 258/4, Johnny Depp cover, *Interview*, vol. 20, no. 4, April 1990, photograph: Wayne Maser, Archives of AWM/AWF

p. 258/5, Madonna cover, *Interview*, vol. 20, no. 6, June 1990, photograph: Herb Ritts, Archives of AWM/AWF

p. 258/6, Denzel Washington cover, *Interview*, vol. 20, no. 7, July 1990, photograph: Herb Ritts, Archives of AWM/AWF

p. 258/7, Courtney Wagner and Stephen Dorff cover, *Interview*, vol. 23, no. 5, May 1993 photograph: Bruce Weber, Archives of AWM/AWF

p. 258/8-9, Francesca Sorrenti, *Rally Runway*, 1996, color photograph, 14 x 11 in. (35.6 x 27.9 cm.) each, collection of the artist, © Francesca Sorrenti

p. 259/1, 2, Katerina Jebb, *Instafashion*, 1996, stylist: Victoria Bartlett, human-life-size color photocopies, 66 x 22 in. (167.6 x 55.9 cm.) each, collection of the artist, © Katerina Jebb

p. 259/3, Sante D'Orazio, *k. d. lang*, 1994, gelatin-silver print, 20 x 16 in. (50.8 x 40.6 cm.), collection of the artist, © Sante D'Orazio

Uptown/Downtown

p. 260, Andy Warhol, *Self-Portrait*, c. 1986, Polaroid photograph, 4 1/4 x 3 3/8 in. (10.8 x 8.6 cm.), AWM/AWF

p. 261, Andy Warhol, *Self-Portrait*, 1986, synthetic polymer paint and silkscreen on canvas, 40 x 40 in. (101.6 x 101.6 cm.), AWM/AWF

p. 262, Fashion feature photographed at The Andy Warhol Museum, *Vogue Italia*, September 1996, archives of AWM, © The Condé Nast Publications, Inc.

p. 263/1, Steven Meisel, *L'Uomo Vogue*, 1995, C-type print, 20 x 16 in. (50.8 x 40.6 cm.), collection of the artist, © Steven Meisel

p. 263/2, Corinne Day, *Rose, Brewer St., London, The Face*, 1993, C-type print, 16 x 20 in. (40.6 x 50.8 cm.), collection of the artist, © Corinne Day

p. 264/1, Andy Warhol, *D. D. Ryan*, c. 1980-82, gelatin-silver print, 10 x 8 in. (25.4 x 20.3 cm.), AWM/AWF

p. 264/2, Andy Warhol, *Bianca Jagger*, c. 1976, gelatin-silver print, 10 x 8 in. (25.4 x 20.3 cm.), AWM/AWF

p. 264/3, Patrick McMullan, *John Samuels IV, Calvin Klein, and Andy Warhol at Studio 54*, 1980, gelatin-silver print, 8 x 10 in. (20.3 x 25.4 cm.), collection of the artist, © Patrick McMullan

p. 264/4, Patrick McMullan, *Andy Warhol and Baby Jane Holzer Outside Linda Stein's House*, 1986, gelatin-silver print, 8 x 10 in. (20.3 x 25.4 cm.), collection of the artist, © Patrick McMullan

p. 264/5, Andy Warhol, *Liza Minnelli*, 1979, synthetic polymer paint and silkscreen on canvas, 40 x 40 in. (101.6 x 101.6 cm.) each, AWM/Dia

p. 264/6, Andy Warhol, *André Leon Talley*, 1982, gelatin-silver print, 10 x 8 in. (25.4 x 20.3 cm.), collection of The Andy Warhol Foundation for the Visual Arts, Inc.

p. 264/7, Christopher Makos, *Elizabeth Taylor and Andy Warhol*, 1981, gelatin-silver print, 8 x 10 in. (20.3 x 25.4 cm.), collection of the artist, © Christopher Makos

p. 264/8, Andy Warhol, *Halston*, c. 1977, gelatin-silver print, 8 x 10 in. (20.3 x 25.4 cm.), AWM/AWF

p. 264/9, Andy Warhol, *Valentino Fashion Show*, c. 1982, gelatin-silver print, 8 x 10 in. (20.3 x 25.4 cm.), collection of The Andy Warhol Foundation for the Visual Arts, Inc.

p. 264/10, Debbie Harry in *Andy Warhol's Fifteen Minutes*, 1986, color 1-inch videotape, 30 minutes, conceived by Andy Warhol, directed by Don Munroe, produced by Vincent Fremont, AWM/AWF

p. 264/11, *Fashion: Kansai in New York*, 1980, color 3/4-inch videotape, 30 minutes, conceived by Andy Warhol, directed by Don Munroe, produced by Vincent Fremont, AWM/AWF

p. 264/12, Andy Warhol, *Valentino Fashion Show*, c. 1982, gelatin-silver print, 8 x 10 in. (20.3 x 25.4 cm.), collection of The Andy Warhol Foundation for the Visual Arts, Inc.

p. 265/1, Patrick McMullan, *Kenny Scharf, Andy Warhol, and Keith Haring*, 1986, gelatin-silver print, 8 x 10 in. (20.3 x 25.4 cm.), collection of the artist, © Patrick McMullan

p. 265/2, Patrick McMullan, *Andy Warhol and Cornelia Guest*, 1985, gelatin-silver print, 10 x 8 in. (25.4 x 20.3 cm.), collection of the artist, © Patrick McMullan

p. 265/3, Andy Warhol, *Diana Vreeland*, c. 1979, gelatin-silver print, 10 x 8 in. (25.4 x 20.3 cm.), AWM/AWF

p. 265/4, Andy Warhol, *John Sex*, 1984, gelatin-silver print, 10 x 8 in. (25.4 x 20.3 cm.), collection of The Andy Warhol Foundation for the Visual Arts, Inc.

p. 265/5, Amina Warsuma in *Fashion: Models and Photographers*, 1979, color 3/4-inch videotape, 30 minutes, conceived by Andy Warhol, directed by Don Munroe, produced by Vincent Fremont, AWM/AWF

p. 265/6, Bob Colacello, *Bianca and Mick Jagger*, c. 1977, gelatin-silver print, 8 x 10 in. (20.3 x 25.4 cm.), collection of the artist, © Bob Colacello

p. 265/7, Andy Warhol, *Jellybean Benitez and Madonna*, c. 1983, gelatin-silver print, 10 x 8 in. (25.4 x 20.6 cm.), AWM/AWF

p. 265/8, Roxanne Lowit, *Andy Warhol at the Ritz*, 1982, gelatin-silver print, 20 x 16 in. (50.8 x 40.6 cm.), collection of the artist, © Roxanne Lowit

p. 265/9, Andy Warhol, *Giorgio Armani*, 1981, synthetic polymer paint and silkscreen on canvas, 39 3/4 x 39 3/4 in. (100.9 x 100.9 cm.), each, collection of Jose Mugrabi, New York

p. 265/10, Andy Warhol, *Sid Vicious*, c. 1978, gelatin-silver print, 8 x 10 in. (20.3 x 25.4 cm.), AWM/AWF

p. 266/1, Roxanne Lowit, *Andy Warhol at the Met*, 1983, C-type print, 20 x 16 in. (50.8 x 40.6 cm.), collection of the artist, © Roxanne Lowit

p. 266/2, Andy Warhol, *Fashion Model*, c. 1982, gelatin-silver print, 10 x 8 in. (25.4 x 20.3 cm.), collection of The Andy Warhol Foundation for the Visual Arts, Inc.

p. 266/3, Christopher Makos, *Liza Minnelli and Andy Warhol*, 1978, gelatin-silver print, 8 x 10 in. (20.3 x 25.4 cm.), collection of the artist, © Christopher Makos

p. 266/4, Andy Warhol, *Carolina Herrera*, 1979, synthetic polymer paint and silkscreen on canvas, 40 x 40 in. (101.6 x 101.6 cm.) each, AWM/Dia

p. 266/5, Patrick McMullan, *Thierry Mugler and Andy Warhol*, 1986, gelatin-silver print, 10 x 8 in. (25.4 x 20.3 cm.), collection of the artist, © Patrick McMullan

p. 266/6, Christopher Makos, *Gang of Four* (Liza Minnelli, Andy Warhol, Bianca Jagger, and Halston at Studio 54 on Liza Minnelli's birthday), 1978, gelatin-silver print, 16 x 20 in. (40.6 x 50.8 cm.), collection of the artist, © Christopher Makos

p. 267/1, Roxanne Lowit, *Sonia Rykiel and Andy Warhol at the Rainbow Room*, 1981, gelatin-silver print, 20 x 16 in. (50.8 x 40.6 cm.), collection of the artist, © Roxanne Lowit

p. 267/2, Russell Todd in *Fashion: Male Models*, 1979, color 3/4-inch videotape, 30 minutes, conceived by Andy Warhol, directed by Don Munroe, produced by Vincent Fremont, AWM/AWF

p. 267/3, Issey Miyake in *Andy Warhol's T.V.*, 1983, color 1-inch videotape, 30 minutes, conceived by Andy Warhol, directed by Don Munroe, produced by Vincent Fremont, AWM/AWF

p. 267/4, Tina Chow in *Andy Warhol's T.V.*, 1981, color 3/4-inch videotape, 30 minutes, conceived by Andy Warhol, directed by Don Munroe, produced by Vincent Fremont, AWM/AWF

p. 267/5, Andy Warhol, from *12 Instant Images*, c. 1980, photograph: Oliviero Toscani, Archives of AWM/AWF, © Oliviero Toscani

p. 267/6, Cris Alexander, *Bob Colacello, Fred Hughes, and Andy Warhol at the Office*, c. 1979, black-and-white photograph, 11 x 14 in. (27.9 x 35.6 cm.), collection of Fred Hughes, © Cris Alexander

p. 267/7, Roxanne Lowit, *Halston Model and Andy Warhol*, 1982, gelatin-silver print, 10 x 8 in. (25.4 x 20.3 cm.), collection of the artist, © Roxanne Lowit

p. 267/8, Paige Powell, *André Leon Talley and Andy Warhol at Christophe de Menil's Dinner Party*, 1986, black-and-white photograph, 10 x 8 in. (25.4 x 20.3 cm.), collection of the artist, © Paige Powell

p. 268/1, Andy Warhol, *Grace Jones*, c. 1985, gelatin-silver print, 8 x 10 in. (20.3 x 25.4 cm.), AWM/AWF

p. 268/2, Roxanne Lowit, *Jean-Michel Basquiat at Palladium*, 1985, gelatin-silver print, 10 x 8 in. (25.4 x 20.3 cm.), collection of the artist, © Roxanne Lowit

p. 268/3, Andy Warhol, *Victor Hugo*, 1978, synthetic polymer paint and silkscreen on canvas, 40 x 40 in. (101.6 x 101.6 cm.) each, AWM/AWF

p. 268/4, Andy Warhol, *Grace Jones*, 1986, synthetic polymer paint and silkscreen on canvas, 40 x 40 in. (101.6 x 101.6 cm.) each, AWM/AWF

p. 268/5, Andy Warhol, *Unidentified Men and Women*; woman (right) is wearing Sprouse clothing, 1984, gelatin-silver print, 8 x 10 in. (20.3 x 25.4 cm.), collection of The Andy Warhol Foundation for the Visual Arts, Inc.

p. 268/6, Andy Warhol, *Jerry Hall*, 1984, gelatin-silver print, 8 x 10 in. (20.3 x 25.4 cm.), AWM/AWF

p. 268/7, Bob Colacello, *Diana Vreeland and Andy Warhol*, c. 1978, gelatin-silver print, 8 x 10 in. (20.3 x 25.4 cm.), collection of the artist, © Bob Colacello

p. 269/1, Patrick McMullan, *Andy Warhol in a Stefano Jacket*, 1985, black-and-white photograph, 5 x 4 in. (12.7 x 10.2 cm.), Archives of AWM/AWF, © Patrick McMullan

p. 269/2, *Chris Stein, Debbie Harry, and Andy Warhol*, 1982, photograph: Ron Galella, Archives of AWM/AWF, © Ron Galella

p. 269/3, *Fashion: Mudd Club Special*, 1979, color 3/4-inch videotape, 30 minutes, conceived by Andy Warhol, directed by Don Munroe, produced by Vincent Fremont, AWM/AWF

p. 269/4, Kansai Yamamoto in *Andy Warhol's T.V.*, 1982, color 3/4-inch videotape, 30 minutes, conceived by Andy Warhol, directed by Don Munroe, produced by Vincent Fremont, AWM/AWF

p. 269/5, Claude Montana fashion benefit for the Grey Art Gallery presented by Bergdorf Goodman, *Andy Warhol's T.V.*, 1981, color 3/4-inch videotape, 30 minutes, conceived by Andy Warhol, directed by Don Munroe, produced by Vincent Fremont, AWM/AWF

p. 269/6, Roxanne Lowit, *Halston and Andy Warhol at Studio 54*, 1984, gelatin-silver print, 8 x 10 in. (20.3 x 25.4 cm.), collection of the artist, © Roxanne Lowit

p. 270/1, Andy Warhol, *Diana Vreeland and Henry Geldzahler*, 1980, gelatin-silver print, 10 x 8 in. (25.4 x 20.3 cm.), collection of The Andy Warhol Foundation for the Visual Arts, Inc.

p. 270/2, Andy Warhol, *Diane Von Furstenberg and Diana Vreeland*, c. 1980, gelatin-silver print, 8 x 10 in. (20.3 x 25.4 cm.), AWM/AWF

p. 270/3, Andy Warhol, *Tina Chow*, c. 1985, synthetic polymer paint and silkscreen on canvas, 40 x 40 in. (101.6 x 101.6 cm.) each, AWM/AWF

p. 270/4, Andy Warhol, *Paloma Picasso*, 1982, gelatin-silver print, 10 x 8 in. (25.4 x 20.3 cm.), collection of The Andy Warhol Foundation for the Visual Arts, Inc.

p. 270/5, Andy Warhol, *Tina Chow*, 1984, gelatin-silver print, 10 x 8 in. (25.4 x 20.3 cm.), AWM/AWF

p. 270/6, Studio 54 VIP pass, c. 1978, Archives of AWM/AWF

p. 270/7, Andy Warhol, *Tina Chow*, c. 1985, gelatin-silver print, 10 x 8 in. (25.4 x 20.3 cm.), AWM/AWF

p. 271/1, Andy Warhol, *Fashion model*, c. 1982, gelatin-silver print, 10 x 8 in. (25.4 x 20.3 cm.), collection of The Andy Warhol Foundation for the Visual Arts, Inc.

p. 271/2, Katherine Hamnett in *Andy Warhol's Fifteen Minutes*, 1986, color 1-inch videotape, 30 minutes,

Notes on the Contributors

Hilton Als is a staff writer for the *New Yorker*. His first book, *The Women*, was published by Farrar Straus and Giroux in 1996. He is the editor of the forthcoming *Our Town: Images and Stories from the Museum of the City of New York*.

Mark Francis is the chief curator of The Andy Warhol Museum, Pittsburgh. He was founding director of the museum from 1989 to 1992, when he was also curator of contemporary art at The Carnegie Museum of Art. He is co-curator with Margery King of the exhibition *The Warhol Look/Glamour Style Fashion*.

Judith Goldman is an author and curator who has written extensively on contemporary art. She is the author of *Windows at Tiffany: The Art of Gene Moore* (1980), and she is currently completing a biography of the art dealer Leo Castelli.

Bruce Hainley is a contributing editor of *Artforum*. His writing appears in *The Nation*, *frieze*, *index*, and the *Voice Literary Supplement*.

Margery King is the associate curator of The Andy Warhol Museum. Her exhibitions include *Andy Warhol: Public Faces, Private Parts* for the 1996 São Paulo Biennial. She is the co-curator with Mark Francis of the exhibition *The Warhol Look/Glamour Style Fashion*.

Richard Martin is the curator of The Costume Institute of The Metropolitan Museum of Art, New York. He is the author of *Fashion and Surrealism* (1989) and *Versace (Universe of Fashion)* (1997) and editor of *The St. James Fashion Encyclopedia: A Survey of Style from 1945 to the Present* (1996). His recent exhibitions include *Haute Couture* (1996) and *Christian Dior* (1997).

Glenn O'Brien is a contributing editor of *Details*. He was editor and art director of *Interview* from 1970 to 1973, editor-at-large in 1989 and 1990, and contributed the column "Glenn O'Brien's BEAT" from 1977 to 1990. The many other magazines he has contributed to as editor and writer include *Harper's Bazaar*, *Mirabella*, *Spin*, *Rolling Stone*, and *Artforum*.

Barry Paris is a biographer, film historian, critic, and Slavic linguist. He is the author of *Louise Brooks* (1989), *Garbo: A Biography* (1995), and *Audrey Hepburn* (1996).

Thomas Sokolowski is the director of The Andy Warhol Museum. From 1984 to 1996, he was the director of the Grey Art Gallery and Study Center at New York University, where he organized the exhibitions *Against Nature: Japanese Art in the Eighties* (1989) and *Interrogating Identity* (1991). He is the author of numerous catalogues and articles on contemporary art including *Don't Leave Me This Way: Art about AIDS* (1995).

John W. Smith is the archivist of The Andy Warhol Museum and organized the *Interview* magazine section of *The Warhol Look/ Glamour Style Fashion*. He is the curator of the traveling exhibition *Candy Darling, Always a Lady* (1997) and co-curator of *All Tomorrow's Parties: Remembering the Velvet Underground* (1996).

Peter Wollen is a filmmaker and film scholar who teaches in the Department of Film and Television at the University of California at Los Angeles. He has written widely on the visual arts. Andy Warhol is a subject of his *Raiding the Icebox: Reflections on Twentieth Century Culture* (1993), and he is co-editor with Colin MacCabe and Mark Francis of *Who is Andy Warhol?* (1997).